Per Olov Enquist

Plays : 1

The Night of the Tribades, Rain Snakes, The Hour of the Lynx, The Image Makers

Per Olov Enquist was born in Hjoggböle, Sweden, on 23 September 1934. He has gained international fame as a playwright, novelist and documentarist. After studying at the University of Uppsula, his debut novel, *Crystal Eye*, appeared in 1961. His third novel, *The Magnetist's Fifth Winter* (1964) received critical acclaim, and his novel *The Legionnaires* (1968) won the Nordic Council's prestigious Literary Prize. Enquist turned to play-writing in 1973 when, as a visiting professor at UCLA, he began to write his first and most famous play, *The Night of the Tribades* (1975). Returning to the novel more recently, Enquist's *The Visit of the Royal Physician* (1999) won several awards including the prestigious Swedish August Prize, and in 2001, *Lewi's Journey* was published.

Gunilla Anderman is Professor of Translation Studies at the University of Surrey. She is also a professional translator of Scandinavian drama into English.

Charlotte Barslund is a professional translator of contemporary and classical Scandinavian drama, including Ibsen, for the English stage.

Kim Dambæk is a translator and scriptwriter. He is also a director and has worked for theatres in the UK as well as throughout Scandinavia.

T0347834

PER OLOV ENQUIST

Plays : 1

The Night of the Tribades
translated by Gunilla Aderman

Rain Snakes
translated by Kim Dambæk

The Hour of the Lynx
translated by Kim Dambæk

The Image Makers
translated by Charlotte Barslund and Kim Dambæk

Introduced by Gunilla Anderman

Methuen Drama

METHUEN CONTEMPORARY DRAMATISTS

Published by Methuen 2004

1 3 5 7 9 10 8 6 4 2

First published in 2004 by
Methuen Publishing Limited,
215 Vauxhall Bridge Road,
London SW1V 1EJ

Methuen Publishing Limited Reg. No. 3543167

A CIP catalogue record for this book is available from the British Library.

ISBN 0 413 77200 4

Typeset by Servis Filmsetting Ltd, Manchester
Printed and bound in Great Britain by
Cox and Wyman Ltd, Reading, Berkshire

Contents

Introduction

The Light from the North

The principle that the universal is often most convincingly expressed when anchored in the particular is much in evidence in the work of Swedish playwright, novelist and political essayist Per Olov Enquist. His roots firmly in the far north of Sweden, Enquist draws on minutely detailed observation from Swedish social and political history in his documentary-based plays and novels. Moving between the past and the present, his writing equally often foretells the future. Among contemporary Swedish writers, Enquist is one of the most 'Scandinavian', observant of the Danish and Norwegian state of the art as well as that of Sweden. And although committedly Scandinavian, he is at the same time a European with an awareness of the whole and its dependence on the sum of its parts.

In northern Sweden, just south of the coastal town of Skellefteå, lies Östra Hjoggböle. Nearby, in the small village of Sjön, stands a green, one-storey house, built by Elof Enquist, who died at the age of thirty-one, soon after the birth of his son, Per Olov, on 23 September 1934. Attached to the gable of the house are some telephone wires. In the winter, when the moon is almost white and the temperature drops far below zero, the cold tightens the wires, turning the building into one gigantic music box as Enquist writes in his 1978 novel, *The March of the Musicians*:

> The music started the winter after the Bell machine had been installed. It was a momentous song that appeared to come from the stars, and it returned, night after night. Always when it was freezing cold. It howled as if the wooden house was a cello and someone out there in the glittering ice cold darkness had pulled a gigantic bow over the strings.

Through the night, an invisible hand draws the bow over the strings that link heaven to earth, filling the cold and the darkness with powerful heavenly music. In *The Hour of the Lynx*, the boy tells how he learned from his grandfather who it was that played the harp:

> Who's singing, I said. I think it's God, he said. Sometimes he sings like that. You *think*, I said, don't you *know*. No, Grandfather said but I think it's him . . .

Throughout his work, ice and cold recur as metaphors in Enquist's writing. 'Now I'm going to tell you the story of the Snow Queen,' says Hans Christian Andersen to Hanne Heiberg in *From The Life of the Rain Snakes*, and he tells her the story about Hanne and her brother Hans, not that different from *The Snow Queen*, the Danish story-writer's own tale. A wicked angel, the story goes, breaks a mirror, making everything that is beautiful ugly, turning warmth into cold and life into death. And as all the little pieces scatter throughout space, one hits little Hanne Heiberg in the eye and she turns into ice. In the snow palace, she tries to fit together the jigsaw puzzle with its pieces made of ice. She tries to put together a word. But she fails. She fails to make the pieces spell the word 'love'. Unable to feel love, Hanne freezes, as do many of the characters in Enquist's plays and novels. In *The Hour of the Lynx*, the frozen state of the boy killer is even equated with evil. This leads to the next piece in Enquist's own jigsaw puzzle of images. Closely linked to 'snow' and 'ice' is the notion of guilt, brought about by sin and the ensuing search for redemption.

During the first half of the twentieth century, the evangelical movements that swept Europe during the mid-nineteenth century continued to exert an influence. In Sweden, their impact was particularly strong in the northern part of the country, including Västerbotten where Enquist spent his childhood and youth. In 1830, George Scott, a Wesleyan Methodist, was sent to

Stockholm as a missionary where he met Carl Olof
Rosenius, the founder of his own Swedish evangelical
movement.

Occupying pride of place on the wall of every Christian
home in northern Sweden would be a colour portrait of
Carl Olof Rosenius, whose gentle, beautiful face framed
by long curly hair was the epitome of the good shepherd
leading his flock. Rosenius's teaching was Lutheran with
elements of a form of German protestant Christianity
which had developed during the eighteenth century in
protest against clerical decadence. Everyone, it was felt,
should be allowed to conduct a sermon as long as their
belief was strong enough. Sermon-like gatherings were
held in individual homes, giving rise to an emotionally
coloured form of religious worship, including a semi-
mystical, near-symbiotic merging with Jesus, the
bridegroom and the object of the adulation. In contrast,
worldly sensuality was frowned upon, ruling out simple
pleasures such as dancing. Enquist tells of the young
people of the village dancing around the maypole, as was
the custom on Midsummer's Eve when the pastor
appeared. 'How would you feel,' he addresses the crowd,
'if right at this moment, Jesus returned to earth and
found you dancing?' Not surprisingly, this put a stop to
any further dancing that evening. Another illustrative
episode tells of a young man whose dream it is to be the
owner of a violin. As the playing of any musical
instrument with the exception of the church organ was
considered a sin, the father of the young man only agrees
to the purchase after his son has promised, hands on the
Bible, never to play dance music. Only then is he granted
permission to buy the coveted instrument.

Even worse were the consequences of greater sins.
Having taken advantage of a young girl, Uncle Aron, the
bachelor, has no other choice than to fill his rucksack
with heavy stones and walk into the deep water of the
river. 'It was a lonely walk he took that night,' Enquist
writes. 'It must've been very quiet. No silence compares

to the one of the soul, forever lost, in the coastland of
Västerbotten, as he walks towards eternal damnation.'

Departure from the northern part of Sweden in order to
study at Uppsala University appears to have inspired
Crystal Eye, Enquist's debut novel which appeared in
1961. This account of young people in what might be
seen as a university town is set against the parental home
and the childhood milieu, and interwoven with
recollections and reflections on the past. As captured in
the scene of the daughter saying good bye to her father,
it is now time to move on:

> We said good bye . . . Father stood there . . . until
> the train left, I saw his face close to the window. The
> window pane was dirty, but his face was strangely
> clear and well defined, I could see every little
> wrinkle, like on a very clear picture . . . see my
> father's face disappear behind a dirty window . . .
> And I realised that . . . I was no longer a child.

In *The Journey*, the 1963 novel that followed *Crystal Eye*,
change is also in the air. The narrator breaks up and
starts looking for a new life and a new world to replace
what he has left behind. Common to both novels is the
interim state that they describe; the narrator is in limbo,
no longer anchored in childhood but not yet having
reached manhood, on his way towards something new
without quite knowing what is in store for him.

Crystal Eye and *The Journey* were followed in 1964 by *The
Magnetist's Fifth Winter*. This novel, in which Enquist's
northern heritage of religious faith is pitched against
logic and pragmatism, contrasting art and imagination
with science and rationalism, marked his breakthrough as
a novelist. Here Enquist treats issues related to guilt and
betrayal which are interwoven into the complex character
of Friedrich Meisner, a man representing the
ambivalence inherent in the notion of 'faith'. Against the
cult of magic and mystery that follows the protagonist
wherever he goes, not dissimilar to the ecstasy of the

world of religion, stands artistic creativity as a possible substitute for the religious ritual. To some, Meisner is the physician who administers his treatment by passing his hands up and down the length of the patient's body without actually touching it. To others, he is the Rainmaker, God's image, leaving in his trail the much-needed rain at the snap of his fingers.

As his model for the character of Meisner, Enquist drew on the 'discoverer' of animal magnetism, Franz Anton Mesmer. According to Mesmer, the rotation of the heavenly bodies exerted gravitational influence on human physiology, analogous to the tidal effect of the moon upon the ocean, which in turn accounted for the periodic incidence of a range of illnesses. However, the combination of his use of unorthodox methods and the not infrequently unseemly behaviour on the part of his patients soon evoked suspicion in medical circles in Vienna, and in 1778, Mesmer was forced to leave for Paris. The arrival of animal magnetism in the French capital was greeted with enthusiasm and, as in Vienna, spectators found the healing events 'mesmerising' with the result that Mesmer became, yet again, a subject of controversy. The medical establishment made every effort to close Mesmer down, and in 1785, two official commissions were appointed with the brief to investigate Mesmer and his medical practices. However, although his personal reputation suffered as the result of official criticism, the cult of animal magnetism flourished and continued to attract clients. Not long after the publication of the French reports, advertisements in the London press announced introductory lectures and demonstrations in the new method 'for healing all known diseases' and by 1786, Mesmerism was thriving in the hands of local practitioners. Although sceptical as to the authenticity of the trances that had been reported, on the night of 13 November 1841, the Scottish surgeon James Braid attended a public demonstration of animal magnetism. After observing the demonstration, he returned and on this occasion felt that he had identified the cause of the mysteriously regular onsets of 'nervous sleep'. Braid was to devote the last eighteen years of his life to the subject, now generally known as hypnotism.

Enquist's Meisner leaves behind an earlier existence that much resembles that of Franz Anton Mesmer, having been branded a charlatan and forced, like him, to abandon the glamorous life of the metropolis. But soon he starts again, attracting the fury of burghers and farmers alike as their wives and daughters fall victim to his seductive powers. Is Meisner then nothing but a charlatan and a seducer? In *The Magnetist's Fifth Winter*, this is the question that Enquist attempts to answer at the same time as he tries to settle the score with the fire-and-brimstone pastors of his northern past.

The conflict between faith and knowledge is further developed in *Hess* which appeared in 1966. In this book, the voice of the narrator switches seamlessly between that of a researcher engaged in the study of the life of Hess and the three scripts that he has allegedly left behind; sometimes it is Hess himself, sometimes someone called Hess or H. When the voice appearing to be that of the researcher is speaking, it is to relate experiences as an air combat fighter in the First World War or as Hitler's representative in the Second World War, while Hess reminisces and recalls events related to growing up in a small town that might be placed geographically in Västerbotten.

In both of these novels of the early 1960s, Enquist spins his events into stories focusing in detail on aspects of the lives of historical characters. However, in a postscript to *The Magnetist's Fifth Winter* the author states:

> It is impossible to certify many of the documents dealing with Friedrich Meisner. They have been created and have ceased to exist together with this novel about him.

A document that has been 'created' for the purposes of writing a piece of fiction and has 'ceased to exist' once the creative process has been completed may hardly be viewed as a document in the ordinary sense of the word, but the approach is characteristic of Enquist's evolving style of documentarism. In his next work, the use of documentary detail was to be taken a step further. In 1968, *The Legionnaires* appeared, which at the end of the decade received the prestigious Literary Award of the Nordic Council and is remembered to date as the major achievement of Scandinavian documentarism.

The documentary trend in fiction and drama that emerged in the late 1960s developed out of the political climate of the times. In Scandinavia, a number of works appeared in Sweden and Denmark and to a lesser extent Norway which drew on information culled from the fields of sociology, journalism and fiction that dealt with aspects of contemporary reality. The genre became known as 'documentarism' and differed from works in sociology and journalism in that it was more than merely investigative, containing dialogue, subjective commentary and descriptive narrative. Often the subject matter was concerned with topical issues.

The time of Scandinavian documentarism coincided with the New Left in Europe and campus radicalism in the United States. Unlike in Scandinavia, in America, journals with large circulations and sufficient funds, and publishers looking for new writing and willing to pay substantial advances, made possible the publication of works such as Truman Capote's *In Cold Blood* and Norman Mailer's *The Armies of the Night*. But while the United States gave birth to the New Journalism and the non-fiction novel, the social democracies of Scandinavia helped to develop political and radical documentary-writing. Still, the United States of the 1960s saw not only the radical chic of the New Yorker, but also the Civil Rights Movement.

In *The Legionnaires*, which appeared in 1968, Enquist lets
the protagonist referred to as 'the investigator' take the
American Civil Rights movement as his point of
departure. In 1966, returning from a Civil Rights
demonstration to the home of friends with whom he is
staying in Jackson, Mississippi, a young Swede is fazed by
the question, 'What do *you* know about the extradition of
the Balts?' Upon his return to Sweden, he decides to look
into the subject, the controversial decision to deport a
group of Estonian, Lithuanian and Latvian refugees in the
summer of 1945. The deportation followed the request
from the Soviet Embassy in Stockholm to hand over the
Baltic soldiers from the *Wehrmacht* to the Red Army. The
Swedish government responded accordingly and, seven
months later, the Baltic refugees were deported.

The research into the history of the event undertaken by
the 'investigator' reveals in brief that 40 of the 146 ex-
soldiers from the Nazi Army were eventually deported,
sentenced and subsequently served time in Soviet
prisons. None was executed and by the 1950s, all had
been released from prison. But, in addition to the
extensive historical research, throughout the book the
author probes the personal motives of the 'investigator'.
While wanting to take part in political demonstrations, at
the same time he ensures that he retains a safe distance.
Returning from an investigative journey from Latvia, he
reflects:

> I'll go on sitting here, not taking part. I'll sit here in
> the sun. All on my own. I'll talk myself into believing
> that I'll never understand. I won't ever understand
> anyway.

While *The Legionnaires* provides historical information
about a political process and, at the same time, is a fully
fledged novel, the subject matter of Enquist's next book
was the history of athletics, intertwined with that of the
Swedish Labour Movement. An accomplished high
jumper and a sports journalist, Enquist had easy access to

inside information for *The Second* which appeared in 1971. This is the tale of Mattias Jonsson, Swedish record-holder in hammer-throwing who was disqualified and had his name removed from the records after having been discovered using a hammer for his successful throws which was four hundred grams lighter than the stipulated weight. Again the author tells a documentary tale. In 1947, Erik Johansson, holder of the Swedish hammer-throw record, was disqualified and his name removed from the records, after having been found to be in possession of two hammers, one considerably lighter than the other. When caught and questioned, he is quoted as having offered the explanation that 'grand competitions require grand results', an answer echoed verbatim by the protagonist of *The Second*.

This account of the political history of the nineteenth century, as reflected in track and field events and in sports arenas, posits three different ideologies against each other: The Communist ideology in the then DDR, East Germany; the Fascist approach of Nazi Germany; and the Swedish model which for a brief period in the 1930s attempted to create a Workers Sports Party founded on the ideology and the values of the Labour Movement. But the parallel, central theme of the novel is the psychology of cheating, a subject as much under debate today as during the first half of the twentieth century. The real-life incident that Enquist describes took place during the 1940s, the true facts coming to light in the summer of 1947. The reactions in the press to this kind of duplicity then as well as now make for some interesting reading. First greeted as a hero, Enquist's hammer-thrower rapidly becomes an object of contempt after the discovery of the deceit. Sixteen years after Enquist's novel appeared, the Ben Johnson incident in Seoul elicited a similar reaction. Sports enthusiasts in the audience from all over the world felt cheated and betrayed, suddenly ashamed of their earlier enthusiasm and ovations.

The year after *The Second* saw yet another publication of a novel on the subject of sports. *The Cathedral in Munich* reports on the events of the Olympic Games of 1972. It was followed in 1978 by *The March of the Musicians,* an account of the early struggles of the Labour Movement in Enquist's native Västerbotten.

The documentary approach that characterises Enquist's work as a novelist emerges as an equally strong force in his plays. When, in 1975, he turned his attention to play-writing, he used as the protagonist for his first play the Swedish writer August Strindberg. In *The Night of the Tribades: A Play from 1889,* Enquist literally sets the stage in the Dagmar Theatre in Copenhagen. In preparation for a rehearsal of Strindberg's one-acter *The Stronger,* Siri von Essen is trying to tidy up in the small theatre when from amongst the shadows at the back of the theatre emerges August Strindberg, her estranged husband. A heated argument soon ensues, interrupted only temporarily by Siri's co-actress Marie David and Viggo Schive, the director of the play. As the rehearsal progresses or, more accurately, fails to progress due to Strindberg's frequent and intemperate interruptions, we learn about the play that Strindberg wrote as well as of past events in the interacting lives of Siri, Marie and August. According to Strindberg, his play *The Stronger* is about the struggle between two women over a man; the recollections of Siri and Marie, on the other hand, corroborate a reading in which it is the man who is desperately struggling to retain the attention of his wife, faced by the threat posed by another, free and independent woman. Thus, with the help of Siri, Marie and Strindberg, Enquist deconstructs *The Stronger,* only to put the pieces together again in new, different constellations, a method of reconstruction easily recognisable to readers familiar with his earlier works of fiction.

August Strindberg and his Finnish-born wife Siri von Essen first met the twenty-year-old Marie David in France, during their second visit to the artist colony in Grez-sur-Loing in 1885. Prior to this meeting, however, an event occurred that had deeply shaken the volatile, delicately balanced Swedish writer. The publication in 1884 of *Married* resulted in a trial for alleged blasphemy. Although legal proceedings against Strindberg were eventually dropped, shouldering the role of the hero of the revolutionary movement and foremost representative of Swedish radical thinking exacted its toll psychologically as well as financially. With the publication in 1886 of the second volume of *Married*, Swedish publishers started getting cold feet, and by the time of Enquist's fictitious meeting of the threesome of August Strindberg, Siri von Essen and Marie David in 1889, Strindberg had been forced to start his own theatre in Copenhagen in order for his plays not to fall victim to censorship. Compounding his problems was the growing sense of isolation resulting from living abroad, a factor also accounting for the plight of Siri von Essen. Living in permanently rented accommodation throughout Europe with her young children, she also felt her aspirations to work as an actress thwarted. Whatever the nature of her relationship with Marie David, given the situation in which she had long found herself, for Siri to have welcomed the company of the younger and independent woman with open arms was hardly surprising.

Changed to the shorter title *The Tribades*, the play opened at the Hampstead Theatre in north London on 8 May 1978 in the translation by Gunilla Anderman included in this volume. It was directed by Michael Rudman with a set designed by Sue Plummer and costumes by Lindy Hemming. Susan Hampshire played the role of Siri von Essen, Georgina Hale was Marie David and Peter Woodthorpe took the part of August Strindberg, with Richard Moore as Viggo Schive.

Following the success of *The Night of the Tribades*, which has been translated into more than twenty languages, Enquist was invited to further extend his research into the life and work of August Strindberg. The six-hour-long series about the Swedish writer, *Strindberg. A Life,* which Enquist was commissioned to write for Swedish television was several years in the making until eventually filmed in 1985. The role of August Strindberg was taken by Thommy Berggren, whose interpretation of the part stressed the stern aspect of the writer gleaned from Strindberg's own photographs, taken during the years that he lived in the university town of Lund in southern Sweden.

The Night of the Tribades is viewed by Enquist as forming part of a triptych. The remaining two plays are *To Phedra,* after Racine, and *From the Life of the Rain Snakes* about Hans Christian Andersen and the Heibergs, the Danish actress and director couple; all are chamber plays that deal with the subject of marriage gone dead and the ensuing struggle for power between the contestants. In 1981, together with *The Hour of the Lynx,* the three plays were published in Swedish in a joint volume.

While in *The Night of the Tribades,* Strindberg and his wife Siri von Essen confront each other, in *From the Life of the Rainsnakes,* it is Hans Christian Andersen, the well-known story-teller and the lauded Danish actress Johanne Louise 'Hanne' Heiberg that take centre stage and mercilessly strip each other of hidden secrets. *From the Land of the Rainsnakes,* which has been referred to as his favourite play by the writer himself, has been staged in translation into a number of different languages. It was also transmitted on Swedish television, directed by Enquist. The idea of the play came to the playwright after reading the autobiographies by Hanne Heiberg and Hans Christian Andersen. The actress and the story-teller did know each other but the meeting of the two is fictitious. Hanne, Jewish by birth, grew up under difficult circumstances during the early part of the nineteenth century and the life of the Danish story-teller was anything but idyllic. Far removed from Danny Kaye's cheerful portrayal, the real Hans Christian Andersen was deeply troubled as well as socially awkward. After a visit to the home of Charles Dickens in 1857, the exasperated family nailed a sign on the door of the guest bedroom: 'Hans Christian Andersen slept in this room for five weeks – which seemed to the family like AGES.'

From the Land of the Rain Snakes is set in the home of the artistic director of the Danish National Theatre, Johan Ludvig Heiberg, and his wife Hanne Heiberg. The drama opens in their solid middle-class drawing room where Hanne is seated at a desk, busy writing her memoirs. She is interrupted, first by her husband, then by Hans Christian Andersen, a friend of the family. While Herr Heiberg comes and goes, Hanne and Andersen talk and it is through these scenes that we learn about the lives of the two. For example, a passage that Hanne has written and reads out to Andersen tells of her childhood in the slums of Ny Ravnsborg in Nørregard in Copenhagen where she would dig up rain snakes or worms. She would then clean them, very carefully, even rinse them several times, to make sure that every little bit of dirt had been removed. Hanne and Andersen shared a common origin, not frequently found among the Danish literati, who, during Denmark's Golden Age, were more traditionally recruited from the ranks of the burghers and the clergy. Both grew up in the 'swamp', the term used by Andersen in *The Swamp King's Daughter* as well as in some of his other stories. As the story in *From the Life of the Rain Snakes* evolves, the past lives of the leading actress Hanne Heiberg and of the brilliant story-teller Hans Christian Andersen start taking shape and a tale emerges of social contrasts and the price paid for changing social class. Initially 'swamp plants', as they open up to the light and develop as artists, their social ascent remains unmatched by emotional growth: the price exacted for social mobility is the sacrifice of warmth for freezing cold and of life for living death.

Under the shortened title of *Rain Snakes*, the play ran at the Young Vic Studio in London from 26 June to 20 July

1996, presented by Nordlys Theatre Company in the translation by Kim Dambæk included in this volume. In the cast were Imogen Claire, Jason Morell, Robert David MacDonald and Sian Thomas, with the set by Kathy Strachan and lighting by Joe Lewis. The director was Kim Dambæk.

'The outsider' is also the subject of Enquist's novel *Fallen Angel*, 1985, the story of a family and their relationship with the boy killer of their child. At the same time, it also tells of the pain of divorce and telephone calls throbbing with speechless loathing between husband and wife. The discussion of the boy, his crime, guilt and search for redemption continues three years later in dramatic form in *The Hour of the Lynx*. The boy is now imprisoned for two criminal acts. This time the victims of his violence are the owners and inhabitants of his childhood home. In prison, he is the object of the attention of two women: a psychiatrist whose task it is to try to help him readjust to the outside world and a pastor whom she has called in to help further her rehabilitative work. The obstacle in the way of further progress, the psychiatrist feels, is the ruling of the prison governor to discontinue the part of the treatment of the boy that allows him to keep a cat as a pet, a decision taken following an incident of alleged misdemeanour. The claim that keeping the cat is to be considered a privilege to be earned is pitched against the view that it is granted by the grace of God. Redemption need not be deserved but is a human right, granted by an all-forgiving God. This is the belief of the cat himself, called Valle after the boy's beloved grandfather who is also, intermittently, addressed as God. For the boy's world to make sense to him, he has to put his belief in the view held by the cat. Hence the play tells of the twenty-fifth hour, outside the twenty-four hours of the night and the day, which, legend has it, belongs to the cat-like lynx. In 1990, *The Hour of the Lynx* was staged as part of the Edinburgh Fringe Festival in the translation by Kim Dambæk included in this volume. The play opened on

2 August at the Traverse Theatre with the part of the Boy
played by Simon Donald, the Pastor by Ann Scott Jones,
and Lisbeth, the psychiatrist, by Carol Ann Crawford. The
production, directed by Kim Dambæk, received a
Scotsman Fringe First Award. A year later, on 14 August
1991, the play was screened by BBC2. Again Simon
Donald took the part of the Boy but this time the Pastor
was played by Eleanor Bron, and Lisbeth by Sylvestra Le
Touzel. It was directed by Stuart Burge.

In his next novel, which appeared in 1991, P. O. Enquist
returned to the subject of his native Västerbotten, again
drawing on documentary material. *Captain Nemo's Library*
is based on the real-life story of two boys, at birth given to
the wrong biological mothers and then raised by them
until age three when one of the mothers started to
understand what must have happened. A lengthy legal
process ensued with the result that the two boys were
brought up in the same family and became brothers. This
allows Enquist's story to be told from the perspective of
two narrators. The first narrator has grown up in a green
house in Västerbotten with an early widowed mother, a
scenario with which we are now familiar. But this time the
narrator's childhood comes to an abrupt end at age six
when he is handed over to another family whose son,
Johannes, is allegedly his mother's child, while he is really
the son of Johannes' parents. This real-life incident is then
fitted into a framework drawn from the science fiction
novels by Jules Verne about the submarine Nautilus and its
captain with the thinly disguised name of Nemo, the Latin
for 'nobody'. As dedicated Jules Verne readers may recall,
this is a mysterious figure, one minute of a kind-hearted
disposition, the next transformed into a vicious killer. In
1993, *Captain Nemo's Library* and *The Cartographers,* which
appeared in 1992, brought Enquist the Eyvind Johnson
Prize, so called after the recipient of the Nobel Prize for
Literature in 1974 for having successfully combined, as
did the title holder of the prize, 'a cosmopolitan
perspective with childhood roots in northern Sweden'.

The subject of the nature of evil and the search for
redemption was one to which Enquist was to return. One
source of documentary information for his literary
dissection of this subject was the chain of events triggered
off on the night of 19 July 1984 in Stockholm which led
to one of the most widely publicised and prolonged legal
cases in Swedish criminal history. The finding of the
dismembered body of Catrine de Costa, a prostitute, led
to a police investigation, the findings of which seemed to
implicate two members of the medical profession. From
the initial arrest of one of the suspects on 3 December
1984, a complex turn of legal events resulted in a
continuation of court proceedings which lasted until 8
July 1988, when the Magistrates Court announced that
the two doctors were not guilty of murder but only of
dismembering the body of the dead woman, a crime now
amounting to double jeopardy and for which they could
no longer be put on trial.

In *Tupilak*, which opened in Stockholm and Copenhagen
in December 1993, Enquist draws on the murder of
Catrine de Costa, incorporating documentary details
from the case into his portrayal of a disintegrating
marriage. 'At the centre of the tragedy there is something
completely incomprehensible and frightening which we
will never be able to interpret' is a comment made early
in the play. It is this 'incomprehensible something' that
the playwright attempts to shed light on by giving it the
name 'tupilak', the symbol of evil. A tupilak is a talisman
of the Inuit people of Greenland. Fashioned from parts
of animal or human bodies, the magic amulet is used for
destructive purposes. It is the evil that sneaks into an
igloo where humans live but it is also the destructive
force in humans. 'Is it in you, in me or only in monsters?'
the author asks.

After Senja's husband, known only as The Man,
announces that he wants a divorce, she starts to receive
anonymous telephone calls. Finally a man appears at her
doorstep. She lets him in and gradually the extent of his

destructive personality is revealed; he turns out to be the
murder suspect in the dismembered body case. As Senja
discovers, the angst and fear that may erupt when the
emotional turmoil of a frozen human starts to 'thaw' can
also turn into violence, the force of which may be strong
enough to kill even the liberator. In this play, as in so
much of Enquist's writing, 'ice' and 'frozen' figure
prominently but here the ice cap rests more heavily on
the human soul than ever before, arguably making
Tupilak appear blacker than any of his earlier plays or
novels. In 1994, *Tupilak* was published in a volume, *Three
Plays*, together with *Maria Stuart*, Enquist's Swedish
version after Schiller and *Magic Circle*, a chamber play
about the Danish Communist Party leader, rumoured to
have sold out the Danish resistance movement to the
Gestapo in 1942. On 14 May 1997, a reading of *Tupilak*
took place at the Traverse Theatre in Edinburgh,
directed by Kim Dambæk and in an English translation
by Anna Paterson.

References to 'ice' and 'cold' and 'frozen' also appear in
the police records of another incident in Swedish
criminal history which shook the Swedish public as
profoundly as the case supplying the documentary
background to *Tupilak*. The event took place in the
summer of 1988 in the small village of Åmsele in
northern Sweden and provided Enquist with
documentary material for a script which, under the
direction of the Swedish director Jan Troell, was turned
into a film. In this film called *Il Capitano* Enquist makes
yet another attempt to arrive at a closer understanding of
the notion of 'evil'.

In July 1988, the Bonnie and Clyde team of Juhu
Valjakkala, known as Il Capitano and Marita Routa, his
loyal 'foot soldier', hid their car in the cemetery in
Åmsele, then set out on one of their customary thieving
expeditions in the neighbouring community. This time,
however, the expedition ended not only in theft (a
bicycle), but also in the murder of three innocent

members of a local family. Whilst Marita was freed, Juhu
was sentenced to life imprisonment. Press coverage of the
events related to the trial showed Juhu, who had been
receiving psychiatric treatment since the age of six,
willingly posing in front of the cameras and basking in
the attention that the case attracted. He showed, in the
words of one of the members of the police investigative
team 'very deep frost damage to the soul'.

In *Il Capitano*, crime, guilt and the search for redemption
and the means to thaw the frost and ice of the human
soul are recurring themes. So is isolation resulting from
the absence of human contact. This may be the fate, not
only of the sociopath, but also of the artist, the observer
of life, the recorder of human behaviour, doomed to
remain an unengaged, objective outsider. It may also turn
into a life sentence for two lonely members of a
dysfunctional marriage.

In the case of *Hamsun*, the film script that Enquist wrote
about the Norwegian writer and recipient of the 1920
Nobel Prize for Literature, the isolation appears to have
been complete on both accounts. The story of *Hamsun* is
concerned with the trial of the Norwegian writer, who,
together with his wife, was taken to court and charged
with treason at the end of the Second World War.
Looking back at the events that led to their ill-judged
actions, the film, again directed by Jan Troell, with Max
von Sydow as Hamsun and the Danish actress Ghita
Nørby as his wife Marie, starts when Knut Hamsun is
already 85 years old. But, at an age when he should have
been enjoying his position as the leading writer in
Norway, Hamsun is called to account for his support of
the German occupation of his homeland. Attempting to
find the underlying reasons for an artist to take such a
deplorable decision, the film examines a number of
possible causes. At the time, the legacy of Romanticism
was still making its presence felt in northern Europe. In
contrast to industrialism and British imperialism, a love
for unspoilt nature and the cradle of culture were seen as

more closely associated with pre-war Germany and its cultural and artistic achievements.

A further factor influencing Hamsun's decision, which is explored in the film, is the Norwegian writer's complicated relationship with his wife Marie who also became a Nazi sympathiser. This is powerfully illustrated at the very beginning of the film in the furious argument between the couple when Marie showers Hamsun with accusations: she was forced to abandon her career as an actress in order to look after her husband and their children, he would leave her alone for months with four young children to immerse himself in the writing of his books. The implication is that, as in the case of her husband, Nazism provided just the right antidote needed for Marie's usurped self-confidence; her thwarted ambitions as an actress and the 'sacrifices' as an artist that she saw herself as having made were at least partially compensated for by the Third Reich's ideology of the woman and mother as the centre of the family. Again, Enquist's theme of isolation and ensuing 'frost bites to the soul' recurs. Hamsun's emotional isolation, resulting from his troubled marital relationship and compounded by his deafness, is seen as a further step towards an act commonly associated with the notion of evil. In the case of Hamsun's wife, there is also a clear parallel with Hanne Heiberg in *From The Land of the Rain Snakes*. Here we have two actresses, one from the nineteenth and the other from the twentieth century, both entrapped by the power of strong men, artists who wanted to turn them into works of art but on their own terms. The result: both freeze and turn into ice queens.

The last play in the present volume, *The Image Makers*, opened at Dramaten, the Royal National Theatre, in Stockholm on 13 February 1998, directed by Ingmar Bergman. In an interview on the eve of the opening night, Bergman tells of receiving the script, described as a play about the creation of a play, only to realise that he had previously met or worked with all the characters appearing in Enquist's documentary material drawn from the silent film era.

The play describes the meeting between four Swedish artists: the writer and story-teller Selma Lagerlöf, recipient of the Nobel Prize for Literature in 1909, a part played in the Stockholm production by Anita Björk; the role of the legendary Swedish stage actress Tora Teje was taken by Elin Klinga; the actor and director Viktor Sjöström, who starred in Bergman's film *Wild Strawberries*, was played by Lennart Hjulström; the fourth role, that of Julius Jaenzon, who pre-dated Sven Nykvist as a pioneer in cinematography, introducing a style of lighting that combined elements of artificial and natural light, was taken by Carl Magnus Dellow.

In his introduction to the 1998 published version of *The Image Makers*, Enquist tells of the meeting between author and director to discuss the film script, prior to the start of filming Selma Lagerlöf's *The Coachman* – the classic novel about the spiritual salvation of David Holm, the Coachman of Death condemned to collecting lost souls for their final destination. Having travelled to Mårbacka, the author's home, Victor Sjöström spent one long afternoon reciting from his script, covering in detail all the 605 scenes of the film that was to be viewed as one of the most remarkable films in cinematic history and the zenith of the era of silent film. Upon completion, the director waited in eager anticipation for comments from the author about his attempt to dramatise her novel. Finally, following a prolonged silence, Selma Lagerlöf spoke: 'Perhaps you'd like a drink,' she asked. True to form, the play that Enquist wrote is his own interpretation of what could be read into that silence, weaving it into the fabric of a story based on information painstakingly culled from available documentary evidence. The English translation of the play included in this volume is by Charlotte Barslund and Kim Dambæk.

More recently, Enquist has returned to the novel. In 2001, his latest book, *Lewi's Journey*, appeared, charting the Swedish Pentecostal movement as its early pioneering spirit turned into firmly cemented dogmatism, and dealing with the rivalry between the two towering figures of Sven Lidman and Lewi Pethrus (to whose American journey in 1941, while war raged in Europe, the book owes its name). But in 1999, prior to *Lewi's Journey*, another novel by Enquist appeared. In *The Visit of the Royal Physician*, now attracting wide international attention since its appearance in translation into a number of different languages, the focus is on the opposition to the Enlightenment from a wider European, rather than exclusively Swedish, perspective. Awarded the prestigious Swedish August Prize, elected the best foreign fiction work by French publishers in 2001, and winner of the Independent Foreign Fiction Prize in 2003, *The Visit of the Royal Physician* is an historical novel. It is set in the 1760s and the sister of George III is married off into the Danish royal family. Shackled to the young troubled King Christian, Caroline Mathilde has an affair with Struensee, the court doctor who has been called in as a trusted advisor to the king. It is the height of the Enlightenment and Guldberg, a manipulative religious fanatic, is determined to undermine the radical ideas that Struensee is attempting to introduce into Denmark. Into a dramatic era in the history of Denmark, Enquist then weaves a wide range of prominent European characters of the period including Voltaire, Diderot, Goethe, Catherine the Great and George III. 'Fierce, direct, imbued with wintry, windswept poetry' according to the *Independent*, Enquist tells his documentary tale of political intrigue and ambition and, as always, of personal betrayal – although this time in translation into more languages and to a wider readership than probably ever before in his writing career.

Gunilla Anderman
Guildford, August 2003

The Night of the Tribades

by

Per Olov Enquist

translated by

Gunilla Anderman

This translation of *The Tribades* opened at the Hampstead Theatre, London, on 8 May 1978. The cast was as follows:

Siri von Essen-Strindberg   Susan Hampshire
August Strindberg   Peter Woodthorpe
Viggo Schiwe   Richard Moore
Marie Caroline David   David Georgina Hale

Director Michael Rudman
Designer Sue Plummer
Costumes Lindy Hemming

Act One

As lights go off, the music starts, late 1880s, heavy but not overpowering. It grows slowly in strength and intensity until it fills the room. The curtains remain closed.

Against the closed curtain slides begin to appear. First they show faces, the faces of nineteenth-century men. Although masculine in the traditional sense, nineteenth-century man looks modern, a purposeful look in his eyes. There are men in uniform, men with firmly set jaws, men looking to the future.

The pictures change to show men in action. There are men on horseback, on hunting expeditions, men who tighten their calf muscles as they are immortalised for posterity. Men who kill, who invent machines and operate them. Men who laugh because they've just had some good news, men who drink, who mount women.

More pictures of men but now giving detailed, specific information. A foot with exact measurements, an arm, cross-section of a muscle with bared nerve fibres. A torso, seen from the front, then from the side. A reclining penis (in a large scale, detailed drawing bearing a striking resemblance to a ship), again with exact measurements. An engine, a rifle, a spade, a locomotive. Suddenly pictures of animals: lions, dogs and elephants. Natives with bulging muscles, a savage, a spear. And then more faces, more faces of nineteenth-century men. The last face is that of **August Strindberg**. *He looks like a young girl. He looks frightened.*

The music reaches a crescendo. The curtain rises and very gently, the music fades away and the lights go on.

Slowly, almost sluggishly, the stage emerges from out of darkness; it gives the impression of being cluttered.

Despite the stacks of beer crates to the right, it is quite clear that we are in a theatre. From the set and props scattered all over the stage, it appears that the most recent play performed at this

*theatre, the Dagmar Theatre in Copenhagen, was some exotic
adventure story. Two badly drawn, fierce-looking cardboard lions.
An elephant. Six roughly drawn natives with raised spears,
perhaps cannibals on some South Pacific island. Against the wall
a ladder. Old, dismounted posters advertise past performances.
Two potted palms. A somewhat scattered and unlived-in but
typically upper middle-class interior – a mahogany writing desk,
some chairs, a writing pulpit, some photographs of the Royal
Family. An enormous bed with a bulging, red eiderdown. For no
apparent reason, a chamber pot, two wash basins and a water
pitcher have been left resting on the bed.*

*The woman is tall, slightly angular, with her blonde hair pinned
up in a bun. She is tidying up, energetically but unsystematically.
She tries to pull the heavy double bed to the side but finds that she
is unable to move it. She removes the chamber pot and the wash
basins from the bed and tries again. She still can't move it.*

Siri *swears primly in a language that resembles Finnish, tries
again but has to give up. She stands there, looking at the bed.*

Siri   What the *vossiha rata* . . . all the bloody *ruppido allat
minnä* . . . *terve sakussat* . . . *umekassat* . . . (*Stops, out of
breath.*) *perkele usti nakasat* . . .

Strindberg (*in shabby-looking clothes steals in and listens
with mounting delight*)   I heard you. Not very nice,
swearing in Finnish.

Siri (*taken by surprise, is embarrassed, but also irritated*)
Good God, you frightened me. Don't try to pretend you
know Finnish.

Strindberg (*encircles her courteously while examining her
critically*)   You were swearing in Finnish! Here we have
the new artistic director of the new Strindberg Theatre in
Copenhagen . . . a charming lady . . . and what does she
do . . . she carts around chamber pots and swears in
Finnish . . . I see. Well, when is the rehearsal due to start?

Siri (*has now regained her composure*)   Little August! The
great man himself is honouring the Dagmar Theatre with

a personal appearance! Who would've thought it . . . and he even deigns to speak to me! I don't believe my ears.

Strindberg   Your eyes.

Siri   What do you mean?

Strindberg   Your eyes! You don't believe your eyes. Not ears! You see with your eyes, you hear with you ears. You're getting careless with your language again. Not very good for your career, you know. Nor does it help you to become financially independent.

Siri (*very formal*)   Half an hour ago.

Strindberg   Half an hour ago?

Siri   Perhaps I didn't hear you right . . . but I'm sure I did . . . (*Searches her memory.*) . . . Didn't I hear you ask . . . when's the rehearsal due to start? I'm positive I did. And that's the answer to your question: it was due to start half an hour ago.

Strindberg (*slightly off balance*)   Well. Well? (*Regains his composure.*) But there's no one here . . .

Siri (*amicably*)   Very astute!

Strindberg   Well?

Siri   We're starting an hour late today. Remember you sent us that little scrap of paper telling us you wanted to attend tonight's rehearsal. That's why we had to change the time. We always try to accommodate.

Strindberg (*glares with suspicion at the pile of beer crates*) Did you drink all that?

Siri   Are you serious?

Strindberg   What the hell are they doing here then? Must be more than ten crates . . . and I know how much you can drink . . . Odd that they've found their way in here, wouldn't you say?

Siri   Not at all, my dear. When there's nothing on, a

brewery uses the theatre to store beer crates. And I'm afraid there hasn't been much on lately. But they'll be gone before long, we can't let them be in the way when we're doing Strindberg, can we?

Strindberg (*restless and worried*)   All right, all right. So when are they coming?

Siri   No idea! But don't worry, they'll be removed.

Strindberg   The actors!! The cast, of course!! You are rehearsing tonight, aren't you?

Siri   They should be here any minute.

Strindberg (*suddenly anxious and worried*)   Listen, Siri, I'd like to talk to you about something before they come . . . It's . . . it's a private matter . . . just between us . . . it's wrong to involve outsiders in family matters . . . A very important principle, I think. (*With some vehemence.*) Something that I feel very strongly about.

Siri   You surprise me.

Strindberg   What do you mean?

Siri   Isn't that how you make a living? By putting our personal problems down on paper and then publishing it, making sure it's known to everyone who's able to read . . .

Strindberg (*roars*)   But that's art! That's literature!!

Siri   Oh, I see, that's art, is it . . . I beg your pardon.

Strindberg   You remember Hansen. I've heard that . . . that case is coming up again. You know, that drunken lout who wanted to kill me just because I got the police on to him. I've heard he's after me, that he's trying to bring up the case again . . . all that about Martha. You know. He won't give up. The whole thing's distasteful.

Siri   I couldn't agree more.

Strindberg   I must talk to you . . .

Siri   I'm delighted.

Strindberg Delighted?

Siri (*exaggeratedly humbly and politely*)   Yes, as I shan't be your lawfully wedded wife much longer, I'm delighted you're still talking to me. Unlike last week in the hotel dining-room . . . you were having dinner with some adoring, sickly-looking fan, if my memory doesn't fail me.

Strindberg My Danish translator!!!

Siri The way he swallowed every word from your lips, I'm sure it couldn't have been good for his digestion. But please accept my humble apologies, I'm terribly sorry I went into the dining-room without permission, that I took the liberty of speaking without being spoken to. You could've wished me good evening, you know, instead of just glaring at me. Christ, you made me feel like a leper. Or a pair of discarded knickers.

Strindberg (*sadly*)   You're using bad language again.

Siri I felt like a *sakutumusset satanas koisternusset valmit markussat*. Something that you with your limited linguistic talent should think long and hard about.

Strindberg (*suspiciously*)   That's not Finnish! You were far too *refined* to learn Finnish. Ladies of noble birth speaking Finnish! Since when?

Siri Like a pair of discarded knickers then!

Strindberg (*with great authority, circles around her, hands behind his back, his eyes fixed on the ceiling*)   Everyone knows that I've disowned you. Everyone knows that I was forced to take action because of all your little slips and indiscretions. And they are perfectly right. I had to. I had to disown you, that's a fact. You're no longer my wife. We can live together. (*With increasing dignity and conviction.*) You can be my mistress. But I have, nevertheless, disowned you. I shall not be seen in public with you. Our relationship is a business arrangement, nothing more. The theatre and the children. That's all.

Siri (*taken aback and amused*)   Good God . . . you're
filled with good news today.

Strindberg   But you are the director of the Strindberg
Theatre in Copenhagen . . . which I founded and to
which I appointed you . . . and therefore I insist . . . a very
modest and reasonable request, I would've thought . . .
that times are kept. Rehearsals must start and finish.
Accounts must be kept. It's hard work, you know, if one
wants to be independent *and* support oneself.

Siri   Anyway, as far as the Martha affair is concerned,
you need not worry.

Strindberg (*nervously*)   What? How d'you know? What
have you heard?

Siri   I mean, what did you expect? First you get that
little tart – under-age probably – into bed. Very nice.
Then you start getting all worked up about her swarthy-
looking older brother. So you report him for theft to the
police. On *very* flimsy evidence. The police come to get
him and throw him in jail. Strindberg's happy and
relieved. But then they find there's no evidence
whatsoever and, after a week inside, the brother's out
again. Livid, of course . . . false accusation . . .

Strindberg (*very distinctly*)   I enjoyed complete . . .
complete . . . legal protection. The girl was *not* under-age.
And she acted out of her own free will. And besides, the
brother's a gipsy!

Siri   Fine. Good. Anyway, he gets out of prison and he's
fuming. And he wants to kill you. And then one evening
he hits the bottle again and tries to get into our
bedroom, screaming and shouting and banging on the
wall with a hammer. Whereupon you, like the hero you
are, vanish into thin air and I'm left to look after a legless
gipsy, his disgraced sister and the whole bloody mess and
to try to stop it all from ending up in court.

Strindberg (*quietly*)   I suffer from claustrophobia, you know that. I can't . . . I can't even think of being in an enclosed room. Every time I think of . . . a cell . . . I die a little. (*Roars.*) And you realised, you scheming little cow, didn't you, that you wouldn't get any more money out of me if they put me away!

Siri   I couldn't care less about you and that girl. That's a matter of supreme indifference to me. I'm not jealous. Did I tell you I talked to the lawyer? More than once. The case has been written off.

Strindberg   You're sure?

Siri   I'm positive, my dear little August.

Strindberg (*sits down, stares vacantly into space*)   Yes. Yes, yes, yes. You're so terribly . . . you're so strong. Yes, yes. You are strong. (*Pause.*) Thank you very much. The way you handled that . . . you're so strong. It was . . . shabby. It was really shabby. I was so frightened. Terribly frightened.

Siri   Why didn't you write about *that* then? Instead of all that libelous nonsense about gipsies you wrote in Tschandala.

Strindberg (*erupts*)   Why?! Why didn't I tell them the truth? Why didn't I tell them I was frightened? That I was scared stiff?! That I ran away?! And that I didn't want to sleep with that silly slut in the first place! Because they would've thought I'd behaved like an old woman and (*Very calmly and matter-of-fact.*) not like a man.

Siri   Oh dear. Oh dear. I see.

Strindberg (*quietly*)And then of course, my study of the female psyche has greatly strengthened my interest in criminal psychology. There's that side to woman's nature too, of course. A side of her that hasn't been sufficiently studied.

Siri (*gives him a long look*)   You'll soon get a chance to study it a bit more. One of those criminals should be here any minute now.

Strindberg (*panic-stricken*)   What? Who? You mean he's coming here . . .

Siri (*angelically*)   No . . . I was referring to the other actress . . . a woman with the criminal psyche that you're so keen to study.

Strindberg (*stiffly*)   Not funny. In rather poor taste, in fact.

Viggo Schiwe *makes an elegant entry, throws off his raincoat, takes a graceful step, opens his arms in an embrace towards* **Siri**, *gives a charming smile.*

Schiwe   Mrs Essen-Strindberg! The enchanting director of the Dagmar Theatre! Late to bed, early to rise! A delicate flower in the lush garden of the theatre! Siri! (*Starts towards* **Siri**, *arms opening in an embrace, is stopped by her warning glance.*) Yes?

Sees **Strindberg** *and hesitates, starts towards him, arms still wide open, stops, hands moving sheepishly in the air.*

Strindberg (*icily*)   And who the hell is this?

Siri   I don't think you've met. Let me introduce you . . . this is August Strindberg . . . and this . . .

Schiwe (*undaunted, makes a fresh start, effusive and grandiose*)   Mr Strindberg! I can't believe my eyes! Mr Strindberg in person! Yes! I ask humbly . . . May I introduce myself, I'm honoured to make your acquaintance (*With increasing formality, a touch of ceremonial speech.*) . . . to make the acquaintance of the greatest poet of our generation – from your pen flow words of truth, wisdom and courage, words that burn their way, like flames, into our hearts . . . if I may put it that way. How I have admired and loved you at a distance. And now we have the honour of receiving you as our guest in Copenhagen, an historical occasion for the Dagmar Theatre . . .

Strindberg (*stiffly but flattered*)   Very kind. Thank you. Thank you.

Schiwe (*now completely wrapped up in his grandiose speech*) If only I could give you a token of my affection! If only I could give you my heart! If only I could find the words to describe . . . if only I could give you . . .

Strindberg   Cash.

Schiwe   What?

Strindberg   Cash. If you want to give me something, I'll take cash.

Schiwe   Yes?

Strindberg   I'm broke. I need cash. However modest the amount, it would be very welcome.

Siri (*hurriedly*)   And this is Mr Schiwe, Viggo Schiwe. Mr Schiwe is a very well-known actor, I'm sure you've heard of him. Mr Schiwe did Jean in *Miss Julie* and has kindly agreed to be our director . . .

Schiwe   Your most devoted admirer!

Strindberg   Well! Well! (*Sourly.*) I've heard of you.

Schiwe (*inordinately flattered*)   You've heard of me? Is that really true? You, Mr Strindberg!? I never would've . . . But yes! Yes! I've met people who consider me to be one of the leading actors in this country. (*Musing.*) . . . *The* leading actor even . . . but you, Mr Strindberg, I never . . .

Strindberg (*coldly*)   People talk. About you and Siri.

Schiwe (*with less assurance*)   People talk, Mr Strindberg . . .

Strindberg   Siri and I have separated, you're right there. But you're wrong if you think she needs a new playmate! Hands off!! Do not touch!! This is a theatre, not a brothel! And after you've grasped that simple fact, I suggest you turn your energy to another, equally demanding task – keep your mouth shut!

Schiwe (*agitated*)   Mr Strindberg! (*From the diaphragm.*) I feel nothing but respect for Mrs Essen-Strindberg, nothing but the most profound respect and admiration . . .

Strindberg (*roars*)   Good! And don't ever try and feel anything else!

Schiwe (*frightened and quickly ingratiating*)   . . . and I shall of course never ever try and feel anything else . . .

Strindberg   And *Miss Julie* . . . nothing surprises me any more.

Schiwe   Surprise you?

Strindberg   That it was stopped, I mean.

Schiwe (*dreamingly*)   Jean . . . What a beautiful part . . . I came to love that part. I felt there was a depth, a purpose that . . .

Strindberg   An old woman by the name of Meyer, clerk to the High Court of Justice, found it blasphemous and stopped it. We could probably get it through the censor if we cut the text. It would make a mess of the whole play but so what, we're doing it for the money. The problem is we haven't got the time. So we have to do something else. *The Stronger. Pariah.*

Schiwe   Any cuts in that play would be a violation . . . a crime . . .

Strindberg   Mr Schiwe! I'm a maintenance machine! I have to support parasitical women and minors! The ladies crave blood and money. I have to keep churning out plays. I can't, I regret to say, young man, afford your sentimental view of my work!

Siri (*gently*)   But they are still immortal works of art, aren't they?

Strindberg   They certainly are! In spite of it all!

Marie David *enters quietly, almost imperceptibly, stops and listens. She is about twenty-five years old, short red hair, a soft round face.* **Strindberg** *is the first to notice her. He stiffens, as*

if struck by lightning. He takes a step towards her, then stops.
Complete silence. **Schiwe** *is perplexed,* **Siri** *looks frightened.*
Marie *looks at* **Strindberg***, tense but calm and in control.*

Marie David   I'm sorry, I know I'm late.

Strindberg (*swivels round, walks agitatedly up to* **Siri**)
And what does this mean?

Siri   I thought you knew.

Strindberg   I knew what?

Siri   There's a non-speaking part in *The Stronger*. Marie
kindly agreed to do it for us.

Strindberg (*slowly, in a low voice to* **Siri**)   I see. Your little
girlfriend has returned.

Siri   So it would seem.

Strindberg (*musing*)   That repulsive, little Danish
lesbian. Well . . . I obviously should've killed her off there
and then in Grez three years ago. It wasn't enough, just
kicking her out.

Siri (*quietly*)   I am free now, you have to accept that.

Strindberg   Was it . . . was it your suggestion?

Siri   That's none of your business.

Strindberg   Isn't it?

Siri   None of your business.

Schiwe   It's true that Miss David's only got limited
acting experience . . . but she has shown evidence of such
a . . . such a wide-ranging, genuine and pleasing register
of expression that I'm sure . . .

Strindberg   Do you *know* Miss David?

Schiwe   Not very well but she's such a charming . . .

Strindberg   I see. You *don't* know her. (*Pause.*) But I do.

Schiwe   The two of you have . . . you've met before?

Strindberg   Unfortunately, yes. A year ago there was a rumour that she had drunk herself to death. Much to my regret, I can see now that it wasn't true.

Schiwe   But Mr Strindberg . . .

Strindberg   (*vehemently, with a threatening glare at* **Schiwe**) Mr Schiwe, anyone who nibbles at my wife will incur my displeasure! Do I make myself understood!?

Marie David   I'm here now, that's a fact. I haven't forgotten what happened but we've got to move on. Why don't we all try and be reasonable about it.

Strindberg *comes to life, walks up to a chair, picks it up, slams it violently against the floor, stares at* **Marie**, *points at the seat of the chair with a finger trembling with fury.*

Strindberg   Here! Right here! During the next few hours Miss David will sit right here. (*Continues to point at the chair with increasing agitation.*) And she will keep her mouth shut! The new play we're about to rehearse – an almost certain disaster if it ever opens – is my own one-act play, *The Stronger*. For the benefit of imbeciles and philistines (*Long look at* **Schiwe**.) I would like to provide the additional information that this *excellent* (*Looks around threateningly, no one dares object.*) that this *excellent* little play has two parts, one of which is silent! Whoever plays that part must not speak! The person in question must remain quiet! Silent! Dumb! 'D' as in dyke, 'u' as in useless, 'm' as in man-hater and 'b' as in bitch. Dumb! And she will sit right here. In complete silence!

Marie David   (*shakes her head resignedly, smiles, sits down on the chair*)   Siri my dear friend, the things I do for you.

Strindberg   (*still pointing, impassioned*)   She will sit right here! And she will exercise the utmost strength of will in a supreme effort to keep her mouth shut for as long as physically possible!

Marie David   (*with friendly interest*)   Mr Strindberg, what have they done to you? When I first met you in Grez, you were so nice and gentle. I don't think I'd ever met anyone as gentle, sensitive, compassionate and . . .

Strindberg (*in an effort to keep calm*)   Listen to her, listen to what she's saying to my face, listen to what I have to put up with . . .

Marie David   . . . I mean vulnerable but yet . . .

Strindberg (*icily*)   The chamberpot, Mr Schiwe, the shit's starting to fly.

Marie David   Why these exceedingly . . . virile . . . eruptions? As if you feel you have to . . . as if you feel you have to or you wouldn't be a man . . .

Siri   Can't you at least try to be civil to Marie. It's all in the past and we did live together in Grez for almost a year. As close friends.

Schiwe (*acutely embarrassed*)   Perhaps I should leave you alone for a minute . . .

Strindberg   As you please. If it causes you distress, by all means feel free to leave. You can always come back when you think it's going to be less painful.

Schiwe   For a brief moment perhaps . . . (*Balances on tiptoe, teetering with indecision, but stays.*)

Strindberg   Although that doesn't seem to happen very often. Just remembering . . . (*Lapses into silence.*) . . . is painful. The departure of the little tribade, how clearly I remember it. Marie Caroline David. Marie Caroline David. Siri as the Queen of the Night. And her as the Queen of the Tribades. I never thought they would meet again. Not after the night of the tribades in Grez.

Schiwe   What night did you say . . . (*Lapses into embarrassed silence.*)

Strindberg (*musing, looks at* **Marie**)   Marie Caroline David.

Siri (*very cheerfully*)   Now, let's get on with it. Come on, let's get down to some work, we've wasted enough time already. All these years I've been waiting to get back to work, there's nothing stopping me now! Let's get on with it! We'll all be nice to each other and August, you'll sit down and watch, like a good little boy, and we'll show you how far we've got.

Schiwe (*relieved*)   Is it *really* that long ago, Mrs Essen-Strindberg? You mean, you've been away from the theatre all these years? What a shame! What a blow you dealt, to the arts and the theatre, when you decided to retire . . .

Strindberg (*acidly*)   The theatre managed to survive remarkably well as far as I can see. And the arts don't seem to be doing too badly either. But she did marry me to make a career, that's true. I was a fool, I was in love with her. She was in love with her career. Simple as that. A delightful woman.

Siri   Rewriting history again, are we! God, you make me livid. You might add, August, my dear friend, that from the start of that marriage I slaved as your scullery maid like a cow for seven lean years. That's what you call my career. Thanks but no thanks.

Strindberg (*delighted*)   That's right. I turned the tables on you!

Marie David   You know, you must've been arguing about this for the last seven years, at least eight times a week. Couldn't you try and think up something a bit more original . . . something new to argue about?

Siri   A new life, that's all I need and I'm sure I can think of something.

Marie David   But what's the point? You're just going over . . .

Strindberg (*sadly, pointing to* **Marie**)   She keeps forgetting. She's not supposed to say anything. Look here, right here, the very first page. That's what it says.

But I can still hear her. I'm afraid, that sooner or later, this will become a matter of controversy.

Schiwe   Quite so . . . it's the face and the body . . . we mustn't forget that this silent part must make use of the face and the body . . . every line of the face can be used to express a range of emotions, pleading, fleeting . . . yet sincere feelings . . . and the hands too can be used to convey an intensity of feeling . . . and the eyes . . . opened wide, they spell fear . . .

Strindberg   (*looks at him with an expression of undisguised distaste*)   Siri, my beloved ex-wife, you're a charming girl, but you show the most extraordinary lack of judgement in your choice of lovers. Just look at this . . . sincere . . . toad. Extraordinary lack of judgement. Commercial travellers and infantile army officers on Baltic crossings and asinine second-rate actors and lesbian ladies in Copenhagen. Will you ever choose someone I can respect!

Siri   (*with rancour*)   I would like to make it perfectly clear, that the relationship between Mr Schiwe and myself has always been strictly professional.

Strindberg   (*musing*)   I sometimes think you . . . quite intentionally . . . tried to hurt me . . . huniliate me . . . by *never* choosing someone that I could respect. *Never ever.*

Siri   Good God, quite a motley crew I seem to have worked my way through.

Schiwe   (*has been working himself up, now explodes*)   I demand an apology! This is going too far! I demand an explanation and an apology! Mr Strindberg, you called me 'a toad'!

Strindberg   (*with surprise*)   Oh no, I didn't, you got it all wrong. A 'sincere toad', I said. I'm sure I did.

Schiwe   (*confused*)   You did?

Strindberg   Yes, I remember it quite distinctly. Ask the ladies.

Siri   Yes, he did.

Strindberg   You see!!

Schiwe   Oh. I see. (*Thinks hard.*)   I . . . I still demand an apology.

Strindberg   But of course. I understand. (*All sweetness.*) I apologise, Mr Schiwe. It was silly of me. (*Puts his arms around his shoulders matily, walks slowly across the stage.*) Mr Schiwe, you are my friend. We must stick together. I can think of a number of people who might find cause to criticise you . . . who might find you a bit thick . . . very thick . . . incredibly thick, in fact. But not me, definitely not me. This is what I'd say – it doesn't matter because you are a man! In this battle, we're on the same side. We must stand united in the battle against the ladies.

Marie David   Now, what's it going to be? A battle against the ladies or a rehearsal? Are we rehearsing tonight or are we not?

Schiwe   She's quite right, we really must . . .

Siri   Yes! Top of page one, will you all sit down please and don't behave like . . .

Strindberg   . . . like ladies . . .

Siri   Top of page one, please.

Strindberg   This little one-act play (*With increasing energy and excitation.*) which at long last is about to have its world premiere is a shattering account of the confrontation between two wenches. They're in love with the same man. They fight over him. The man is not present but nevertheless, he dominates the stage in his absence. As is so often the case. Eventually one of the ladies triumphs and returns to the man. A very simple set. A corner of a ladies' coffee-room. Two little iron tables, a red velvet-covered sofa and a couple of chairs. Siri enters . . . correction, Mrs X enters. She is dressed in winter clothes . . . hat and coat and she is carrying an elegant

Japanese basket. At one of the tables sits . . . let's call her
Madame Y. Now, I had thought of her as a rather
(*Delighted, walks around in happy little circles.*) *repulsive*
woman, red-haired and flabby, hooked nose . . . (*Retracts
after warning glances from* **Siri**.) Anyway! She is sitting at
the table with a half-empty bottle of beer, reading a
woman's magazine. Perfect. Excellent vignette! Her two
favourite occupations! Extremely well captured! The beer
bottle in particular (*Musing.*) . . . quite extraordinary, the
amount of beer . . . must've been twenty beers a day . . .
and frequently more if I remember correctly and my
memory is usually very reliable . . .

Siri   August . . .

Strindberg (*happily*)   As I was saying. Miss David sits
there in silence, with a woman's magazine, drinking beer.
The moment she finishes one, she starts on another –
another magazine, I mean, of course.

Schiwe (*annoyed, feels he is being ignored*)   Some stage
directions perhaps at this point . . . sincere although with
obvious signs of hidden tension . . . unassuming and
relaxed monologue . . . warmth and . . .

Strindberg   Begin!

Schiwe   And Miss David, a calm but feeling expression
would seem most appropriate during the first few . . .

Strindberg   Enough bloody talk. Begin! Begin!

Siri (*braces herself*)   'How are you Amelie, dear? It makes
me so sad to see you sitting here all alone on Christmas
Eve, no cosy little home and family waiting for you.'

Marie David *looks up from the paper, nods and continues to
read.*

'You know, it really hurts me to see you here; alone, all
alone in a café and on Christmas Eve. It hurts me as
much as that time in Paris, when I saw a wedding party in
a restaurant where the bride was reading a magazine

while the bridegroom played billiards with the witnesses. Oh dear, I thought, not a very good start! Playing billiards on his own wedding night! – You mean, she wasn't much better, reading a magazine? Well, that's different, I think.'

Strindberg (*chuckling*)   It certainly is . . . a damned sight worse. At this point, the dipsomaniac continues to guzzle her beer while a waitress brings a cup of hot chocolate for the other lady. Mr Schiwe, with your experience as Jean from *Miss Julie*, perhaps we could use your mastery of *servility* for this part today. Just pretend you're setting out a cup. (*Benignly.*) Intense concentration, now, Mr Schiwe, calm and sincere gestures, pleading and expressive!

Schiwe (*with dawning realisation*)   That could be interpreted as sarcasm, Mr Strindberg.

Strindberg   Correct, Mr Schiwe, correct! (*Now cheerfully on the offensive.*) Oh, Miss David, by the way, I'd better warn you that the day we open, it won't be a man bringing the chocolate. Instead there'll be a pretty little girl! That's important to remember, Miss David, we don't want your passions to run riot! Hands off the girl! Don't touch her up! Leave her breasts alone! No endearments! No passionate glances! That just wouldn't be consistent with the logical structure of the play.

Marie David (*quietly through clenched teeth*)   That's enough, Mr Strindberg. There are limits. That was cheap and unworthy of you. I'm not going to put up with it.

Strindberg (*delighted*)   I've offended you! You're going to walk out in a rage! And never come back!! Are you really!!?

Siri (*lets the manuscript drop to the floor in a gesture of despair*)   Oh yes. I knew it. It's so typical. Now, when I've finally got the chance to work again. In my profession. First time in years. Then he sabotages it. No qualms whatsoever, that's him.

Strindberg   What? What? What have I done?

Marie David   Siri, you're not surprised, are you?

Siri   I s'pose not. But it upsets me just as much every time it happens.

Strindberg (*slightly worried, walks guiltily around* **Schiwe**) I find it very difficult to work with women. They never stick to the point and the slightest excuse and they'll take things personally. Never able to be objective. You are a man. You know what I mean. (*Roars.*) You know what I mean!

Schiwe (*startled and nervous*)   Of course, I know . . . (*Trying to find a way out.*) Perhaps a different acting style at this point . . . more warmth . . . more expressive body movements . . .

Siri   Marie. Please, Marie.

Strindberg   Middle of page two. Waitress leaves and does not return. The vivisection continues. Start, please. Mrs X, Siri, you're on.

Siri   I would like to play this part. I've been waiting so long for this chance to get back to work. I'd very much like to see if I could do this.

Strindberg (*almost apologetically*)   Middle of page two . . .

Marie David *walks quietly up to the chair, gives* **Strindberg** *a long look, sits down.*

(*To* **Schiwe**.) See what I mean. Another uncalled for interruption. Good thing I remained calm and in control.

Siri   'You know, Amelie, I'm beginning to think it would've been better if you had stayed with your fiancé. I told you to forgive him, remember? You could've been married now with a home of your own. Do you remember last Christmas, how happy you were when you visited his parents in the country . . . '

Schiwe　Here, Miss David, perhaps I may suggest that an expression of *pain* passes over your face . . .

Strindberg　Can one just go on helping oneself to beer like that? It's like stealing, isn't it? Some black coffee on the other hand wouldn't be a bad idea. Real coffee, not the stuff they used to serve up in Grez. (*Paternally.*) And Mr Schiwe, enough of this nonsense. Expression of pain! Quite absurd and inaccurate! Miss . . . Miss Y once had a fiancé', that's true. Poor bugger, he couldn't have had an easy time of it. But once he managed to get out of the trap, they're both free. And don't for a minute think she feels any pain! She's happy! That's her nature.

Schiwe (*confused*)　But according to the script, she's supposed to . . .

Siri　This is unbelievable!

Strindberg　For this lady, there is no greater pleasure than seeing the number of men on this earth decline. (*Conspiratorially to* **Schiwe**.) When she's depressed, all she needs is to take a stroll to the cemetery. Just seeing the gravestones of dead men puts her in a good mood again. The names of men. The names of dead enemies . . . We must face facts, Mr Schiwe . . . Such is the calibre of our opposition!

Schiwe　But . . . the script . . . you're very difficult to . . . (*Anxiously.*) You're joking, Mr Strindberg?

Marie David　What's it going to be? Is it my life we're discussing? Or this play and this woman who's quite a different person. According to the script anyway.

Strindberg (*wistfully*)　I would love a cup of black coffee. Perhaps . . . I wonder, Mr Schiwe . . . having played Jean, in *Miss Julie* . . . you must . . .

Schiwe (*exasperated*)　. . . now have mastered the art of servility, I know, yes, I'll see what I can do. You know, we've been at it nearly an hour now. If we continue like this we'll still be here tomorrow morning.

Siri   Before I have a nervous breakdown, can we agree what this play's all about? This is how I read the script. Two women haven't seen each other for a long time. They meet again. At one time they were both in love with the same man. There's a confrontation. The stronger triumphs, then returns to her husband. Yes?

Strindberg   Correct. The man, though not present, is the centre of the attention. They both love him and they fight over him. (*Lightly.*) As women tend to do.

Siri   Good. And if that's the script, darling, why don't we stick to it Why then do we have to get Marie's ex-fiancé involved ?

Strindberg   Who does?

Siri   You do!!!

Strindberg   Who? Me?

Marie David   There's something strange about this play. It's like . . . it's like it's pretending to be something that it isn't. Like something's covered up. As if everything that's important is outside the text. When did you write it?

Strindberg   Not long after . . . after you left Grez.

Marie David   Is that when you wrote it?

Strindberg   Yes, that's when I wrote it.

Schiwe   (*busy with the coffee, curious*)   When did you write it, did you say?

Strindberg   (*examines him contemplatively*)   Mr Schiwe. Schiwe. You probably have a first name too, Mr Schiwe.

Schiwe   Viggo.

Strindberg   Really! Viggo. (*Gloomily.*) Viggo Schiwe. Well, not much you can do about it I s'pose. (*Composes himself.*) Still, you are a man. I can talk to you. Criminals, baboons and women, they're all governed by instinct. But with a man, it's different. With a man you can hold a conversation. Right?

Siri   Just nod, that'll make little August happy. We don't mind.

Schiwe, *extremely ill at ease, tries a smile, shakes his head equivocally and looks wistfully at the door.*

Strindberg (*very matter-of-fact*)   I sat down and wrote the play the day after I'd kicked Miss David out of our respectable house and home in Grez. Her and the other lesbian lady, her little girlfriend Sofie. (*Suddenly blurts out with delight.*) I've got it! The fairy tale! *Little Viggo's Adventures on Christmas Eve.* That's it. I've got it. (*Completely calm.*) That's when I wrote the play. It's as simple as that.

Schiwe (*confounded*)   You kicked them out? But why?

Siri (*completely resigned*)   Go on, for God's sake, let's have it then. Tell them your story! It improves with age, gets more fascinating every time I hear it.

Schiwe   But . . . you didn't actually use force, did you? . . . That would have been rather discourteous, Mr Strindberg . . .

Strindberg   Mr Schiwe, you must try and understand (*Addressing himself more and more to* **Schiwe**, *entreating, his eyes tightly shut.*) what it was like, all those years. Isolated from everyone and *abroad*, like living in the dark . . . and everywhere all these women, like bats, flapping their wings, just waiting to strike . . . (*Appealing.*) Mr Schiwe, I was scared, you can understand that, can't you? . . . You're scared too sometimes, aren't you? (*Roars.*) I know you are, I know just how scared you are, that's why you're spouting all these fancy emancipated compliments . . . (*Quietly.*) Yes, just like bats in the dark. (*Pulls himself together, very businesslike.*) Anyway. There we were living in Grez, and then this couple came, from Copenhagen, to stay with us. Marie and Sofie Holten (*Scornfully.*) Little

Ollie! That's what she wanted to be called. Ollie! These
damned feminists, always insisting on using men's
nicknames. Both are tribades. One thinks she's a writer.
The other one dabbles in paint. And then Mr Schiwe,
then it happens. *They take my wife away from me.*

Schiwe   But Mr Strindberg.

Strindberg   I suffer their company. (*Calmly, but with
effort.*) I live with them. I put up with my wife's lengthy
and passionate tributes to Miss David's wonderful body
. . . her breasts. All these . . . embraces . . . I don't
understand. They kiss, they spend every minute together,
they talk . . . as if I *didn't exist* . . . (*With almost childish
hurt.*) They never tell me what's wrong with me . . . I even
begin to think there isn't anything wrong with me . . . I
just don't *exist!* And then the children start to like her.
Marie . . . Marie . . . they never stop talking about Marie.
And then this sexual perversion . . . I must talk to
someone about it . . .

Marie David   You're right. We must talk about it. I'm
beginning to realise that we must talk about it.

Schiwe   Must we really?

Strindberg   Why not?

Marie David   Yes, we must.

Siri   But why? Does it help us understand the play we're
working on?

Strindberg (*roars*)   All this rubbish about
understanding the play. Stop it! It's about a man
although he doesn't appear in the play. Shut up and get
on with it!

Marie David   That's right. No longer holding centre
stage.

Strindberg   And then came that night. The situation
had become impossible, it was dangerous. Marie had to
get out of Grez . . . she'd got mixed up with some girl, the

locals were all up in arms, she had to get out. (*Almost desperate.*) I could've had her put away, it's an offence punishable by law, but I decided against it. For the sake of my wife really . . . And then, on the night of the farewell party . . .

Schiwe (*incredulous*) You had a farewell party?

Strindberg   Of course, we had a farewell party! We were close friends! And that night . . . I shall always remember that night . . . a light, gentle drizzle throughout the night, it didn't stop until dawn . . . (*Lapses into silence, hesitates.*) It was painfully obvious that my dear Siri . . . I'm sorry, I didn't want to implicate you . . . although you deserve it. I don't feel any qualms. My dear wife's passionate love for the enchanting Marie Caroline David.

Schiwe   Mr Strindberg! Mr Strindberg!

Strindberg (*quietly, almost chanting*)   It rained almost all night but in the end, I went outside and just stood there, all on my own . . . and the window . . . the window looked just like a painting. And I think I must've stood there for some time. And then I went back. And there they were, all of them. Her too. You should've seen her, the object of my wife's burning desire. I remember her so clearly. Marie Caroline David. I can still see her. Red-haired and flabby, hooked nose, double chin and yellow eyes, cheeks puffy from drinking . . . she never stopped drinking . . . flat-chested, claw-like fingers . . . the devil himself would've taken fright at the sight of her. Double chin . . . yellow eyes . . . bloated from all the alcohol . . . drooping mouth . . . yellow eyes . . . puffy cheeks . . .

Schiwe (*incredulous*)   You're talking . . . you're talking about Miss David?

Strindberg (*with increasingly desperate monotony*)   And Siri sang a ballad, 'Mignon', I seem to remember, in her sweet and rather beautiful voice . . . and when she'd finished . . . she started to cry. And then she got up and walked over and sat down next to this monster and then

this Danish monster gets to her feet, takes her head
between her hands and devours her lips with her open
mouth. Hardly what one might call spiritual communion,
I thought to myself. (*Lapses into silence.*) And then, when I
looked out, it was almost light.

Schiwe   So what did you do, Mr Strindberg?

Strindberg   I drank the old hag under the table.

Schiwe   You mean . . . Mrs Strindberg?

Strindberg   I don't very often call my wife an old hag.
Except when I've got good grounds, of course. I meant
Miss David, naturally.

Marie David   Thank you.

Strindberg (*looks at* **Marie**, *continues almost affectionately*)
I remember, we had to go outside because you felt sick.
And then, down by the road, you fell. You were on your
knees and you looked up at me with those wide,
frightened eyes and you were letting out these silly little
yelps.You were trying to lean against . . . a gate post, I
think it was. And then, suddenly it was light. And you
were throwing up. (*Musing.*) Never, ever have I
encountered such an unappealing representative of the
human race.

Marie David (*gets up, walks over to* **Strindberg**, *looks at
him in silence*)   Is that the way you saw it?

Strindberg   I've had strong doubts about the wisdom of
women's emancipation ever since.

Schiwe (*does not speak, everyone is silent, he finally asks in a
shaky voice*)   Is this true?

Strindberg   Ask the ladies.

Schiwe   Is it true?

Siri   There are two categories of writers, Mr Schiwe.
One tells lies by piecing together fragments of the truth.
The other tells the truth by using an assortment of lies.

Strindberg   And which kind am I supposed to be then?

Siri   Whichever is worse.

Schiwe (*still shaken*)   . . . But what did you do, Mrs Strindberg . . . how did you . . .

Siri   I didn't do anything, I was very upset.

Strindberg (*quietly, almost apologetically, addresses himself directly to her*)   Siri had lost her lover. She was unhappy and troubled. She'd go for long walks, sing sad songs and visit her girlfriend's favourite spots. She cried and she pined. That's true, isn't it Siri?

Siri   For four long years we'd been living out of a suitcase . . . in exile in this European wilderness, fighting and arguing . . . I'd been living with this panic-stricken child, pretending to be a titan . . . And no one, absolutely no one, wanted me for what I was . . . or could've been. There I was, waiting for better times to come. And I wait. And I wait. And I grow older. And then this woman appears from the Danish city of Copenhagen in northern Europe. And she's completely independent. And she talks to me as if of course there's a part for me to play in this life. She tells me it's not too late! Of course I loved her!

Schiwe   Of course.

Siri   I couldn't help it. I got very upset when he kicked her out. I liked her.

Strindberg *looks at her in silence, does not know what to do, wants to say something, remains silent.*

(*Explodes.*) Here's this free and independent woman but that one-eyed bastard's only interested in one thing! He has to prove she's a lesbian alcoholic! So what! Who cares?

Strindberg (*astonished*)   But it's a fact worth mentioning, isn't it?

Siri   You have already! More than once!

Schiwe   Now, I'm inclined to agree with Mr Strindberg here. I would've thought it would be almost impossible to ignore the fact that . . .

Siri   Marie had something else you see, that was much more important to me.

Strindberg   Let me tell you something, Mr Schiwe, let me tell you something in complete confidence. *Do you know* that every single evening for a whole year that diabolic threesome wanted to play whist! But not *one* of them knew how to play! Not one of them ever bothered to learn the rules! Mr Schiwe, that's how I learnt the meaning of true suffering!

Marie David   I remember you once said something about your father . . . you said you hated his 'Icelandic nature'. You never wanted to be like him, you said. You must've changed, what's happened?

Siri   Why do you even bother to ask? The battle was lost a long time ago. When he's not the centre of attention, he panics, his whole world collapses and he gets as dangerous as a frightened rattlesnake.

Strindberg (*astonished*)   All these unintelligent and uncalled for attempts to analyse my psyche. Hands off Siri! My psyche is the sole preserve of future scholars.

Marie David   Might a repulsive, red-haired, flabby lady with a double chin be granted permission to ask a question?

Strindberg   Permission granted.

Marie David   Was it after that night that you decided to write a play about . . . the reunion of two women in love?

Strindberg *remains silent.*

Marie David   And that's supposed to be . . . this play?

Strindberg *nods.*

Marie David (*to herself*)   Then it's lost on me.

Siri (*exaggeratedly humbly*)   Do you think it might be a good idea . . . may I suggest . . . may I humbly suggest that we give a bit of attention to the play . . . that we start rehearsing? Anyone else think that might be a good idea?

Strindberg (*relieved*)   You're right! Let's start! This will be fun. Let's start! Let's do the reunion of the tribades.

Siri (*acidly*)   That'll give free rein to his imagination.

Strindberg   Enough talk! No more interruptions! Energy and enthusiasm. Force and feeling! And perhaps some more coffee! Mr Schiwe . . . with your experience as Jean in *Miss Julie* I am sure you're now . . . (*Stops short after a murderous look from* **Schiwe**.) . . . perhaps you could . . . Thank you, Mr Schiwe! Quite right! Coffee for the gentlemen and more beer for the ladies! Let's start!

Marie David (*quietly, stares at him*)   Mr Strindberg. Now I remember.

Strindberg   Yes?

Marie David   Now I remember. Now I remember when I really started to like you. Why I liked you so much. Now I remember.

Strindberg (*completely still, expressionless*) Yes?

Act Two

Music.

A slide projected against the curtain showing a man with the head of a bird.

The stage is dark, lights come on slowly. **Siri** *is engrossed in her manuscript,* **Marie** *is opening a bottle of beer.* **Strindberg** *is standing not very far from* **Siri**, *looking at her, teetering on tiptoe, apparently wishing to say something but hesitates.*

Strindberg   How are the children? Are they all right?

Siri (*without looking up*)   Yes.

Strindberg (*hesitates*)   Does Karin ever use that camera I bought her?

Siri (*curtly*)   I don't know.

Strindberg   Maybe they could . . . (*Tentatively.*) Maybe this summer they could come and stay with me for a couple of weeks on the island, then you'd . . .

Siri   No.

Strindberg   . . . then you'd get some time to yourself . . .

Siri   No.

Marie David *sits down with the open beer bottle in her hand. She gazes melancholically into space. She gives a sigh.*

Strindberg   How's your drink, Miss David? Not finished, I hope.

Marie David *looks at him without smiling.*

Come on, have another one. Just one more. I'm sure you need one. A little drink once in a while never hurt anyone . . .

Marie David   I like having a drink, Mr Strindberg. And more than once in a while. You see, Mr Strindberg, I have never – in Grez or at any other time – made a secret of the fact that I am an alcoholic. Because I am. Nor have I tried to make any excuses for it.

Strindberg (*slightly off balance*)   Well. In that case.

Marie David   Exactly.

Strindberg   Well . . . Cheers then!

Marie David   Cheers.

Strindberg (*now walking around in circles, gathering his strength, working himself up*)   The evidence is now overwhelming . . . time after time it's been proved that I'm right . . . in spite of the allegations of lies and distortions. We now have proof! What did I say about the drinking!! No one present could've failed to have heard that admission! You heard it, didn't you Mr Schiwe, and that's what matters because you're a man and not a compulsive liar like the ladies. And you heard it, didn't you?

Marie David   Perhaps you'd like it in writing. It might be a useful reminder for you when you write about me. Because you will sooner or later, won't you?

Siri   Good God, yes!

Strindberg   What!??

Siri   Good God, that's all I can say. All that stuff about women vampires. Who's the vampire, I wonder. More a collection of self portraits, I would've thought. Mr Strindberg's cunning little method of self analysis. My God, are you a vulture! Anything human and you'll devour it.

Strindberg   Describe it, my dear! There's a difference.

Siri (*with a graceful pirouette*)   Allow me to introduce . . . for your entertainment . . . the gastronomic miracle of Swedish literature! Voila! Time after time devoured and

digested in the acclaimed works of the great maestro.
Forever alive! Forever willing to be devoured anew!

Strindberg (*agitatedly*)   You cow! I've turned you into
an international celebrity and you haven't even got the
grace to thank me!

Siri   Thank you! For what? For being battered in public?
For lying there with my heart bared, bleeding, on the
floor? Should I thank you for that?

Strindberg (*lecturing*)   Just remember, when you're
lying there, battered, covered in blood, your heart bared,
bleeding – then you only need to say to yourself: but for
me, literature would be much the poorer!

Siri (*getting increasingly agitated*)   You eat people alive. You
think they're there for your consumption! You should've
seen him that night poor Viktoria tried to kill herself. As it
happened, we were staying at the same hotel and soon
enough poor Lundegård came banging on our door to tell
us all about it. Typical, isn't it, for a man not to keep his
mouth shut. And you should've seen him. Didn't Mr
Strindberg lap it all up! Oh. Mmmm. (*She circles round him
imitating a ravenous animal in sight of its prey, eyes wide open,
tongue hanging out, licking.*) Mmmm! What a juicy story! The
expression on the face of the Great Artist . . . the look of a
merciless vulture! . . . and all the gory details, how he
gobbled it all up! A woman who tried to kill herself!
Unrequited love! Deserted! Knives, blood . . . gulp . . . gulp
. . . perhaps . . . perhaps material for a play? Slurp! A lady of
noble birth . . . on Midsummer's Eve . . . an affair with a man
. . . he left her . . . slurp . . . slurp . . . slurp . . . a razor . . .
those ice cold, piercing eyes, taking note and recording
every minute detail.

Marie David   But Siri . . . Why d'you say that? . . . You
know the empathy in that play's extraordinary . . . Why
worry about the expression on his face?

Siri   You haven't been mauled as often as I have. That's
the difference!

Strindberg (*infuriated*)   Of all the women in this world, why did it have to be her? Why did I have to fall in love with this woman, this traitor, this parasite. Terrible. Terrible.

Marie David (*amazed*)   You mean you love her?

Strindberg   Of course, I love her and I always will do . . . but that's got nothing to do with her . . . falling in love, that's just something that happens to you . . . like cancer. Or bubonic plague.

Marie David   I see . . .

Strindberg (*now very serious*)   Why did it have to be her? That's what's so infuriating. That I had to fall in love with someone that I dislike so intensely.

Schiwe   You dislike so intensely . . . ??

Strindberg   It just isn't fair!!!

Siri (*icily*)   So? You're still a vampire.

Strindberg   Yes, that's probably true. (*Very calmly.*) You're a parasite, you suck my blood and spend my money playing the mistress and bossing the maids around while you dream of a career that you never had the talent for. And I'm a vampire sucking your blood. Sounds like pretty normal family life to me.

Schiwe (*bewildered, to himself*)   I wonder . . . I wonder what there is about writers that's supposed to be so remarkable?

Siri (*categorically*)   Nothing!!!

Strindberg   I'll tell you. We commit words to paper, that's what's so remarkable.

Schiwe   Is it really?

Strindberg   I record other people's feelings and fears, long before they even know them themselves. A year, ten years, a hundred years before. But when those words and

feelings are down on paper, and you can read it all, then
you get anxious and annoyed. Not at the war of terror
that the ladies are waging against us. No, you get annoyed
with the messenger. With me, who tried to warn you.
That's what I find most extraordinary!

Siri How do you like that, Marie. Not like Grez. Little
August's back in fighting form. What vitality!

Marie David Which could be put to so much better
use. If only it could be used to fight for the emancipation
of women . . .

Strindberg (*furious, screams*) Balls, Miss David, balls!!! If
you know what that means??? (*Regains his breath.*) Yes. Yes,
yes, yes. I'm sorry. It was silly of me. I said that, didn't I? I
did apologise! Does it have to be in writing??? (*Quite calm,
disillusioned.*) Now, my dear friends, here we were in Grez,
living together in friendship and misery, but how exactly?
Month after month, night in and night out, I have no
choice but to play whist with two Danish lesbians and a
wife who is working hard at making it three. Not one of
them knew how to play, not one of them ever bothered to
learn the rules! At night they lie there nibbling at each
other. And then, during working hours, these three ladies
of high social standing expect me to carry them on my
shoulders while I fight for the emancipation of women.
My answer is: NO.

Schiwe (*plaintively*) But the rehearsal, Mr Strindberg
. . . the rehearsal . . . the play . . . What are we going to do
about the play?

Marie David Siri, could you get me another beer,
please?

Strindberg (*gets out the manuscript, furious*) Page two at
the bottom, Miss David listens in silence while Siri sings
the praises of domestic bliss. Begin!

Siri Where?

Strindberg 'There's no place like home.'

Marie David   That's just what my pox-ridden father used to say after he raped my mother. Every Wednesday and Friday evening as he closed the bedroom door behind him.

Strindberg   'There's no place like home.'

Siri   'Yes, Amelie, dear, there's no place like home – after the theatre, she means – and the little ones! Well, I couldn't expect you to understand that!'

Strindberg   That was awful. Terrible. (*Pleading.*) With conviction, Siri, with conviction. You're talking to an emancipated baboon, who's betrayed everyone and everything, who has no aim in life, just spouts a lot of twaddle about freedom! You're in the right! Persuasion! You've got to persuade her. (*Agitated, to* **Schiwe**.) Hardly surprising, there's never been a successful woman horse-trader in history! They lack fire!

Siri   Yes, darling. (*Opens her basket and shows her Christmas presents.*) 'Look, what I bought for my dear little piglets.' (*Takes out a doll.*) 'Look at this, I bought it for Lisa! Look, she can close her eyes and turn her head! Look! And this is for Maja! A toy pistol! (*Loads and fires at Y.*)'

Marie David *lets out an amused giggle.*

Schiwe (*with concern*)   At this point, it might be preferable to use some slightly more graceful and expressive gestures to . . .

Strindberg   She's supposed to look frightened!!!

Marie David *makes a rather elaborate gesture of fear.*

(*Resigned.*) Good God, this is going to be some performance.

Siri   'Did I frighten you?' (*Takes out a pair of embroidered slippers.*) 'And this is for him. With tulips that I embroidered myself. I loathe tulips, but he has to have tulips on everything.'

Marie David *looks up from the script, curious, gives a sarcastic look.*

Schiwe (*tentatively*)   I s'pose we don't have any doubts . . . I s'pose we all feel this is a good play?

Strindberg   It's an excellent play. (*Hurt.*) A sure classic, if it's ever performed. But with all this gibberish . . . all these women jabbering . . . we'll never get anywhere. It would only take one person to keep her mouth shut now and then and we might get somewhere.

Siri   May we continue, maestro?

Strindberg   Yes!

Schiwe (*worried*)   I do hope you understand, Mr Strindberg, I wasn't expressing any doubts about the artistic quality of the play, I was merely . . .

Strindberg   Don't, Mr Schiwe, don't express anything. Make a supreme effort to suppress it!

Siri (*inserts her hands into the slippers*)   Look! Bob's got such tiny feet! Look! And you should see the way he walks! So elegant! You never saw him wearing slippers, did you?

Marie David *laughs out loud.*

Siri   'And when he gets angry, he stamps his foot, like this: Those diabolical maids, they never learn to make proper coffee! Yak! And those cretins, now they've forgotten to cut the wick again! And that draught from the floor makes his feet turn into ice. Ouch, it's cold, and those idiots, why can't they keep the fire going!' (*She rubs the slippers together, the sole of one against the leather top of the other.*)

Marie David *laughs, partly with genuine amusement, partly under the influence of the beer.* **Schiwe** *is amused too.* **Siri** *gives a well-captured caricature of* **Strindberg**: *his fat little hips, his dainty gait, his somewhat effeminate movements: both women take great pleasure in her impersonation.*

Strindberg (*face clouds, more and more hurt*)   That's an incorrect reading of the script! These are endearing little mannerisms that the wife is describing with affection! Not ridicule! That's wrong! These two women are fighting over the same man. He's not present but he's still the centre of attention! Affection! That's the script!

Siri   Yes, my love. 'And then he gets home and starts looking for his slippers that Marie has put away under the chest of drawers!!! Oh, but shame on me for making fun of him. He's a kind man, he's a good little man – if only you could find someone like him . . .'

Siri *erupts into giggles,* **Marie** *too finds it difficult to remain serious.*

I'm sorry, I'll do it again . . . 'He is a kind little man . . .' (*New eruption of laughter,* **Siri** *now begins to make anatomical references through discreet but suggestive movements of her little finger.*) . . . My little man . . . 'Oh' I'm sorry . . . I'm sorry . . .

Schiwe (*embarrassed but at the same time amused, red-faced, looking at* **Strindberg** *and the ladies in turn*)   Ladies . . . ladies . . .

Siri   '. . . a little man, a slender little worm . . .' (*Gaily hums a well-known risqué song.*) 'Oh, oh, this teeny weeny worm he's got . . . it couldn't do an awful lot . . . not only was it far too . . .'

Marie David (*still laughing, tries to pull herself together*) But Siri . . . now you're going . . .

Schiwe   Mrs Strindberg!

Strindberg *puts down his manuscript slowly and with deliberate care then stands still, looking straight into space. His face is tired and expressionless, but twitching nervously. The two women gradually calm down, everyone becomes silent, increasingly embarrassingly silent.* **Strindberg** *does not move.* **Schiwe** *rocks backwards and forwards on his heels, heel-to-toe, heel-to-toe. He looks nervously at* **Strindberg**, *at the women, at the ceiling.* **Strindberg** *remains silent for some time.*

Strindberg   Siri, you promised. More than once. (*Very quietly, as if speaking to himself.*) But I always knew I couldn't trust you. I knew you'd grasp every possible opportunity. Because you know it hurts. And it would happen, over and over again. I could always see it coming. Sometimes to my face, sometimes behind my back. Because you knew I . . . I couldn't get over it. You knew I couldn't sleep. It's incredible! And you knew it. I did what you wanted – the lover always does – I did everything to please you. I played the servant. And the child. Whatever you wanted. I was gentle . . . I let you . . . And then you spread the venom behind my back.

Siri   Now, now, my little August. It happens to all of us. What makes you think you'd be spared?

Strindberg   I haven't been.

Siri   We all get our fair share. And then as we start losing our self-respect, little by little, we turn into beasts. It happens to all of us. You're lucky, you can always turn it into *literature*.

Strindberg   Yes, I still can. But not because of what happened. In spite of it. In spite of what happened. (*Quietly, with growing fury.*) At parties, late at night among friends, after her fifth beer, that's when she'd start. I was so naïve. I was a gentle and considerate lover, I thought she wanted it that way. That she loved me like a child. But she didn't, in secret she despised me. Now, this last year, I've changed – love at forty – I've become cynical, coarse, lewd and now she loves me as . . . a man. A man! (*With increasing revulsion.*) I have become a man. Doesn't matter if I beat her up, not as long as she gets what she wants! Talk about ideals!

Schiwe   . . . Mr Strindberg . . . that little remark about . . . your size . . . it was only meant as a joke . . . not to be taken seriously, Mr Strindberg . . .

Siri   Next, I suppose, you'll regale us with the story of you and that seventeen-year-old Martha . . .

Strindberg (*furious*)   You don't think I diddled that little tart out of my own free will, do you?

Siri   Oh, you didn't . . . I see . . .

Strindberg   And it happened over and over again. Little pinpricks. My beloved wife would smile and joke and drink. And then she would do it again. My dear little Siri . . . you little cow . . . you charming little cow, with your glassy, alcohol-sodden eyes and your risqué little jokes . . . (*Roars.*) . . . Why must it be the bolt? Maybe the nut's too large!! . . . And everyone would lap it up! . . . *Interesting*! . . . Remember Grez, Miss David? I'm sure you do. (*Silent.*) With my genitals tingling with fury, the next morning I boarded the train for Geneva and got a doctor to come with me to a brothel. And I proved my manhood! – And not for the first time either I might add! All strictly scientific and in the presence of a medical expert! *The Abduction of Proserpine!*, Mr Schiwe, inspired by Bernini's statue! Freestanding group without support! And a fertility test! Evidence that my sperm's fertile! And I had it measured! When aroused, Mr Schiwe, it's sixteen by four centimetres. Sixteen by four. Medically certified, under strictly controlled scientific conditions!

Schiwe (*somewhat sheepishly*)   Sixteen by four?

Strindberg (*triumphantly*)   Exactly!

Schiwe   Sixteen by four . . . four centimetres, that's the circumference, is it?

Strindberg (*explodes*)   The diameter, you idiot! Sixteen centimetre's the length, four's the diameter! The *diameter*!

Schiwe   Oh, I see, the diameter, I see . . . (*Thinks hard.*) I never thought of measuring across . . . but I s'pose I should really . . . I'm sure you're right . . .

Strindberg (*with friendly interest*)   You arrive at the circumference by dividing the diameter by two which gives you the radius which in turn is multiplied by two according to the formula two pi r.

Schiwe   Two fi . . . r?

Strindberg   Two times pi times the radius. Pi equals 3.14, it's a constant. The radius in this particular case happens to be two centimetres. Hence the circumference must be two times 3.14 times two, which works out at 12.56 centimetres. The circumference is 12.56 centimetres. That's quite a difference!

Schiwe   Oh yes . . . yes of course . . . yes, that's quite a difference!

Strindberg   A *circumference* of four centimetres would be this big! The size of a pencil!

Schiwe   Oh yes, of course. Of course.

Strindberg   (*matter-of-fact*)   My circumference is 12.56 centimetres. I know that's correct, I've checked it.

Schiwe   I'd never question . . . never . . . (*Repeats, tries to memorise.*) Two times pi times the radius . . . two times pi times the radius . . .

Marie David   Good God, what are they doing?

Strindberg   Mathematics!! (*Quietly.*) Sixteen by four . . . That's how conclusions are drawn on untested hypotheses! (*Falls silent.*) But her little insinuations never stopped. Her own affairs (*Gives her a dark look.*) – all those second-rate actors and cross-eyed Finns – outright moral crimes with potentially fatal consequences – illegitimate children! Syphilis! – for that she had a ready-made excuse – that was all because of . . . of what she called . . . my weakness.

He is now pacing back and forth, among the props and the scenery, restless, increasingly overcome by agitation and suppressed despair. Against the background of cardboard lions, savages with bulging muscles and native Americans, he looks very small, almost like a child.

So I'm supposed to be *weak*! Me! I covered the whole of France with an enormous rucksack on my back! In twenty-one days! And in a third class compartment! I climbed mountain peaks! I rode a horse from Vevey to Lausanne and back again in twenty-four hours! (*Now with overt despair, tears of unjust injury in his eyes.*) Last summer I risked my life swimming across the Vierwaldstaetter-See! Ice cold water, I was braving death! And I've been all on my own in a tiny dinghy in the Baltic! Thirty-four kilometres, that's how far I had to row. Etcetera, etcetera, etcetera. And I'm supposed to be weak! Why did I do it then?

Marie David　Good question.

Schiwe　But Mr Strindberg, calm down, Mr Strindberg.

Strindberg (*sits down, his head in his hands, his whole body trembling*)　I know . . . I know I'm making a fool of myself. I know it's humiliating, Mr Schiwe, I know I shouldn't be doing it, why are they making me do it? It's all wrong . . . I shouldn't have to! It's strange . . . it's the male inside me. When he's attacked, the pain's so strong. (*He is silent, still seated, his body rocking back and forth.*) I s'pose, she's right, I'm not all that big. I can't really call myself big . . . Not under normal circumstances. But average when I'm aroused. It only became important because . . . because everybody was talking about it. All the time. When I was young, back in Stockholm, it was so . . . important. They all used to laugh at me. (*With increasing irony and distaste.*) So, one time, I decided to hold an open-air cock inspection. In the presence of witnesses – including a harlot of good repute – I didn't get a distinction but she awarded me a clear pass.

Marie David　Mr Strindberg, please. Stop now, please.

Schiwe (*has now managed to find a pencil and a piece of paper*)　I wonder . . . perhaps you could let me have that mathematical formula again . . . two times fi . . . do you think you could let me have it again, please . . .

Strindberg (*furious, pointing at* **Siri** *and* **Marie**)   Forget it! Women of the future won't need us, Mr Schiwe. We won't be of any use to them! Just look at them. Don't think it's just my prick, Mr Schiwe, they're as unenthusiastic about yours! We're in the same boat, Mr Schiwe. We all are.

Schiwe (*perturbed and deeply shaken*)   But I'm sure that can't be true . . . Mr Strindberg, how can you say that (*His hand goes out in an appeal to the ladies.*) . . . I'm sure that *can't* be true . . .

Strindberg (*energetically*)   Big prick! Small prick! Average prick! Slightly less than average prick! Makes no difference whatsoever!!! We're no use to them any longer! (*Circles around* **Schiwe**, *restless, his hands opening and closing.*) I can sniff it out. Something's going on. I always sense it long before anyone else. I've got a built-in alarm system in my genitals! Buzzzz. The system's been alerted! Buzzzz! Change! Change! Danger! Buzzzzzzzzzz! Danger! Danger!

Siri   Just look at him . . .

Strindberg (*angry*)   Just wait, it'll happen to you too! You'll be redundant too! (*Worried and increasingly confused.*) All these new demands . . . the female organs of today aren't satisfied with just the male member, they require much more according to the latest research . . . all the rules are changing . . . Mr Schiwe, nothing is certain any more. (*Roars.*) They call me vindictive! Yes, I do not wish to fall victim to the ladies! (*Cunningly.*) Attack calls forth counter-attack, that's self-defence. And if I'm vindictive, it's because I've been wronged. Therefore I must be right which means someone else must be wrong. Hence the ladies are wrong!

Marie David (*amused*)   Mr Strindberg, I don't know anyone who's got such a highly-developed sense of feminine logic as you do. No one I've met, no one I've ever read about.

Strindberg (*reserved*)   Women do not possess any powers of logic whatsover.

Marie David   See what I mean. But not only that, you also manage to express this 'feminine logic' in such an amusing way. Your very lack of logic assumes . . . an almost aesthetic quality.

Strindberg *glares, sulkily and exhausted.*

(*Amicable and curious.*) There's a fine little woman there inside you, Mr Strindberg.

Schiwe (*agitated*)   'A fine little woman' . . . How can you say such a thing to Mr Strindberg . . . ?

Marie David   A gentle, intuitive, mysterious little woman that you will not stop harassing.

Schiwe   Honestly, that's quite enough, now I really feel I must intervene on Mr Strindberg's behalf. Such crude insults . . . 'A fine little woman' . . . you shouldn't have to listen to such . . . it's . . .

Strindberg   It's not me, it's you. You won't stop harassing me.

Marie David   Who? We won't?

Strindberg (*very quietly*)   You never allowed me to be the one I was. That's why I hate you so much. Or hate them, I mean.

Marie David   That's why . . .

Strindberg   Yes, that's why.

Marie David   I think that I know, from my own experience, what you're . . . what you're trying to say.

Strindberg   Do you? (*Looks at her in silence.*) Yes.

Marie David *gets up, gets another beer and opens it.*

Your fourth.

Marie David Correct.

Strindberg You'll drink yourself to death.

Marie David In all likelihood.

Strindberg But you're free, you do live your own life. You know something . . . (*Looks around timidly, lowers his voice.*) . . . If you promise you won't take it any further . . .

Marie David I promise. You can talk.

Strindberg You know, I like you in a way. I respect you. With you it's different. It's not just talk. You live by what you preach.

Marie David Thank you.

Strindberg (*now becoming interested, confidentially*) You know, it's now 1889. For years, these confounded emancipated ladies have been talking about the liberation of women. But they don't *do* anything. More than half of the world's population are women. But look at those whingers! What have they done to set themselves free? History is full of tales of oppressed men who seized power and set themselves free. Women just whinge. That's what drives me crazy. I walk into my room, sit down at my desk and six months later, I've written two plays, one novel and fifteen articles. But what have they done? They haven't moved. There they are, in the same salons, still jabbering. Any oppressor that they've killed? Throats they've cut? Prisons blown to smithereens? Any riots that they've organised? Any walls covered in blood? No! The baboons go on jabbering. The day they seize their freedom, that's when I shall respect them!

Marie David And support them in their struggle?

Strindberg (*extremely surprised*) *Of course* not! I shall fight them even harder! But with respect.

Marie David Respect you call it . . . this machismo . . .

Strindberg You are frightened of being free!

Marie David   We are?

Strindberg   And when the baboons are set free, they'll drink themselves to death!

Marie David (*completely dispassionately*)   I'm afraid I shall have to disappoint you, Mr Strindberg, but I don't find your views on women particularly reactionary. It's just that you've never quite understood . . . what prison's like . . . or what freedom's like.

Strindberg   But this whinging and whimpering . . . A hundred years from now and there won't be a man on the face of the earth, the whinging will have made them all jump off the nearest cliff. The battle of the sexes will be over.

Marie David   That wasn't very funny. (*Gets up to get another beer, opens it.*)

Strindberg   Your fifth.

Marie David   Correct.

Strindberg   You'll drink yourself to death.

Marie David   In all likelihood.

Strindberg   A pity in a way.

Marie David   You won't feel that way in the morning.

Strindberg   What made you start?

Marie David   Well, it didn't have anything to do with freedom, that's for sure.

Strindberg (*encouragingly*)   Just plain weakness of character, probably. Maybe genetic. Bad blood most likely. (*Looks at her with curiosity.*) I heard somewhere that George Brandes . . . the writer . . . the *great* writer according to some . . . was your father? He was a frequent guest in your house when he was younger, wasn't he? And he had a relationship with your mother although, of course, she was married? That's true, is it?

Marie David   George Brandes, champagne socialist and drawing-room radical . . .

Strindberg   Oh really? (*Brightens up.*) You seem to have sound literary judgement if nothing else. So that's where you got your weakness of character from.

Marie David   I wonder, Mr Strindberg. (*Pensively.*) If you had met my mother. Illegitimate child from 185 Dybergade, promoted to the rank of plantation slave to the Copenhagen aristocracy. Dear Mr Strindberg, if you should ever wish to write about servants' daughters . . . But you wouldn't, would you?

Strindberg (*doesn't listen, walks around with his hands behind his back*)   It's almost uncanny. George Brandes' daughter, the scourge of my house . . . I always thought that Brandes . . . He writes about your mother somewhere, doesn't he . . . about this oppressed woman who showed him the prison that is family life . . . that's right, isn't it? Brandes, the darling of the women's leagues . . .

Siri (*from the bed in the background*)   Conspiracies and women's leagues. Now you've really got him started.

Strindberg   Like father, like daughter. I should've known.

Marie David (*now under the influence of the beer*)   George Brandes, the great writer. A radical and educated man. A *highly*-educated man. (*With slight sarcasm.*) He held all the right opinions about everything but that wasn't much use to my mother, was it. He'd never met anyone like her. She refused to knuckle under to anyone. It was so exotic, he thought, nature's own child in fetters! A bird in a cage . . . he was so taken by her . . . and he worked hard on her and finally she did it. She got up, took me and my brother and got out. Like you read in a book, it made for great literature. But then, of course, he was stuck with her and that's when it started to get a bit embarrassing . . .

Strindberg   And the husband, deprived of his wife, left with the loss and the pain . . .

Marie David   Brandes must have seemed like freedom to her . . . a new life . . . she must've thought it was possible to escape. But Brandes was never in love with her, he was just *compassionate* . . . a beautiful woman, oppressed by her aging, syphilitic husband. What a tragedy! What great literature! (*Musing.*) She really was beautiful. The most beautiful slave-girl on the whole plantation. (*With increasing intensity.*) But she didn't know anything! She'd never learnt anything. Her whole life had been spent parading around looking beautiful . . . and then, after her escape, her freedom became a bit of an embarrassment. She'd never read any books . . . never seen any plays . . . she had nothing to talk about . . . she was still a prisoner. And Brandes, of course, was such a highly-educated humanitarian . . . with such compassion . . . for the oppressed . . . but once my mother was free, it all became a bit of an embarrassment . . . for everybody . . . So it didn't work out.

Strindberg   I take it she drank herself to death.

Marie David (*musing*)   When I think about all the radical, highly-educated, unprejudiced humanitarians I've met, it's nice to meet a real bastard like you, Mr Strindberg.

Strindberg   So Brandes was your father! And the poor, aging . . . husband . . . deceived by his wife! . . . had to work to support illegitimate children and a parasitic wife while lampooned in Brandes' books . . .

Marie David   Don't worry, Mr Strindberg. George Brandes was not my father. All my mother was unsure of was whether I was the result of my syphilitic, legal father's Wednesday or Friday rape. He was a man set in his ways, you see!

Strindberg   Two rats in a pit.

Marie David I only remember her after she was . . . free. Freedom became an obsession with her. She'd got this fixed idea, you see, that she wasn't a baboon, with a criminal psyche, whose sole function in life was to provide copulation on demand. Those sorts of ideas finish women off pretty quickly, Mr Strindberg!

Strindberg Yes.

Marie David What broke her, she told me once, was that in this new world of freedom, there was no part for her to play. Her freedom was . . . it wasn't any . . .

Strindberg (*quietly*)   . . . Any use. I know.

Marie David (*slightly drunk, examines him closely*)   Do you? (*Pause.*) Do you know something, Mr Strindberg? You know that night when we had our little farewell party in Grez? (*Very matter-of-fact.*) How nicely you expressed it. Such terribly elegant words. 'A light, gentle drizzle throughout the night.' That bit . . . 'the Danish monster took her head between her hands and kissed her lips' . . . and then, at the end, that nice bit about 'grey dawn'. 'The Night of the Tribades.' I just wonder if you ever thought about how I felt? How I felt being kicked out, courteously and amicably. 'While we gave a farewell party for our friends.' How terribly civilised!

Strindberg Don't drink any more. (*Pained silence.*) Yes, I remember.

Marie David You drank that red-haired monster under the table, you said. Yes, come morning and it wasn't all that civilised any more. No one was pretending, everyone was just terribly . . . terribly honest. I remember we'd gone outside, we were down by the road. It was Siri. And me. And you. You remember, don't you.

Strindberg Yes.

Marie David Yes, you do.

Strindberg *in an icy-blue, cold, hazy light, he moves as in a* *dream while* **Marie** *is talking.* **Siri** *is with him. They move very slowly, shouting and speaking soundlessly, white-faced, their mouths wide open but all that is heard is* **Marie**'s *voice barely audible above the low but intense music, relating the events of that morning in Grez.* **Strindberg** *and* **Siri** *dance their slow, inexorable ballet in the blue-white light round* **Marie**. *It is a bad, slow-moving dream.*

I was so sick. I was lying with one arm around . . . it must've been a gate post, I think, and I was throwing up. And I got it on my dress. I was so sick. And Siri was running round and round in silly little circles, crying and shouting. And I was throwing up and I got it on my dress. It was awful. I was leaving. And Siri was crying. It was like trying to separate a pair of Siamese twins with a meat cleaver, did you know that? Did you know that?

Strindberg, *icy-blue face, mouth wide open, his body stiff from fear, moves slowly round her, pointing at her, while* **Siri** *moves around* **Strindberg** *in a wider circle.*

You were standing close to me. I was very drunk, but I could see your face and I saw your mouth move. Soundlessly. I couldn't hear anything but I think you were shouting at me, telling me what you thought of me. And I was so sick. And there were some children standing there, staring . . . they must've come from the village. But all I could see was your face. It was grey. Your mouth was like a black hole opening and closing, but I couldn't hear a word. And then, suddenly . . . Suddenly I just liked you so much.

Strindberg *stops in the middle of a movement, the light decreases in intensity, the music reaches a crescendo and stops. His mouth closes, his eyes open and stare vacantly into space.*

I thought I knew you. You and I, we'd never been able to play the parts we should've played. It seemed like that grey, manic face with that black hole in the middle was my own face . . .

Strindberg   (*in a hollow voice*)   Yes. Yes.

Marie David   We must've caused a terrible scandal in Grez.

Strindberg *pained, remains silent.*

Schiwe (*uncertain what to do, wants to ease the tension, braces himself, walks up, hesitantly*)   Now for me a woman is like a flower . . .

Strindberg   What?

Schiwe   Don't you think that woman's nature . . . Don't you think we should try at least . . . to look upon a woman as a flower . . .?

Strindberg (*in a hollow voice*)   Good God, is that halfwit still here . . .

Schiwe   And we have to wait for the photographer. He said he'd be coming tonight.

Strindberg   The photographer?

Schiwe   Your picture, Mr Strindberg. You and the Dagmar Theatre Company. For the benefit of posterity.

Strindberg   Posterity? That too.

Schiwe   Shall I go and have a look . . . see if he's coming?

Strindberg   Yes.

Siri (*has been lying on the bed, gets up and walks over to the others*)   We don't seem to be getting very far, do we? I s'pose, I might as well say goodbye to a career in the theatre.

Strindberg   An irreparable loss to the theatre.

Siri   Well, I have to admit I'd been hoping. (*Looks at* **Schiwe** *as he walks out.*) Even he seems to have sense enough to leave.

Marie David   This is it, then?

Strindberg (*sits down, very tired but determined*)   No, no.

We must carry on. I've got bills to pay, I can't borrow any more. We all need money. This little theatre is all we've got, no other theatre will do my plays, no publisher will take my books, my articles aren't accepted anywhere. No one's got a good word for me. Ten years now, it's been going on and this is where they've got me. Here. Down here. The Dagmar Theatre and this damned play, that's all we've got. Not much, but it's better than nothing. We must carry on, there's still something we can do. We must finish the rehearsal of *The Stronger.* It's as simple as that.

Siri   So what do we do?

Strindberg   We continue.

Marie David   Yes.

Strindberg (*with an effort*)   Page five, top of the page, 'When I first met you, it was very strange.'

Siri   'When I first met you, it was very strange.' (*Pauses, gives* **Marie** *a long look.*) Yes, it certainly was.

Strindberg (*accommodatingly*)   Go on.

Siri   'When I first met you, it was very strange – I was so frightened of you, I didn't dare let you out of my sight. I organised my life so I'd always be close to where you were – I had to become your friend because I didn't dare be you enemy.' (*Icily.*) A complete lie. (*Continues abruptly.*) 'But I could feel the tension every time you came to see us because I could sense that my husband didn't like you.' True enough . . . It didn't take him long to realise that freedom is contagious. 'And I felt so uncomfortable, I felt as if I was wearing ill-fitting clothes – and I tried to talk to him, I begged him to be nice to you but it was no use – until you got engaged. Then, suddenly the two of you became great friends. It almost seemed you now felt it safe to show your real feelings'. Safely imprisoned and locked up, he means. Ingenious distortion of the facts, I must say. It's poor Sofie who's supposed to be the fiancée, is it? . . . And if she and Marie were together . . .

but as it happened, my darling, it was you who were jealous of . . .

Strindberg (*extremely irritated*)   All these irrelevant comments! This extraordinarily *personal* interpretation of literature . . . this extraordinary arrogance and self-preoccupation . . . the *assumption* that everything centres around you and your bloody baboons . . . as if you were the centre of the universe . . . Just act and stop talking! You're here to act, not talk! Keep your mouth shut and act!

Siri   What shall I do then? Have my lines come out of my ears?

Strindberg   Shut up and act!

Siri   But it's so bad. And it just isn't true, I can see it now when . . . when we're all here. Only chance of success in Copenhagen for this play is to do it in Finnish and tell everyone that it was written by Ibsen!

Strindberg (*enraged, raises his finger at her*)   You! You! From now on I won't write a word about you! I shall silence you! That will be your punishment!

Siri   Help! I'm dying! Help! Did I really hear you right!

Marie David   Do we have to discuss what's true and what isn't, it's a *play*, isn't it . . . ?

Strindberg (*furious, points at the manuscript*)   It's the truth! Every single word! Don't try to lie your way out of that! You tell me, didn't the tension in our marriage start when that cow arrived?! Isn't that when it started?! Just as I've recorded here!!

Siri   My dear little August, when you see a free woman, like so many other men, you just panic. That's what triggers off your alarm. That's when your willie starts trembling. Buzzzzzzzz! Danger! Buzzzzzzzz! That's when you fear for your life and start shouting 'lesbian'. Buzzzzzzzz . . .

Strindberg   Well! Isn't she a lesbian then? Isn't she?

Marie David   If she is, so what?!

Strindberg (*emphatically, impassioned*)   A free woman does not frighten me, I wouldn't want a woman to be any other way, you know that. But I also want a free woman to *work* and to be *nice* to me, and *not* talk a lot of rubbish and make fun of my willie!!!

Siri   For you a woman is most certainly not like a flower.

Strindberg   A poppy in that case. All beauty on the surface but pure poison underneath. Like opium! Addictive! Intoxicating and enslaving. (*Delighted with his nice image.*) A woman is like a poppy!

Siri   God, this misogyny . . . I can't understand it . . .

Strindberg   God, this rubbish about my misogyny. (*With great pathos, and a degree of self-pity.*) I have nothing, absolutely nothing against women. (*Points a finger accusingly.*) But would you, I ask, would you want your daughter to marry one!!?

Siri   Oh yes, what a relief that would be.

Marie David   What sort of world is this? If people like you . . . if a man like you feels he has to stand there and scream and shout and measure lengths and diameters and feel frightened and think of women as opium and . . .

Strindberg (*doesn't listen, his voice suddenly very lonely, like that of a child*)   Siri, I know I won't see you again, I know this is the last night of our life together. I'll never see the children again. I know you won't show me any mercy, I won't see Karin . . . Greta . . . Putte. It's a fact, Siri. And for me it's life or death. *I cannot live without a woman.* That's what's so terrible . . . I am going to see Öhrwall at the maternity hospital. He'll get me a young woman with a small child, father unknown. About twenty-five, she doesn't have to be beautiful, as long as she has a pelvis and two breasts. I'll look after the child and bring it up and I'll mount the woman and make new ones. I must have children. I can't live without the sound of children's voices.

Siri   That's the way he thinks.

Strindberg   I'm not the only one!!

Siri   Exactly! Just get a new slave! We women have been oppressed . . .

Strindberg   Oppressed!! Who? For centuries women ruled the Swedish household. They worked on the land. They looked after the money. They ran the house. They had responsibility for the education of the children. They acted as the highest religious authority in the family. They controlled virtually *everything* while the men laboured at their work and submitted to their rule! That's the situation for the majority of women, Miss von Essen! And here we have this bloody Finnish virago with a title before her name who hasn't done a stroke of work in her whole life and she talks about 'we oppressed women'! You have no right to speak for those who really are oppressed! If my mother had heard you, if my quiet, patient, charming, oppressed and hard-working mother had been here now, she would have *bitten your arse off*! In complete silence and without any irrelevant comments!

Marie David   Unconvincing argument, Mr Strindberg. Your logic's definitely feminine.

Strindberg (*roars*)   But my intuition's far superior to yours! I know what's true! I can sniff it a mile off. I go after it and I get it!

Siri (*restless, walks up and down*)   You two seem to be enjoying this conversation . . . but I'm afraid I don't find it very amusing. I've heard it too many times. His intuition and his dead mother. This quiet, hard-working woman . . .

Strindberg   Don't you dare! Don't you dare touch her!

Don't you dare touch her sacred memory! Don't you dare . . .

Siri   Oh dear, oh dear, I won't, I won't. I'm only interested in one thing. Am I, or am I not, going to appear on the stage of the Dagmar Theatre on the ninth of March 1889?

Marie David   Siri is right.

Strindberg   Yes. Yes, she is, strange as it may seem. It's late and we're all tired but she's right. We really must try and finish this. We must . . . concentrate . . . let's do the most difficult part. Perhaps we should do page eight. Page eight, please. The long monologue where she expresses her hatred because she now realises that her girlfriend once tried to take her husband away from her.

SIRI I don't believe my ears! 'Ears', notice! Hear – ears! Right? I got it right this time, didn't I?

Strindberg (*pretends not to hear*)   It's all in the script! The script's sacred! And according to the script, these two women are fighting over the same man. He's not present but even in his absence he still dominates the stage. They both love him and they fight over him. It's all in the *script*!

Siri   Yes, darling. Of course, we love him. Passionately. Perhaps we should have a picture of him and I could kiss it at regular intervals? Wouldn't that be . . . ?

Strindberg   Page eight. Top of page eight, please. 'That's why . . . '

Siri   Let's get on with it. You're on, Marie.

Strindberg   'That's why'! Why the hell don't you start!

Marie *leans wearily over the foot board of the gigantic bed,* **Siri** *sits down gently by her side. Calm, almost resigned, she starts to read, completely contradicting the essence of her lines; her voice is warm, intimate, almost caressing.*

Siri 'That's why I had to embroider tulips on his slippers. I loathe tulips, but of course you like them.' (*Takes* **Marie***'s hand and caresses it gently.*) 'That's why we had to spend the summer on the Mälar Lake – because you couldn't stand the Baltic; that's why my son had to be called Eskil – because it was your father's name; that's why I had to wear your colours, read your books, eat the food you liked, and drink your favourite drinks, like that chocolate drink. That's why – oh God – it's terrible!' (*Very warm, very gentle, with a little smile.*) 'It's terrible, when I think of it, terrible . . . '

Strindberg (*confused, pleading*) But Siri, that's not right, you're doing it all wrong. You're supposed to hate her, Siri! Hate her! You must show how much you hate her!

Siri (*continues as if she has not heard*) 'Everything, everything came to me from you – even your passions. Your soul bored into mine like a worm into an apple, it ate and it ate, until only the husk was left and some fragments of black powder.' (*Gradually giving free rein to her feelings, now caresses* **Marie***.*) 'I tried to escape but I couldn't – with your black eyes you hypnotised me like a snake – I tried to spread my wings but only to be pulled down again – I was in the sea and my feet were tied together and the harder my arms tried to swim, the deeper I sank, way down until I reached the bottom and there you lay, like a giant crab, your claws reaching out to grab me – and that's where I am now.' (*Extremely quietly, gently.*) 'I hate you, I hate you, I hate you.'

Strindberg (*the manuscript has fallen out of his hand, he stands completely still in the middle of the floor, rocking back and forth. He starts to speak in a thin, childish voice*) Siri, that's not right . . . Siri . . . you're doing it all wrong . . .

Siri*'s manuscript has dropped to the floor and she clutches* **Marie** *tightly and caresses her. Their embrace becomes increasingly more intense. Suddenly* **Siri** *begins to cry. She cries more and more desperately and desolately. She presses her head* *against* **Marie***'s breast, caresses her, cries convulsively but yet happily.*

Siri   Oh Marie, Marie. I've been so lonely.

Marie David (*eyes closed, holds* **Siri** *in her arms as if she were a child, rocks her quietly*)   My little Siri. Little Siri. Just cry. It's all over now.

Strindberg *walks with very, very tiny steps up to the chair and sits down. His grey and vacant face is twitching. He looks out at the audience. He is silent. The bed with the two women is in semi-darkness, their bodies can barely be seen, the only sound to be heard is* **Siri***'s sobbing which slowly dies out.* **Strindberg** *remains silent. The music starts, very gently.*

Marie David (*frees herself, walks across the stage, up to* **Strindberg**. *She pulls up a chair and sits down next to him. She speaks to him in a very calm and friendly voice*)   Mr Strindberg.

Strindberg (*does not answer, almost imperceptibly his body is rocking back and forth, through his tightly closed lips comes an almost soundless groan, a sort of tuneless hum*)   Mm mm m m m m m m m m m m m m m m m m m m m m m m m m . . .

Marie David   Mr Strindberg.

Strindberg   Mm m m m m m m m m m m m m m m m m m m m m m m m m m m m m m m m m m . . .

Marie David   Mr Strindberg, your play is not altogether clear, I'm afraid.

Strindberg (*suddenly becomes silent, waits, then in a barely audible voice*)   I know.

Marie David   Sometimes it doesn't seem . . . true. But then, at other times, it seems . . . very, very true, almost *despite itself.* The truth escapes through the cracks. Where you couldn't close the gaps.

Strindberg   I know.

Marie David   Yes. Of course, you do.

Strindberg   After that night – I knew I'd lost. And I wanted to write a play about what it would be like . . . when the two of you met again.

Marie David   After the operation, you mean? After you tried to separate us with a meat cleaver?

Strindberg   Yes.

Marie David   So you wrote a play about two women who are in love with the same man and . . .

Strindberg   Yes . . .

Marie David   But you knew . . .

Strindberg   I knew I'd lost. But when I wrote the play, I wrote it the way I wanted it to be.

Marie David   The way you *wanted* it to be?

Strindberg   Sometimes you have to write about things the way you want them to be. You never know, it might make them happen.

Marie David *looks at him attentively, does not answer.*

(*With almost childish astonishment.*) I feel completely empty. Weightless, like a shell. Completely empty.

Marie David   Mr Strindberg, I always thought that what you wrote about marriage was so true. And I thought you were the most truthful man I'd ever met. But all the time, you'd tell these lies . . . I just couldn't understand . . .

Strindberg   You lock up two rats together, Miss David, and they'll start to scream. And they'll start to tear each other apart. It's as simple as that. I'm screaming, Miss David. Why don't you help me out?

Marie David   I understand.

Strindberg   No, you don't. Because I loved it too.

Marie David *remains silent.*

Siri and I were probably just like everyone else. We

thought we owned each other and spent our whole life nursing our hard feelings. If we'd spent it nursing our good feelings, it might've worked out differently

Marie David (*nods, hesitates, starts tentatively*)   Perhaps you . . . I s'pose you realise that Siri and I . . . that now we'll be living together.

Strindberg (*long silence*)   Yes, I do realise that.

Marie David   Something else that I'd like to tell you.

Strindberg   Yes?

Marie David   I do not altogether dislike you.

Strindberg   Thank you. (*Remains silent for a while.*) I don't altogether dislike you either. (*Very simply and in a friendly voice.*) You do realise, don't you, that I shall now have to fight you.

Marie David   Of course, I realise that.

Strindberg (*in the same friendly voice*)   I shall have to fight you with all the weapons I have at my disposal. I shall have to . . . hound you, discredit you and fight you. I don't have a choice. I'm forced to, you know that, don't you?

Marie David   I realise that. And I accept it.

Strindberg (*apologetically*)   That's the way it has to be.

Marie David   I know. We cannot change the rules.

Strindberg (*takes a deep breath. He is tired, stares vacantly into space, looks at her and passes his hand over his eyes*)   I s'pose we should finish the rehearsal.

Marie David   Yes.

Strindberg   We can't stop now. We've got a lot of work ahead of us. We can't stop now.

Marie David   No, There's a lot more work to be done.

The **Photographer** *comes in quietly, unnoticed, through the*

*door, suddenly stands there with his camera under his arm –
tripod, cloth, box. He looks around, then, without surprise in his
voice:*

Photographer   Have I come to the right place?

Siri *who has been huddled up on the bed in the background, gets
up – she is now completely calm. She fixes her hair, straightens
the creases in her dress, fastens a button in her bodice.*

Siri   Yes. You've come to the right place. We're ready for
you.

Strindberg (*gets up, walks to the front of the stage, speaks
straight to the audience in a very calm voice*)

After the rehearsal that night in March 1889 at the
Dagmar Theatre in Copenhagen it all came to an end.
On the ninth of March, *The Stronger,* starring Siri von
Essen, had its premiere. It was a complete fiasco and
closed after only one performance. August Strindberg
returned to Sweden and he and Siri von Essen were
divorced. Siri von Essen and Marie David then lived
together, first in Sweden, then in Finland where Marie
contracted tuberculosis and, after only a few years, she
died. But Strindberg was to meet Marie Caroline David
yet another time. It happened, by chance, on the twenty-
fourth of June, 1891 in Lerkile. On this occasion, they
did not have the chance to exchange a single word as, in
a fit of violent fury, Strindberg attacked her and pushed
her down a flight of stairs. She had a bad fall, but escaped
serious injury. In the trial that ensued, Strindberg was
found guilty of assault and ordered to pay a fine of 135
crowns. It was their last meeting. He never saw her again.

Photographer (*has now quietly and skilfully mounted his
camera*)   I'm ready.

Siri *walks up to* **Strindberg** *and takes his arm. He moves
obediently, walking in step with her, like a well-disciplined dog.*
Siri *holds him by one arm,* **Marie** *by the other. They walk up
and stand in front of the camera.*

Photographer   The gentleman in the middle, please.

They help to put him in the right place. **Strindberg** *is now standing in the middle.* **Siri** *is on his left. She leans gently and affectionately against his shoulder.* **Marie** *is on his other side. She stands with her head lowered, slightly turned to the side as if in deep thought or as if wishing not to be part of the group.*

Strindberg *in the middle, straight and completely rigid. He stares into space.*

An extremely strong flash, followed by an icy-blue cloud that makes their faces deadly pale. The stage darkens and the photograph that has just been taken is projected at the back of the stage, in a large scale blow-up. The music increases in volume.

Rain Snakes

by

Per Olov Enquist

translated by

Kim Dambæk

This translation of *Rain Snakes* was first performed by
Nordlys at the Young Vic Studio, London, 1996. The cast
was as follows:

Johan Ludvig Heiberg   Robert David
                                             Macdonald
Johanne Louise Heiberg (Hanne)   Sian Thomas
Hans Christian Andersen (HCA)   Jason Morell
The Old Bald Woman (OBW)   Imogen Claire

Director Kim Dambæk
Designer Kathy Strachan
Lighting Designer Joe Lewis
Producer Charlotte Barslund

Act One

A portrait at the back is the first thing to be seen as the lights come up. It is a portrait of a woman. She stands by a window staring out, the light shines in through the window; afternoon, tristesse, melancholy.

Or are we mistaken? Is it perhaps just a scene of calm waiting? The painting is W. Marstrand's famous portrait of Johanne Louise Heiberg.

There are two people in the room. A middle-aged woman. And a very old woman, who, strangely enough, has been tied to her chair. She is completely bald and dozing.

But first, the room. We appear to be in the mid-nineteenth century, a well-kept and solidly bourgeois Copenhagen during the years that were later to be known as 'The Golden Age'. A desk dominates the stage. The middle-aged woman sits at the desk, facing us. She writes, head down, in deep concentration. A piano stands to one side.

*The middle-aged woman wears her hair up and has a slightly prominent nose. She writes. Her name, incidentally, is Johanne Louise Heiberg (**Hanne**). The one on the canvas. The work of art.*

The old bald woman in the chair could be in her seventies, is of gruesome pallor, wrinkled and wearing a subdued blueish-white dress. A wide band ties her to the back of her chair (so as not to fall forwards) and both her forearms are tied to the arms of the chair. No coarse or rough rope. Long strips of material have been used. Knotted in bows.

In her sleep (is she really asleep?), she occasionally stirs. Little fleeting smiles cross her shrunken mouth. A small content gurgling, as from a sleeping child.

The woman at the desk does not look up. She just continues writing.

Quiet.

A man enters swiftly through the side door. It has been raining and he shakes his coat having taken if off. Swiftly, but not in a hurry. His hair is very thin, brushed back at the temples. A sharp profile. His name is **Johan Ludvig Heiberg**.

The woman writing does not look up.

Heiberg (*very collected and without raising his voice*) Catastrophic. Absolutely macabre.

Hanne *looks up from her work, staring at him without surprise or curiosity; silent.*

Heiberg   It's Andersen. He . . . (*Goes to the window, looks out.*) So soon. There he is. That torrent of tears is about to gush down upon us. It's my fault.

Hanne (*long pause, she looks at him attentively, but without surprise and says coldly*)   Really?

Heiberg   At times he's not all there. It was a scandal. Afterwards he was in such a state of despair that I felt obliged to invite him over. You'll have to comfort the creature.

Hanne   Me?

Heiberg   You. For you he has some sort of . . . I don't quite know what. But I promised.

Hanne (*starts writing methodically once more, and says coolly*) Whatever the calamity may have been, I have no time whatsoever.

Pause.

So what happened?

Heiberg (*pensive*)   To think that God should have wished to pour genius into a *vat* as unstylish and unrefined as Andersen's.

Hanne (*without looking up, lightly*)   Yes, that was rather thoughtless. To some God grants style. To others genius.

Heiberg (*turning his head and looking at her, a faint but slightly tense smile crosses his lips; ironic*)   Very clever, Hanne dear.

He walks past the portrait, looks up at it and straightens it: was it really hanging crooked? Impossible to say. He walks up to **Hanne** *from behind, quietly, but she senses him. She stops writing, lifts her gaze slightly, wary, she hardly moves, just waits, the pen trembling quietly in her hand. She feels his face ever closer. From behind her shoulder he stares at what she has written.*

Hanne?

Hanne   Yes, dear?

Heiberg   Hanne, dear . . . what have you written here . . . rain snakes?

Hanne *slowly and quietly, carefully and very disciplined lays the pen down along the right-hand side of the paper. She does not answer. Is she thinking of the question? She turns her head and looks at him. Silent.*

Heiberg   Hanne?

Suddenly, through the silence there is a knocking on the door, giving **Heiberg** *a start.*

There he is. I cannot bear hearing it once more. You look after him. He needs a little sympathy, a little 'there, there, there' and then get rid of him as quickly as possible.

He leaves the room, swiftly.

Hanne (*distinctly.*)   R . . . A . . . I . . . N . . . (*But he has gone, the door closes to. She looks at the door pensively and adds:*) . . . Snakes.

More knocking. **Hanne** *lifts her pen slowly, holds it close to the paper, as if writing. She sits, completely still, pen in hand, her gaze focused on the paper. Another knock. The door opens, carefully.* **HCA**'*s long horse's face is seen in the door opening, already full of deep melancholy. The long body executes some* *peculiar movements, slithers in graciously and commences a preliminary bow. And then he sees her. His face contorts into a joyful smile and then once more into one of unspeakable sorrow. He enters, shuts the door and crosses to her. A magnificent entrance full of pathos, despair and happiness.*

HCA (*dramatically*)   You've already heard! You'll understand my despair! My shame! The shame of it all, which will . . .

Hanne   Come in.

HCA (*stares at her, still with an expression of deepest despair which gradually changes to one of confusion, and he says, in a quieter tone*)   But I already have! I am here!

Hanne (*resigning herself to the fact, she says sharply*)   You shouldn't come in, Andersen, until I say come in.

HCA   Aha? (*Slightly ill at ease.*) Shall I go out and try again?

Hanne   For God's sake, no!

HCA (*suddenly anxiously aware of a problem having arisen*) I've bungled, Mrs Heiberg. No, don't! Don't say anything! I can see it on your face! Don't say anything! I've bungled. If it's so, tell me straight away. Have I bungled??

Hanne (*with some effort*)   Yes.

HCA (*deep despair overpowers him again, he wrings his hands, his face an ocean of pain and emotion*)   I knew it. I've bungled again. I won't sleep a wink tonight. Everything! Everything happens all at once! The King. The catastrophe. The despair. The dentures. The dust. And the Queen patting me on the head.

Hanne *stares at him in disbelief, but no further explanation comes out of* **HCA**, *who has just caught sight of the* **Old bald woman**. *The* **OBW**'s *head rests lightly to one side, a joyful smile across her toothless mouth with little discreet whistling noises coming from her lips. He restrains his anguish and crosses to her, bowing politely.*

HCA   Oh, do forgive me! I did not see that . . . please
excuse my impoliteness . . . may I introduce myself . . .
Hans Christian Andersen . . . poet! How enchanting to
make your acquaintance!

*He grasps her hand, and, to his surprise finds it tied; thinks of a
solution, leans forward, kisses her hand, which seems to bring
the* **OBW** *out of her mercifully dark and happy slumber.*

OBW's *eyelids twitch, a gigantic toothless smile lights up her
face, her eyes open wide, a little saliva trickles from the corner of
her mouth, she looks at him, smiles mischievously, seductively
flirtatious like a young girl. Then a noise comes from her mouth,
first guttural, then more songlike, indeed, like a wave, a song
swells up from within her, like some ancient memory.*

OBW   . . . Eeeeee . . . eeiiiiiin . . . eiiiiinnnnn . . .
kooommt der faaaaa . . . ssssssoooooibbbber-eer waaaar . . .
schwännnnnnnnwchen . . . eeeeerrr schlaaag . . . im tisch
. . . eeeeiiiiinn kommt de muttrrrr . . . eeein sollst duu
fitttachen du schlägst . . . fi . . . so ein kusssss . . . e . . .
(*Laughs quietly, then repeats.*) eiinnn . . . iiiinn . . . he came
. . . cuuu . . . nnt . . . slammed the table . . . .aeee . . . don't
hit the baaaalls . . . that into my cuuuuuunnt . . . eeeee . . .

*Her voice quietens down to a long, whining tone, an
inarticulate animal whimper.* **HCA** *has watched her, as if
paralysed, but* **Hanne** *does not appear to have heard or else she
is completely indifferent. She has not turned around.*

HCA (*still seems to be in conversation with the* **OBW**, *and
says, politely*)   How charming and interesting to make
your acquaintance . . .

Pause, he does not know quite what to do.

Très enchanté, madame!

Distractedly he crosses to **Hanne**.

Perhaps she speaks French?

Hanne   Not lately.

HCA   Who . . . is she?

Hanne   What was this catastrophe? Do hurry, I haven't much time.

Suddenly reminded of his misery, sorrow and melancholy overcome **HCA** *yet again, but he commences with a certain amount of determination.*

HCA   I shan't sleep at all tonight! I shan't sleep! Only cry and . . .

Hanne   So you've said. But what happened?

HCA (*collecting himself*)   At the palace. The entire court assembled. The King. The Queen. I mean the Countess Danner. Princes. Princesses, foreign ones at that. His Excellency the Lord Chamberlain Holstein. Everybody. And I, a guest of honour. I have been asked to give a short speech. A recital. For all these people who proclaim to love me! Such incredible charity! Imagine my delight. That the King. The Queen. I mean the Countess Danner. Princes. Some of them foreign. Everybody. I have forgotten some . . .

Hanne   My husband.

HCA   Your husband! How could I forget him!

Melancholy overpowers him again.

A nightmare.

Hanne   My husband?

HCA   Whom I admire above all else! No, no! There I stand before this dazzling audience. Before the King. He looks at me with his radiant eyes, his warm smile. His gracefully sculpted . . .

Pause.

Well. And the Queen. And everyone else. Your husband was also there. (*Dramatically.*) Your husband!

Hanne (*lightly*)   There, there.

HCA   And I think to myself: how far you've come, Hans Christian Andersen. The son of a simple shoemaker. I've decided to give a short extemporised speech to their majesties. About love. I had thought of the title to the speech myself. 'Amor Omnia Vincit'. Love conquers all. Then I allow myself a short artistic pause, so as to heighten the suspense. I open my mouth to take flight and my dentures drop to the floor.

Hanne   God!!!

HCA   Quite! The Queen's very words!

Hanne   (*sceptical, but showing interest for the first time*) You're joking, surely.

HCA   (*agitated and reproachful*)   One does not joke about such things! Have you ever heard anyone joke about dentures??

Hanne   (*thinking it over*)   Yes, as it happens. Although not in our circles.

HCA   Wretches forced to wear dentures, however, do not joke about them. And besides, mine hurt! They don't fit properly. (*Very factual and concentrated.*) The problem, Mrs Heiberg, is that if the upper arch is too . . . flat . . . it diminishes one's ability to suck. But if the arch is too high, it may cause an abscess. So one has to alter, lower the palate. It's called the palate. But the sore that I have, in the actual palate vault, can you imagine a church, Mrs Heiberg?

Hanne   (*curious*)   A church??

HCA   I like to think of it as the vaulted ceiling of a church. And here, where the palate reaches its . . . here, in the actual . . .

Hanne   (*turns away impatiently*)   I don't wish to know!

HCA   (*sorry and hurt*)   You don't wish to know? Aren't you interested?

Hanne   Yes! But . . .

HCA   Imagine my mouth as a church. There, where the vaulted ceiling reaches its highest . . .

Hanne   I don't want to know! I do not want to know!

HCA (*helpless*)   If an abscess develops, it's painful.

Hanne (*tries gaining control over the situation*)   If you don't get to the point, I shall have to call my husband!

HCA (*brightening up*)   Well now, that would be very kind . . . perhaps he is interested? If you . . .

Hanne (*extremely collected*)   Before I go completely crazy; you were saying; you are about to give your speech. Love conquers all. And then you drop your . . . them. Whatever happened next is all I wish to know, nothing else!

HCA   I dropped them right down on the carpet! Do you know what that means??

Hanne (*thinks*)   I have no idea.

HCA (*his entire body becomes very plastic*)   I just stand there! Paralysed! I bend down. Try to pick up the . . . them. Put them back. The entire court before me. I feel, with my entire body, how compassion and sympathy streams towards me from all sides. But also . . . yes, giggles. Perhaps I'm mistaken. But just the thought of someone giggling at my misfortune. There's mumbling. Do you understand, there's mumbling. This mumbling! You cannot distinguish a single word, but the mumbling is awful, it's booming in my ears! I pick them up, put them back, but then! Then! I feel dust! The carpet was dusty! Fluff in my mouth! There's dust and fluff on my false teeth! Fluff from the carpet! I try to begin my speech again. A poet's tribute to the royal couple and to love. I say, 'Amor Omnia Vincit, love conquers all.' But it is impossible to recite an ode to love with fluff on your dentures!

Hanne (*gripped*)   Yes, yes. Of course it is.

HCA   Gritty! Dusty! Fluffy! There I am, a poet standing before their majesties! It's a nightmare! And then I burst into tears.

Hanne   I quite understand. I would have done the same.

HCA   They lead me to a chair. Give me a glass of water.

Hanne   You should have had a cognac.

HCA (*guardedly*)   I never drink when performing!

Continues.

A glass of water. They bathe my brow as if I were ill. The King strokes his hand gently over my head and urges me to stop crying. The Queen assures me that she was very fond of the speech, as far as it went. I fall to my knees, kiss her feet, assure her that I am touched and grateful for her . . .

Hanne (*rises in agitation*)   Her! She is no Queen! She's a floozy! And you kissed her feet??

HCA (*weakly*)   No, she was wearing shoes.

Hanne   Well, you were lucky, Andersen, believe me.

HCA   But I still can't continue the speech. Something's gone wrong. It's as if I . . .

Hanne   Set off on the wrong foot.

HCA   Foot? Yes, something like that.

En passant.

Of course, the incident with the dentures was not the best of beginnings.

Hanne   That's enough. Stop.

HCA   But to think that the royal couple . . . and the whole court . . . still show such indulgence towards me. No matter how bad things get.

Hanne (*harshly*)   You being a world famous genius
might just have a little to do with it.

HCA   Do you really think so?

Hanne   Well, it is only a guess.

Violently.

That an artist of your calibre should . . . lick the feet of
that cow. I can't believe it. It can't be true. It's degrading
– to all of us!

HCA (*looks at her sadly, like a dog that has wet the carpet, sits
and says gloomily*)   I'm sorry.

Pause.

You're right. There were always the King's shoes.

Hanne   Oh!

HCA (*after a moment's deep thought*)   But I am world
famous for the wrong reasons!

Hanne   Wrong reasons?

HCA   Yes, children's fairy tales . . . they are not . . . they
don't count. They're not real literature. What counts is to
be performed at the Royal Theatre. Real plays. Tragedies.
And such.

Hanne (*stunned, then angry*)   I can't bloody believe it . . .

HCA (*can't believe his ears*)   Sorry? Mrs Heiberg?

Hanne   At times I don't think you're all there. You're so
totally lacking in judgement that you ought to be stuffed
and paraded in a travelling circus!

HCA   But surely fairy tales don't count in the same
way?

Hanne   So much of what counts as literature is rubbish!
Tons of it! That's the problem. And then you wish to
make matters worse by writing some pretentious drivel
for the Royal Theatre. We've got plenty of that, thank you

very much; stick to your fairy tales, Andersen, that is great art; one simple story may change a person's life. But you'll never be a playwright; never, ever!

HCA (*emptily*)   Why?

Hanne   You are far too feminine by nature.

HCA (*his legs helplessly entwined, he looks down, and finally says, quietly*)   Perhaps it's true. I have never boasted of having a masculine nature.

Pause, melancholic.

If only I could write as good a play as your husband . . . that would count . . .

Hanne (*quick*)   He doesn't write any more.

Explodes.

So why did you write those stories if you don't think they count? Why . . . for what purpose?

HCA   Oh, them. For no purpose at all. I only wrote them because I was happy.

Hanne   And the plays because they are literature and count.

HCA   Yes, something like that.

Hanne (*brutally*)   Perhaps that is why they are so incredibly awful.

HCA (*disconsolate*)   Don't say that, you mustn't say that, dear, sweet Mrs Heiberg. You, our leading actress; you and your husband who decide what's good and what should be performed, won't you think more kindly of me. It's nasty of you, it's nasty of you, dear . . .

Hanne (*also agitated*)   You mustn't beg like that! You make me ill begging like that. Why this humility? No reason, whatsoever!

She paces the room, out of control.

I'm infuriated and I don't know why . . . As though I had some sort of responsibility for you. As if we were brother and sister! Oh! To kiss the foot of that . . . of her. (*Almost to herself:*) And that fat imbecile whom she pulls around by the nose.

HCA (*deeply shocked*)   Mrs Heiberg!?? The King?!!

Hanne   You might have learnt the rules of the game by now. Otherwise they'll never take you seriously.

HCA   The game?

Hanne (*harsh and quiet*)   I had to learn. Our sort have to, Mr Andersen.

HCA (*curious, slightly guarded*)   Our . . . sort?

Hanne *turns, stands by the window, quiet.*

HCA   Mrs Heiberg?

Pause, she doesn't answer.

Do you dislike me?

Pause.

Mrs Heiberg. Someone like me. Born in a sewer. The sewer is dark and full of rot and decay. It stinks. And I'm a small weed in the sewer, a sludgy plant that has never set eyes on the sun. There's an awful stench and smell and the sewer plant has never ever seen the sun. But it wants to reach up. Towards the sun! Trees surround the sewer, their branches reaching out across and covering it. And the sewer plant reaches upwards. Have you ever seen a sewer plant, Mrs Heiberg? Ugly things, ugly, ugly, no charm, no grace. But they reach upwards.

Hanne   I know what the sewers are like.

HCA   But sewer plants?

She doesn't turn, she's silent.

Suddenly; a dark bellow comes from **OBW**, *increasing in* *volume, like an animal in despair, far away, strangely dark in its tone. Her eyes are still shut, even as the dark song dies away.*

OBW   . . . öööööööööööööööööööööööööö . . .

Heiberg *in his dressing-gown, crosses calmly and routine-like to the* **OBW**. *He holds a small metal bottle in front of her mouth and forces it between her lips. She struggles against him for a few seconds, then drinks in quick gulps. He removes the bottle. The fluid trickles down her cheek. Black. He wipes. Her eyes remain closed.*

Heiberg (*looks at her pensively*)   It seems to be more frequent now.

HCA   Is she . . . ill?

Heiberg (*scrutinising* **HCA** *calmly and critically*)   I see you're feeling better now, Andersen.

HCA (*dramatically*)   I've told your wife everything!

Heiberg   Everything? One should *never* do that.

Hanne   Mr Andersen will be leaving shortly. He's told me of his latest recital for the King and Queen.

Heiberg   Yes, that attracted a lot of attention.

Hanne *has sat down by the desk, he moves over to her, almost shyly.*

Hanne? Will you be writing tonight?

Hanne   Yes.

Pause.

And you? Are you sitting and . . . waiting?

Heiberg   Yes. Precisely. As usual.

Pause.

I have almost forgotten what it feels like to write.

Pause.

But Mr Andersen! (*Light aggression, almost jolly.*) Mr Andersen! You are so . . . creative! A child of nature. Creative children of nature are so extremely popular right now.

Cold, to **HCA.**

But there's one thing I'd like to know. What was that speech actually to have been about? If you hadn't dropped your Demosthenes' stones, so to speak.

The atmosphere is slightly tense, **HCA** *looks from one to the other.*

HCA   About love, that is what it would have been about. About the family. I would have tried to formulate my . . . dream about love.

His face radiates with a joyful smile, he has had a thought.

I actually think . . . it would have been . . . about you! About the Heiberg family! Amor Omnia Vincit!

Hanne (*almost unintentionally*)   Good God. I'm beginning to think we were lucky.

HCA   A family portrait from 1856! About a marriage like yours – erudite, wise and warm. It's perhaps even better than the royal couple. The Heiberg couple.

He claps his hands together, maniacally, paces up and down, agitated and happy.

How stupid I am. I didn't see. But what if it's not too late. What if you were to help me? Chance has led me to your matrimony. I shall . . .

Stops, says quietly:

A family portrait from the middle of the nineteenth century.

Heiberg   A fine thought. Don't you agree, Hanne?

Hanne (*forced*)   That was kind, Andersen. But I think we ought to change the subject now. Besides, it's late.

HCA (*very quiet*)   The family. Love. Which conquers all.
An ideal. Perhaps I could do it in the shape of a play.
They ought to be able to perform it at the Royal Theatre?
An ode to love . . .

Heiberg   Then mind you don't drop your teeth again.

Hanne   Leave him in peace!!!

Heiberg (*he looks at her surprised, says coldly and quietly*)
Such . . . power of emotion. You seem to have found one
another.

Amiably to **HCA**.

Mr Andersen. You are so . . . ebullient. Like a jolly baby
elephant that has found himself a pristine porcelain
boutique. Just mind you don't smash anything.

HCA   How do you mean?

Heiberg   I mean – I don't think it would make a good
play.

HCA   Oooh. (*Dully.*) Then you don't want *that* one
either.

Much more apathetic and quiet.

I urged Mrs Heiberg not to be so heartless in her verdict
of . . . it might not prove too helpful.

Bursts out.

You are hard, Mr Heiberg. Hard! Hard! You are so
incredibly . . . hard! . . . so . . .

Heiberg   Mr Andersen?

HCA   Yes??

Heiberg   May I interrupt you?

HCA (*naively puzzled*)   But you already have?

Heiberg   I understand you think I'm a blackguard.
That's your business. But there's one thing I have to

make absolutely clear. There's something called 'good taste'. It's based on eternal values. Do you follow?

HCA (*obediently*)   Yes. Good taste is based on eternal evaluations.

Heiberg   Eternal values! Good taste is not something one learns in the slums. The language of the slums and taverns is at the lowest level; the language of the haphazard, the ephemeral . . . occasionally the language of fairy tales. Of the common man. But we, who defend good taste and enduring art, must brandish the sword of castigation. Take up battle against common language, against bad taste. Against waning self-control. Against the coarseness of popular speech. That's our duty. To nail down what is beautiful and what is ugly.

HCA (*melancholic*)   I've felt pain every time you've nailed me down.

Heiberg   Can't you be content with your . . . fairy tales? They enjoy such popular success. Why must you, by hook or by crook, write for the theatre?

Hanne (*stands quietly under the painting and looks up at it*) Perhaps he's malleable. Can be formed. Like I was.

Heiberg (*hears the irony which hurts him, says quietly*)   Yes, Hanne, I've taught you the meaning of good taste. You are my finest work of art.

Concentrating, the sentences flow from **Hanne**'s *mouth almost complete, almost perfect, as if translated from German.*

Hanne   And yet only the connection between fault and perfection in a person, the relationship between the two, creates a person, creates that which is personal in a person. For are we not, deep down, as finely nuanced as the plants, among which we seldom find a purely white or purely black leaf, nay, all things considered, does not the whitest of lilies have some of the other hues in its shading?

Heiberg (*very alert, speaking to* **HCA** *yet looking at* **Hanne**)
Isn't her language beautiful, Mr Andersen. Almost
complete, like a petal. And yet deep inside there's a tiny,
pretty and dangerous dagger. That was lovely, Hanne.

Hanne   And am I right?

Heiberg   It . . . was so lovely that I forgot to listen.

Hanne (*an odd stillness between the two*)   Shall I . . .
translate?

Heiberg (*short pause, then embittered to* **HCA**)   Even the
Englishman, with his curious popularity, Mr Shakespeare,
can only be performed if his plays are rewritten. The raw
Shakespeare certainly has his merits. But he must be
adapted! Adapted! To harmonise with good taste. He
describes a raw reality, that's true. Describes, indeed. But
is it necessary, I wonder??

HCA   No, it's quite obvious that . . .

Heiberg   Mrs Beijer's adaptations of his work have a
completely different elegance to the originals.

Hanne (*uncertain*)   She makes them sound quite
charmant . . .

Heiberg (*sharp glance at her, which side is she on? Then with
bite*)   Style and taste are eternal. Constant. Constant!
(*Quietly to himself.*) Like the archival metre.

HCA (*naively*)   The what?

Heiberg (*very loud*)   The archival metre!!! (*Quietens
down and speaks slowly and patronisingly as to an idiot.*) The
archival metre is the standard measure for measurements
defined as being one tenth of a million of a meridional
quadrant of the earth. Called a *metre*. (*Scrutinising without
hope* **HCA**'s *gaping face.*) Defined as the distance, at zero
degrees centigrade, between the ends of that metre-ruler,
the prototype, kept in a vault in the Breteuil pavilion in
Paris. The archival metre. The metre of all metres. The
ur-metre.

*No smile on **HCA***'s *face.*

All metric measurements stem from this prototype. These
measurements are eternal. And so too in art. Thus we
measure. Thus we judge. The measure of good taste.
We judge by these . . . invariables. According to a
constant.

HCA (*breathlessly interested*)   Now I understand!! The
archival metre!

He is about to embrace **Heiberg**, *thinks better of it, shakes*
Heiberg's *hand, almost tears of joy in his eyes.*

Oh, you are so clever. You've read everything. You've
known all of that all along haven't you?

Heiberg *slightly flattered, but the enthusiasm is a bit too much.*

HCA   One ten millionth of . . . may I jot this down?
(*Draws out his notebook.*) . . . The Earth . . .

Heiberg   A meridional quadrant.

HCA   A constant. Invariable. Good taste. Just like a
connoisseur. (*Stiffens, opens eyes wide, his horse's face starts to
quiver.*) Like you! (*Pointing at* **Heiberg**.) Like an archival
metre! Like you!

Heiberg   Like me?

HCA   The archival critic! Whoever decides good taste,
must be invariable, the archival critic!

*Fumbling with his notebook – putting it away, pulling it up
again, he continues enthusiastically.*

Imagine if I could write a tale about the archival critic!
The invariable archival critic. It begins in Copenhagen.
He's standing in King's Square. Outside the Royal
Theatre. Then he falls victim to an awful series of trials
and disasters. He's shanghaied by buccaneers.

*Deep concentration, carried away, his face is a mass of
contortions.*

There is a blizzard, he's shipwrecked. Close to drowning!
He's washed ashore, and there he's attacked by wild
creatures.

He winces out of horror and sympathy.

Serpents! Scorpions! He escapes, then new storms; he
lands in the middle of a war, he's shot at! A field hospital,
he's struck by the plague, boils all over his body, the
hospital burns down, everyone around him dies! Locusts!
A pack of mangy, ferocious, rabies-infested hounds set
upon him, he escapes. A snowstorm, Indians on the
warpath track him down, capture him, scalp him. He's
trampled down by a stampede of buffaloes . . .

*He hesitates, desperately searching in his rich catalogues of
disasters, brightens up.*

The bridge collapses! But in the end, the archival critic is
back in Copenhagen! Once more he stands in King's
Square and he is exactly . . . exactly . . . the same!
Unchanging!

Fumbles for his notebook and he notices **Heiberg***'s stony face,*
HCA*'s enthusiasm slowly dies.*

. . . Unchanged . . . ??

Heiberg *studies* **HCA** *with very cool eyes. He's intelligent
enough to realise that this is a complicated story. There is not a
trace of a smile on his face. Then gently and elegantly he brings
his heels together, bows slightly, smiles faintly ironically and
turns to go. Stops in the doorway, looks at* **Hanne**.

Heiberg (*quietly*) Hanne?

Hanne No!

Heiberg I understand.

Pause.

I'd better leave you then . . . to yourselves. (*And he calmly
leaves the room.*)

HCA (*miserable*)   Did I say something wrong, Mrs Heiberg?

Still looking at the door, where her husband left, **Hanne** *scrutinises* **HCA**.

Hanne (*friendly*)   You are not so easy to grasp, Mr Andersen.

HCA   I think I did say something wrong. Hurt him somehow.

Hanne   He's only been confirmed in his belief that no one needs him any longer. Not even his opinions.

HCA (*in disbelief*)   Mr Heiberg???

No answer, he sits.

Everyone finds me so naive. But . . . I only want people to like me. To be loved.

Hanne   Most unusual.

Standing with her back to him, says quietly.

And how do you imagine love then, Mr Andersen?

HCA   You know. I'm not so experienced. (*Pause.*) But I think of it almost constantly. And then I imagine it to be – well, like a painting. As if you and Mr Heiberg were sitting here one evening. Conversing. So lovely, so warm. I would like things in my life to be just like they are in yours. And I would want my beloved and I to sit like that, each in our own armchair. With the lamp aglow. In the evening. First my beloved would read something from a book. And then, in her own words, she would say something similar to what you just said, something like 'Are we not like plants amongst which one seldom finds a purely white or purely black leaf?' and I would answer with something witty or refined, then she would reply in her elegant voice, and then it would be my turn again, and then she'd say *this* and I'd say *that*, and we would continue in this way, sitting by the lamp conversing all evening. That is how I imagine love, Mrs Heiberg.

Hanne   Dear God.

She turns, looks at him, shakes her head. But it's as if she can't stand still, paces the room briskly, suddenly crossing to a cupboard in the bookshelf, she takes out a bottle with a light-brown liquid. She pours a small glass and empties it expertly and quickly, looks at the empty glass.

You don't want any, do you? No.

Returns the bottle and glass to the cupboard, looks at him sharply.

Cough mixture. An actress must nurse her instrument.

Pause.

You did say you didn't want any, didn't you? That's what I thought.

Pause.

That was a splendid idea you had, wasn't it? Love conquers all. About the Heiberg family.

Pause.

So you know what sewers are like, do you? And sewer plants. I read your memoirs last autumn, but obviously they were not straight from the horse's mouth. Only nice, moving stories. Mama was poor and noble. Papa was honest and noble. Grandmama was poor and noble, staying at the poorhouse surrounded by jolly and noble people. Grandpapa was a simpleton, but noble all the same, apparently. There was a weeping willow growing in your garden. Where do you get it from?

HCA *is silent.*

Hanne (*brutally*)   Something's not quite right, is it? But it's the same old story. No one dares touch their sore spots. (*Pause.*) And eventually it's impossible to do so. And then everything is . . . gone.

HCA   Sore spots?

Hanne   Oh. Piss off. (*Friendlier.*) I'm sorry. But you see
it's like this, Mr Andersen. I'm slightly impatient. On
edge. There's a smear campaign against my husband and
I. We're thought of as having too much power. We're
being slandered. My dearly beloved friend, the actress
Anna Nielsen, died recently, who for most of her life had
schemed to have me booted out of the theatre, but was
too talentless to succeed. She wasn't suitable for leading
roles. I was forced to oppose her for the sake of our art. A
small bouncy and jovial character like her shouldn't play
tragic parts. And anyway, she was far too old. Some are
just born too old.

HCA (*like a wounded animal*)   She played the lead in my
first play!

Hanne (*critically*)   Quite.

Pause.

She hated me. Before I wouldn't have shed a tear if she
contracted the bubonic plague. But then she goes and
dies. And I become . . . melancholic. She lingers on,
somehow, like a question. Why did we do all those things?

Pause.

So much hate. Everyone says that I'm a witch. I wasn't
like that before. How has this happened?

HCA (*agitated*)   But you don't have any enemies!

Hanne   How droll.

HCA   Everyone loves you.

Hanne (*amiably*)   Except those who persecute me
purely for artistic reasons.

HCA   Artistic?

Hanne   Artistic reasons. Everything that happens at the
Royal Theatre happens purely for artistic reasons. For
example, there's Doctor Ryge, our leading actor and
member of the board of directors. He has, purely for

artistic reason, been my enemy all his life. He thinks I am arrogant and lack talent. He's thought so since the day when I was still only thirteen and he dragged me into a closet at the Royal Theatre, unbuttoned his fly and wanted me to suck him off. That's what I call a children's fairy tale, Mr Andersen!

HCA (*deeply shocked*)   Mrs Heiberg! What a way to speak!

Hanne   Surely you mean – what a way to behave?

HCA   Yes . . . of course.

Hanne   But don't worry. I got away.

HCA   Well . . . that . . . was lucky!

Hanne   And because of that, the doctor started thinking ill of me, purely for artistic reasons. I was too quick. But in the theatre you have to be very quick at times.

HCA   But if Mr Heiberg . . . heard you say this! With his . . .

Hanne (*icily*)   . . . disgust of anything that's coarse? But Mr Heiberg can't hear us. And you won't tell him. Mr Heiberg is incredibly sensitive to slander of his wife. It would hurt his pride. And that makes him very disagreeable. Just like me.

HCA   When you talk like that . . . it frightens me.

Hanne   Calm down. Love conquers all.

HCA   I don't feel very well . . . I . . . perhaps I should leave.

Hanne (*after a short pause, in an odd tone of voice*)   No. You're not quite ready. Not yet. When I want you to leave, then you'll leave.

HCA   Mrs Heiberg. (*Pause.*) I don't know what you want. Is it me? You don't want to hurt me, do you? (*Stares ahead, emptily.*) I feel you're going to hurt me very shortly.

Hanne (*breezily*)   No one wants to hurt you, surely.
You're so adorable. Have you actually ever met real
evil?

HCA   All my life.

Hanne   Of course! Everyone is after you. Rabid dogs.
Herds of buffaloes. Indians. Collapsing bridges!

HCA   When mother sent me to the mill in Odense, I
couldn't get the other workers to like me. So I thought,
perhaps if I sing a few songs. And dance well.

*He starts dancing slowly, almost without noticing himself, with
small shuffling and clumsy steps, deadly serious.*

And I sang. (*Pause.*) With my high clear voice which was
greatly admired.

Hesitates, staring straight ahead.

Then they said that my voice was so high that I had to be
a girl. And then they grabbed me. And undid my trousers
to check. And examined me. In the end they let me go
because I screamed so horribly. I still dream about it.
They chase me in my dream. They're out to get me. And
then I'm so ashamed.

Pause.

You're not out to get me, are you, Mrs Heiberg?

Hanne   I'm not out to get you. (*Pause.*) On the
contrary, you're adored in every palace throughout
Europe. Everyone's little darling. There seems to be an
enormous demand for booby geniuses like yourself.

HCA *nods, stares at the floor, wrings his hands, his horse's jaws
grinding at imaginary hay, but he's silent.*

Hanne   You're exactly how they imagine an artist
should be. It's just that . . . It's too obvious. It pains me to
see.

HCA   What's too obvious?

Hanne   I can't tell you. But it is.

Paces restlessly, aiming towards the small cupboard, hesitating, she then reaches for the bottle.

A real artist shouldn't prostitute himself so obviously. And clumsily!

HCA (*despairing*)   But I could never do it as elegantly as you!

Hanne (*stops, a quick, uncertain smile*)   As I??

Pause, lightly.

No. Probably not.

Grabs the bottle, quick and routined drinking ceremony.

Cough mixture. An actress must nurse her instrument. You don't want any, do you.

She's really evil now, calm and contained, her fangs gleaming.

To drop your dentures is only human. But what you did with that madam. I knew her when she was just a ballet pupil. She danced poorly and was a hussy even then. Ach.

Slams cupboard, giving **OBW** *a start. The* **OBW** *opens her eyes and mouth, calling a name, growing in clarity.*

OBW   Heee . . . mannnnn . . . ! Hermann! Hermann!

Hanne (*brutally matter-of-fact*)   He's not here!

HCA   Where . . . is he?

Hanne   He's dead!

HCA   Oh . . . what a shame . . . (*Reflective.*) Who is Hermann?

Hanne   An older gentleman who adored little girls. Papa and Mama ran a public house. In the evenings there'd be dancing. Papa drunk. Then Hermann came and lifted me down off the billiard table. His fatal mistake.

Stands indecisively in front of **OBW** *who appears to have fallen asleep again, says softly:*

Do you follow?

HCA (*thinking*)   No. Not at all.

Hanne (*explaining*)   He liked small green fruit. I was one.

HCA (*fearful and with terrible foreboding*)   Did your father . . . kill him?

Hanne (*agitated*)   Papa? Are you crazy? Papa *never* beat anyone but Mama!

HCA (*relieved*)   Oh! You had me worried.

Hanne   And the children too, of course.

HCA   Of course.

Hanne   Actually, no. Strangely enough. He always beat my brothers and sisters, but never me. He'd be drunk every night and would beat them. But never me. He was a gentle and sensitive person really. For example, he'd always feel sorry when he'd beaten them. He'd wake up with a hangover, feeling sorry. Then you'd have to comfort him and say that it didn't matter. Day after day. We tried locking the door between the bar and the kitchen when he got drunk, but then he'd kick the door down, take off his belt and start beating. Next morning. Tears and comfort, tears and comfort. Papa was so proud of his girls. My sisters and I had to dance on the billiard table. I cried and cried, but we had to. And all the drunks and whores sat around staring and screeching. All the filthy comments. About little knickers and things like that. Papa was blind drunk and didn't understand a thing. Babbling about his little stars. Until the day Hermann came and lifted me down off the billiard table.

HCA   But . . . did that kill him?

Hanne (*irritated*)   No. Why should it?

HCA   That's what you said.

Hanne (*mechanically*)   'When the setting sun of life, shines on childhood memories, they assume a golden glow, a glimmer which warms and reconciles.' As my husband puts it. Perhaps that's the way it should be. Life cleansed of the filth of existence.

Pause.

A curious thought.

Pause.

Papa was impossible that night. Up we went, we had to dance. And I cried and cried. There was a man sitting at a table, all alone. His name was Hermann. I was nine, all the whores sang, it was winter, snow, I cried and cried and danced, and then this Hermann got up and lifted me down off the billiard table. And said she shouldn't be forced.

Pause.

Actually he lifted me out of one life. And into another. I wonder if he ever knew.

Pause.

At first I thought he wanted to . . . fondle. But he didn't. Not then. He just stood there staring at me with his large moist cow's eyes. Talked to Mama. Papa was too drunk.

Pause.

He wished to be my benefactor, they said. He would pay. Do you know what a benefactor is, Mr Andersen?

HCA   It's someone who . . . whom one must be very grateful to.

Hanne   Who drags you up out of the sewer. But you pay for it, don't you? Haven't you paid your benefactors, Mr Andersen?

HCA *is silent, she moves in close to him, whispering almost.*

Hanne   Oh yes. Sooner or later. One always has to pay. One way or another.

Crosses to the cupboard, quickly, same ceremony, drinks rapidly, looks into the empty glass, says tonelessly:

Life was sunny, life was gay, life was flowers and a roll in the hay. As they say.

Pause.

Hermann had large moist eyes full of longing and a big fat kisser and he would come to fetch me whenever I had to go to the theatre. I was a ballet pupil. A long, wet kiss. Then holding little Hanne's hand, off we went.

With disgust.

I heard all the jokes about us. Hanne with her boyfriend. What we did. It was as if everyone knew. And the sense of shame was great. Every time he came he wanted his long, wet kiss. Little Hanne, how sweet you are. Little Hanne was to be educated. Not to be vulgar like . . . like the whores! Not to know dirty jokes! Not to dance on the billiard table!

She circles **HCA** *as if wanting to provoke him, reach into him.*

I heard so many fairy tales as a child! Mr Andersen! Do you know this one? Boy and girl lying on the ground in the woods, having fun. The boy gets up, pulls up his breeches and says: 'Had I known you were a virgin, I would have taken more time!' Then the girl gets up, straightens her dress and says: 'Had I known you had more time, I would have taken off my silk knickers!'

HCA *stares at her as if paralysed.*

Hanne   Oh! Don't come over all prune-faced with me. Surely, you can't be that innocent, you must have seen and heard a few things? A little bird told me you have an aunt in Copenhagen who runs a brothel. You must have stayed there a few times. Am I right?

HCA *looks at the floor, wrings his hands.*

Hanne   What does it matter? (*Comforting.*) All of Copenhagen's a whorehouse.

Pause.

Hermann paid. I was to become elegant. Holding hands. Kissing his wet lips in the parlour. And shame, shame, shame.

Pause.

Little ten-year olds are so strange.

HCA   I would like to leave now, Mrs Heiberg. I don't wish to hear any more. I'm frightened.

Hanne (*not listening or caring*)   It was so strange. Tied to someone you loathe or despise. And you know that everyone is staring and talking. It's like going for a never-ending walk through hell. Hand in hand with Uncle Hermann. You walk hand in hand through hell and hear everyone laughing behind your back. And then it's as if you become one.

Pause.

No, you melt together. Fused together by degradation. Because he could also hear. What they said. You both melt into one. It's almost like . . . love.

HCA   Love?

Hanne   Loathing and attraction and shame. And love.

Pause.

Then Heiberg came along. He was so different. Although similar in some respects. You could recognise them by their eyes, their tone of voice.

HCA   Who?

Hanne   The masters. Who shape our lives. Imagine all the masters I've had. And they shape . . . and mould . . .

and no one understands that you always have to take the last step yourself.

HCA   Heiberg? Also Heiberg?

Hanne   He was also very fond of little green fruit. But for slightly different reasons.

Pause.

For seven years Uncle Hermann paid for me. For seven years we carried on like that. Then I turned fifteen. That's when it all ended. (*Sits wearily.*) I think Hermann actually wanted to kill me. He knew it was over. He didn't stand a chance. I think he wanted to take a carving knife and slice me away from the rest of the world, so he could keep me. Like a lump of meat.

Pause.

When Heiberg entered my life, Hermann became obsessed. Spying on us everywhere. The little green fruit was almost ripe, and he'd lost his hold of me and he became desperate. I could see him following us everywhere. Disguised as an old man with a beard and a cane. He moved through Copenhagen like a ghost. I saw him everywhere, in a carriage, crouching behind a fence, in a window, without a carriage, walking, at dusk, in the mornings, I didn't want to speak to him any longer. I began to understand what I was worth. Little girls who radiate sensuality learn very quickly how much they're worth. He came to us and cried and wanted me to speak to him. But I wouldn't. He cried and said that I was killing him. I didn't say a word. Then he said that he wanted to die. When Heiberg's letter of proposal arrived I let Hermann read it, while I calmly sat looking at his face. I wanted it to hurt so much that he would burn up. He read the letter, completely ashen-faced and left. He was like someone in a fever. He came almost every day, stared at me for a few minutes, and left. Our relationship had lasted seven years, I couldn't break away. He would come, lie down on our kitchen bench with his coat on, cry desperately and then fall asleep. I would sit on the floor, resting my head on his arm, which hung down quite still, smelling of wet wool. Listen to him sleeping, saw the street lantern reflected in the ceiling. When he woke he'd try to stroke my hair, and I'd scream that he was a filthy pig, rush out and lock myself away. I didn't want to show him that I'd cried. I was afraid he might understand that if you've gone through hell, hand in hand, then you melt together. And you can never free yourselves of each other. I'd been a little dog he'd dragged around. Now he was a dog. I enjoyed tormenting him, it was necessary, for if you melt together then love is like that. He howled like a dog. I locked myself away and he left.

Next day the same. He arrived, fell asleep on the bench, I sat on the floor, in the dark, stroking his arm. I had chased out all the others, Mama thought I was ill, everyone was frightened of me. When he woke up I'd scream that he was a pervert who would fiddle with little children. I was very fond of him and felt ill when I saw him. I looked at his sleeping face, the light from the street on the ceiling, his face was bloated and pasty like that of a corpse that has been in water for so long that you can pull off bits of skin and flesh from the face. The skin thick and pale and the face bloated, a rotting corpse in the water, a dead man still breathing with regular breaths. He woke up, tried to stroke my cheek. Then I bit his hand, he bled. I still remember the taste of him. I screamed that he stank, that he should wash his greasy old underwear. He just looked at me, like an animal and said he loved me. And I just screamed. Then he said he wanted to kill himself. 'Do it, you old bastard,' I said softly, so he would believe me, very softly and calmly, 'are you thinking of drowning or hanging yourself?' I was fond of him. I was actually very fond of him.

Pause.

The odd thing was . . . that I even felt . . . lust for him. Lust.

Pause.

He said: 'I'm going to kill myself, but first I'm going to write you a long letter, and explain everything so you'll understand, little Hanne.' I said, that's typical, always some excuse, you can never be trusted. He just stared at me silently, said he was sorry and left.

Then they came and told us he was dead. He'd put a pistol in his mouth and blown away the back of his skull. I saw him. He had a charm around his neck, and in it was a lock of my hair. So strange. The back of his head had been blasted away, only his face with his disgustingly pleading eyes remained intact. I looked at him and was completely calm. It was as if a thin layer of ice began to mould around me. I think that was when I started to die.

HCA (*quiet*)   You hurt each other badly, Mrs Heiberg.

Hanne   The odd thing is that he was actually only twenty-seven when he died. We were both quite young when we died.

HCA   Why did you hurt each other, Mrs Heiberg?

Hanne   It's difficult to explain. The awful thing was . . . the lust.

HCA   The lust?

Hanne   What sort of a life is this?

HCA   What a horrible way to . . . leave you.

Hanne   No, no. He's still here. Don't you see him?

HCA   Mrs Heiberg . . . I can't quite understand you . . .

Hanne   Don't be frightened, come closer. Then you'll see him. Weren't you going to write about the love that conquers all? Well, then you have to get very close. So you can see.

She is very close to him.

I'm also curious, Mr Andersen. Look closely. Don't you see him? My bodyguard.

The room is very quiet.

HCA   Bodyguard?

Hanne   You'll see him soon. When you do, we can begin.

Complete silence, she is very close to him, then she suddenly breaks away, a smile, a laugh which grows and then dies away.

Let us begin!

She takes a graceful dance step, testing him, stops, looks at **HCA** *as if she wanted to ask him something she dares not talk about, and says:*

At last we dance together once more. Let us dance the minuet from 'Mount of Elves' together. Come on, come on, Mr Andersen. Come on.

Act Two

Darkness. Out of the darkness comes a rhythmic, melancholic melody played on the piano. It is the minuet from **Heiberg**'s *musical drama 'Mount of Elves'. Someone is playing the piano, someone not quite sure of the notes but full of enthusiasm. A woman. She plays and sings full of enthusiasm and gay abandon.*

Hanne   Tra lalala la lalala . . .

Yes, it's her. She makes the occasional mistake, but on the whole it is quite good.

More light.

The eyes of **OBW** *are now open, her mouth grinning a toothless smile. Her hands beat the rhythm. As her forearms are tied down, only her hands can actually move. But she does her best.*

The one attracting attention, however, is **HCA**. *He's dancing with extreme concentration. Almost all his steps are correct and he dances with serious gravity. His face is a landscape – a correct step makes him radiate with dramatic joy. A wrong step throws him into an abyss of despair. He moves his arms like Pavlova's father did late in life.*

Hanne *comments and plays.*

Hanne   Wrong! Wrong! Wrong! Wrong! Wrong!

HCA   But I've . . . forgotten . . .

Hanne   You have to remember the minuet from 'Mount of Elves'! We must all know it! It expresses our national character! The soul of the nation!

HCA   . . . Yes, I agree . . . but I am trying . . . da dada . . .

Hanne   Again! Again! Position! Compliment to the King! Not too deep!

HCA *bows slightly towards the imaginary royal box, smiling aloofly.*

Hanne   Good! Just right! And then . . . now! Da dada da da dada da . . . that's it.

HCA (*panting slightly*)   To think that we . . . once danced together!

Hanne   What a blessing you didn't continue! Da dada da . . . what a great play this is! The greatest and most successful political drama ever written in Denmark! Or ever will be written!

HCA   . . . I thought . . .

Panting.

. . . Political? I thought it was a . . . comedy?

Hanne   . . . da da . . . and compliment! Compliment!

He bows again.

Too deep! You must be precise! Brief! This is where the King appears and unites the couples, rescues love, rights all wrongs and is the hearty father of the nation whom everyone adores. God, I remember that opening night, Andersen. It was incredible. Women cried and men wiped their noses and it was like a wave of love, a wave! Of love breaking from the stalls on to the stage and further, right up into the royal box. That's what I call political theatre at its best, Andersen. Now that was a tribute to the King! Heiberg certainly knew how to pull it off!

HCA (*gloomily, almost to himself*)   And he didn't drop his dentures either.

Hanne   But what thanks did he get!!! (*She bashes out a chord and spins around.*) What thanks did Heiberg get?! Just look at that royal imbecile. He lets his ignorant mistress persecute Heiberg and myself and helps our rivals and gives money to the Court Theatre – that's the thanks he gets. And then you go and kiss the feet of that slut.

HCA (*almost bitter*)   I *have* apologised! Several times!

Hanne   Unforgivable.

HCA (*with a hint of wit in his voice*)   To have written 'Mount of Elves'?

Hanne   It's a masterpiece! It's a tribute to the King, a real tribute, only we have the wrong king! If we had a real king, it would be the right tribute! Now, it's wrong! Do you follow?

HCA (*thinks long and hard*)   Absolutely. Right. And wrong.

Hanne   Good! Let's do it once more.

She strikes a chord, a somewhat boisterous and excited start. And then sharp knocks are heard on the wall to the adjoining room. One, two . . . three, four . . . The room grows quiet. No more knocks.

HCA   What was that?

Hanne   That was God knocking.

HCA   I thought it was Heiberg.

Hanne   Same difference.

HCA (*reproachfully*)   Doesn't he like 'Mount of Elves'??

It is as if some of **Hanne**'s *joy has gone, she leaves the piano, seeming to be slightly cold, she fetches a blanket, holding it hesitantly for a few seconds and then wraps it round the legs of the* **OBW**. *The room is very quiet.*

Hanne   On nights like these he sits in the attic staring out of the window at the stars. Alone in the dark. He doesn't move. As if he were turned to stone.

Pause.

Only ice and ice cold stars surround him. No one can reach him. He is so anxious . . . so lonely.

HCA   But why? He has such . . . power?

Hanne   He doesn't care about that any more.

Pause.

I think sometimes he'd rather be a brilliant village idiot. If only the ice . . . would crack.

Pause.

HCA   That was him knocking?

Hanne   With his cane. With that hideous cane. The handle is the head of a wolf. Ivory. The jaws gape wide open, its teeth exposed, like a rabid wolf. That's how things have turned out for him. Everyone has fangs. Everything stinks of death.

Suddenly she hides her face in her hands and with a rattle, gasping for breath, she says:

What have we done to him? Am I to blame? Is it me??

Calms herself, brushes her hair back, almost mechanically and indifferently.

We do such strange things to each other, Mr Andersen. It's not much fun turning to ice.

Suddenly exploding with fury at the dumbfounded **HCA**.

He used to write comedies! Wonderfully amusing and joyful little pieces which you could . . .

Collects herself.

Forgive me.

HCA   (*perplexed, then he blurts out*)   You are so alike.

Hanne   Alike?

HCA   Same shape of face, same nose, same forehead,

same ears, same . . . it's as if you were . . . brother and sister.

Silent, **Hanne** *looks intently, but guarded at him.*

HCA (*trundles on naively*)   Although he's so much older than you, twenty years perhaps. It may be more like father and daughter.

Hanne   Aha. Here we go.

HCA   Just think, your names are almost the same. Johanne Louise. Johan Ludvig. As if your mother had named you after him! Perhaps she admired him.

Hanne (*quick*)   How?

HCA   Read his poetry . . . or . . . had he already had his debut then? . . . Perhaps she knew him?

Hanne (*striking like a cobra*)   Shut your bloody gob! She hasn't done you any harm. I'm proud of her. One of the most remarkable women I've ever known. (*Very soft and emphatic.*) My mother's no bloody concern of yours, Mr Andersen.

HCA (*frightened*)   But what have I said?

Hanne   No bloody concern. Do I make myself clear???

HCA   I can't stand people speaking harshly to me! I start to cry!

Hanne   I don't give a damn. Save your tears for someone else. I can't stand seeing someone I'm fond of being picked upon.

More aggressive.

You shouldn't be ashamed of your parents, Andersen. Of course it's very nice that you write such lovely things about your mother, but you shouldn't lie about her. You're ashamed, and so you lied.

HCA (*extremely upset*)   I lied?!

Hanne   Wasn't she a little old boozer who got delirious and drank herself to death in the poorhouse? Of course she was. Everyone knows it. Nothing wrong in that. But you should have visited her once in a while instead of slithering around Europe licking aristocratic arses.

HCA   I'm not ashamed! That's a lie!

Hanne   Not at all! You embellish and lie.

HCA   . . . She . . . she . . . she . . .

Hanne (*ruthless*)   She died in a stupor, something you found slightly embarrassing. Why? Nothing to be a shamed of. My father died the same way. And I don't try to disguise the fact. We who are born in the sewers mustn't disgrace ourselves. Mustn't be ashamed. Mustn't degrade ourselves.

HCA   Of course, you've had such fine masters. You know everything . . .

The atmosphere grows venomous and hostile.

I admire you, Mrs Heiberg. You never made a fool of yourself. And then, of course, you're members of the ruling elite, possessing the sharpest of perceptions.

Hanne   Quite. I've learnt to climb like a man. And that's not respectable. Is that what you meant to say, Andersen, dear?

HCA (*he moves closer to her and almost screams:*)   I wasn't ashamed of her!!!

Hanne   Don't spit on me. It's . . . disgusting.

HCA (*gradually losing all self-control*)   Oh, Mrs Heiberg! How can you insult me like that! Insult me! I'm not ashamed of her! But you are heartless! Heartless! Well, take heed! Take heed!! Right now you're looking down on me, insulting me. But suddenly the tables will turn. And then I'll . . . then I'll (*Stamping his foot in convulsion, as if trying to trample a snake.*) . . . I'll . . . crush! I'll crush you! I'll . . .

Hanne (*calm but curious*)   Aha . . . dear, dear, dear!! The little children should see you now, Mr Andersen! Not a saint after all, are you?! You can be quite . . . malicious! Quite vicious! How entertaining!

HCA (*despairing*)   But you provoked me! I'm not really like that! Not by nature!

Hanne   Pathetic.

HCA *tries to collect himself, but the hostility between them, although less intense, still burns.*

HCA   We all do what we have to do, Mrs Heiberg. Each one dancing his own way.

He stands in the middle of the room, his arms outstretched assuming the starting position. Then he begins to dance the minuet again, but extremely slowly now, ritualistic, almost slow-motion and dreamlike; and softly, almost threateningly, the music starts, slightly altered to a darker and more frightening tone.

You have to learn the steps. And . . . you . . . also . . . have . . . to pay.

Pause; three steps to the left, three steps to the right – as if in a dream.

Do you know when I saw you for the first time? No, it wasn't at the Court Theatre. No . . . No . . . No . . . It was the same autumn that I arrived in Copenhagen, September 1819. I saw you in the Deer Park, a little girl, a little girl, how old can you have been? Eight perhaps? But you were such a striking child. Did you know that?

Hanne (*watching him suspiciously – what is he up to?*) What are you getting at?

HCA's *face calm, the steps slow and not at all ridiculous. No more flailing about – this is a different dance.*

HCA   It was . . . during the pogroms.

She is immediately quiet, but remains controlled. She's on guard now.

Hanne Aha.

HCA It felt as if . . . all of Copenhagen . . . was a gaping wound. All at once . . . everything was ablaze. Violence. Violence everywhere. At first I didn't understand what was happening. I thought it was war. There were gangs of men with sticks. The hunt was on. For the Jews. Windows shattered. Small shops suddenly on fire. No one knew how or why. Then larger stores. Painted symbols. I don't know how it happened, but suddenly one day I found myself out in the Deer Park. There was howling and screaming. They'd found a woman who sold sausages in a tent.

He stops mid-step, but the strange and threatening music continues, and he looks at her for the first time since the dance began.

It was awful.

Pause.

I was from the country. Didn't know anything. It was the strangest, most frightening experience of my life. They had grabbed her and held her arms twisted behind her back. And then the fun began. Rings of sausages were fished out of her pot and hung in chains around her neck. She screamed and everyone laughed because they thought it looked so comical and stupid. And no one knew why she screamed. Not until later. Because the sausages were boiling hot. They let go of one arm, because she screamed so terribly, and she snatched and grabbed at the sausages to get them off, but they were boiling hot. They'd melted to her skin. Black and bloody sausages. They'd melted into her skin. And she screamed and grabbed at them to get them off. And finally people stopped laughing and it was silent. That was when I saw you.

Hanne (*softly and almost controlled*)   That's a damned lie.

HCA It was so disturbing. And so . . . comical. That's why I remember you. A little girl squeezing in past the people watching, right next to me. As if she wanted to hide, was afraid. (*Pause.*) Or was ashamed. (*Pause.*) And the one with the sausages just kept on screaming and snatching and scratching at her chest and crying out a name . . . as if for help . . .

Hanne *crosses to him, resolutely, and slaps him across the mouth. He staggers backwards, almost sitting down – he's in pain, his hand to his mouth.*

Hanne (*hisses*)   What are you on about? How dare you talk like that? These lies; how dare you?

HCA (*stares at her frightened*)   . . . She . . . was ashamed . . .

Hanne   Filthy lies. I recognise those stories. My enemies make up new ones each week. They know my mother was Jewish, and start bitching. You too. What sort of rubbish is that? I was seven in 1819. As if you could remember a seven-year-old girl you'd never seen before. And in a crowd in the Deer Park.

HCA   But three years later, when we were ballet pupils . . . I recognised . . .

Hanne   That's a lie. But I suppose you have your reasons for this slander.

She paces restlessly to the little cupboard, takes a quick gulp, slams the door shut, crosses to the **OBW** *and starts tugging determinedly at one of the ribbons, without undoing the knot.*

It's time for bed. It's time for bed. It's time for bed. It's time . . .

She stops mid-sentence, stares blankly straight ahead and says quietly and mechanically:

I've had a completely normal and respectable Christian upbringing.

Pause.

HCA (*cutting through the silence*)   She screamed Hanne, Hanne, Hanne . . .

Hanne (*softly*)   If you persist with your bloody lies, I swear I'll persecute you with all my strength and power and all my heart, for as long as you live. And believe me, I know the art of persecution.

HCA   But when it comes to my mother you . . . lie! Lie! . . .

Hanne   Go back home and crawl under your mother's old whoring sheets, and stop talking rubbish about things you don't understand. You have no idea of a little girl's feelings when she realises she was born a pariah.

Pause, then soft and intense.

But I swore that that would never, ever, happen to me. Not what she . . .

Pause.

But enough. My mother was a great woman. She saved our entire family. Including me. Whom she loved.

Suddenly quiet, her aggression draining away, she says, almost with a smile:

Mama had so many funny expressions. Of me, she'd say: 'Hanne is no mere mortal. She's a fision.'

HCA (*can't quite follow*)   Fision?

Heiberg (*suddenly standing in the doorway, in his dressing-gown*)   Vision. Yiddish accent.

Hanne (*tense silence, then ironically*)   I knew you'd be back. Sooner or later.

Pause.

And how are the stars tonight?

Heiberg   As always. Very clear. Very cold.

Hanne   Then surely it's a shame to desert them.

Heiberg (*uncertain of her tone*)   Perhaps I'm intruding. You seem to have . . . found one another.

Hanne (*lightly*)   Does that frighten you?

Heiberg   Not at all.

Hanne (*almost too kind*)   You just wondered what we were talking about. What we were up to. And so you come in . . . isn't that right?

Heiberg   I'll leave if you prefer.

Hanne   Do you know, Mr Andersen, I do think he's slightly frightened of you?

HCA (*upset*)   Frightened?? Of me?

Hanne   Extraordinary, isn't it? He thinks you're somehow going to corrupt me. With your curious . . . fision. But it's too late, my friend. I cannot be corrupted. Mr Heiberg has such respect of . . . corruption.

Heiberg   Hanne, you know that I'm only afraid of one thing.

Hanne   Of becoming invisible? Yes, of course. So is everyone else.

HCA (*tries breaking the tension*)   Do you study the stars, Mr Heiberg? How interesting . . . how exciting!

Heiberg (*close to* **HCA**, *looking at him as if wishing to solve a mystery*)   Do you dislike me, Mr Andersen?

Pause.

I'm sorry. That was stupid. I . . . don't study them. I only sit and look at them.

HCA   Nothing else?

Heiberg   No. Just that. (*To himself.*) At times one can find a sort of comfort in the fact that so many of the stars one sees – are actually dead. Extinguished.

HCA   But surely you can't see them then?

Heiberg   Yes. You can. They've been dead for thousands of years. But their light takes time to reach us.

So I see their light as it was before they died, although they themselves are dark and have extinguished. It's a sort of comfort.

HCA Comfort? Why?

Heiberg A comfort for me, at least. And increasingly so. It makes death . . . it makes the stars a little more like us.

Hanne Such slight comfort. Would you like me to come and sit next to you?

Heiberg (*a sharp, ironic smile*) I'm not sure. Perhaps I do.

Hanne But you are not bothered?

A smile appears and fades again on **Heiberg***, he's silent.*

The layer of ice?

Heiberg (*softly*) The layer of glass, rather.

Pulls himself together.

How is your great play coming along, Mr Andersen? Amor Omnia Vincit? Have you been . . . creative?

HCA (*quiet*) I have . . . understood. That I can't write it.

Heiberg What a pity. A play about Hanne and myself. (*Crosses to* **Hanne***.*) It was a beautiful thought, Hanne. A beautiful thought.

Hanne *suddenly hiding her face in her hands, as if in sorrow or fury, her head shakes as if having a fit.*

Heiberg (*calm*) Control yourself, Hanne.

Hanne No. No. No.

Heiberg No matter how bad things may be, one must control oneself. (*Her head still shakes in fits, he adds softly:*) Hanne . . . you haven't been taking your . . . cough mixture again . . . have you?

Hanne (*exploding*)   Oh, shove it up your arse!!

Heiberg (*after a pause*)   I see.

He stands in front of her slightly irresolutely, steps towards her, changes his mind, shakes his head quietly, then he crosses to **HCA** *and with a sudden and totally irrational outburst of fury, he almost spits the words in* **HCA**'s *face.*

You know nothing about death. Death!! Nothing! Nothing!

He collects himself, straightens his dressing-gown, adjusts the cravat, looks around and says in his old friendly and controlled voice:

Hanne? Your portrait.

Hanne   Yes?

Heiberg   It's hanging crooked again. You ought to straighten it.

Hanne (*after a pause*)   Yes, father.

The portrait actually hangs slightly crooked. That's obvious now. She rises and looks at the monumental portrait of herself. She adjusts the painting, although to the wrong side. Now it's very crooked. She looks at the result calmly, without a smile.

Is that better?

Heiberg   Yes. I'm sorry.

Hanne   Johan. (*Close to him, softly.*)   We promised each other. We decided once and for all, never again to wander around in this desert of ours being sorry.

Heiberg   I forgot.

Hanne   No apologies, no blame, no accusations, no forgiveness, no mourning over things that don't exist.

Heiberg   Or ever could exist. Yes. That's true.

Hanne (*stroking his arm awkwardly*)   Are you going to bed?

Heiberg   No. I think I'll sit up tonight. It's so clear. (*Pause.*) It's such a sharp, cold and clear night.

Walks irresolutely over to **HCA**, *and says almost childishly:*

I think of you a great deal.

Pause.

Love conquers all. That was a fine thought.

There is a slight twitch at the corner of his mouth, the veneer is about to crack, and he asks quietly:

And what is . . . the answer???

HCA *quiet and confused, arms hanging limp, shakes his head perplexed.*

Heiberg *gives a slight melancholic smile, almost embarrassed at having revealed too much. With ironic haughtiness he looks at his shoes and says, as if to himself:*

In which case . . . what is the question?

Turns, crosses to the door, stops by **Hanne**, *and looks very lonely all of a sudden.*

If you need me, I'm in the . . .

Pause.

No, of course not.

He exits.

HCA   Have I been very naive?

Hanne   It's naivety he lacks. That's why he's ever so slightly frightened of you.

HCA   I don't believe that.

Hanne   Not frightened perhaps. He longs for that little bit of naivety that keeps us alive.

HCA   I feel so stupid.

Hanne   He *dreamt* of creating a person . . . like a work of art. Out of nothing. Mould, shape, perfect. I was the work of art. It's actually an horrific thought.

HCA   Yes it is. And it is probably an horrific thought for him too. That when the work of art is complete, the artist is no longer needed.

Hanne   Or that the work of art can feel a sort of . . . shame. My husband and I have a somewhat complicated relationship, Mr Andersen.

HCA   I've begun to realise.

Pause.

Why did you call him . . . father?

Hanne   Did I?

HCA   Yes. You did.

Hanne   What of it?

Suppressing her fury.

So you've heard that filth as well. I might have known. So innocent . . . 'You are so alike . . . ears, nose' . . . You should be ashamed of yourself. You should be ashamed of yourself!

HCA   What?? I think you've . . . Why should I be ashamed??

Hanne   Oh, stop it. You know exactly what I mean.

Pause.

This . . . this . . . this slander. This backstabbing. You should see the dear little anonymous letters I've received. Short notes. Unsigned. Saying he knew my mother. They had an affair at Little Ravnsborg. And I'm meant to be the result. At times the letters have been smeared with excrement.

Matter-of-fact.

Mr Andersen . . . do you know the punishment for incest?

HCA   But . . . Mrs Heiberg! I've never . . . never! Thought along those . . .

Hanne   Death. Strange how a story like that begins. At times I think of it like this: it's been noticed that our marriage . . . is unlike any other. It . . . deviated. That is true. But people jump to all sorts of conclusions.

HCA   On my word of honour! I've never heard anyone insinuate anything like that.

Hanne (*circling the* **OBW**, *she adjusts the blanket and says softly and pensively*)   I wonder what goes on inside her. In this slumber. Now when it's too late, I wish I'd asked. She's dreaming, her whole life must be there, in this dream. Like . . . an enormous cauldron. And every so often . . . a tiny bubble rises from the bottom.

Pause.

People understand so very little. About love.

HCA (*turned away*)   Yes.

Hanne (*not cruel, but friendly*)   Mr Andersen and his project. The power of love. The project. Of course, you write so much about your infatuations. And none are ever realised. Your love either leaves you. Or you leave her.

To his back, he doesn't move, doesn't turn around.

You're frightened, aren't you? You don't wish to reach her? You'll never find your way if you *want* to be lost. Are you frightened?

HCA *is silent.*

Hanne   It's nothing to be ashamed of, being frightened.

HCA   I'm sorry . . . about the . . . gossip.

Hanne *is noticeably tired now, she crosses to the desk, sits and looks at the paper, lifts her pen but doesn't write, just sits still.*

Hanne   I'll try to write a little.

Pause.

One must try to understand why things happened the way they did. Why I died.

Pause.

I write down everything and try to string it together. Try to . . . make connections . . .

Suddenly the atmosphere is very mellow and warm.

HCA (*shyly and modestly*)   I understand. It's like that game we played as children. You draw masses of dots on a piece of paper. And then you number the dots. And then you let . . . well perhaps your little sister . . . try to discover the pattern. You draw a line from dot to dot. One. Two three four. Five. Six. Finally you have a picture. (*A smile, almost joyful.*) It's usually an elephant!

Hanne (*with a slight smile*)   It's usually a donkey.

HCA   An elephant. A baby elephant. As Mr Heiberg said. One that clomps about in fear. And smashes things in the porcelain shop.

Hanne (*looks at him silently, nods*)   I'm actually very fond of baby elephants.

Pause.

I wonder what my picture will be. When I finish drawing the line. But I've had fine masters. They certainly taught me the steps. How to carry oneself. The game. This whole . . . career. They taught me everything and I was incredibly clever. Incredibly hard as well.

HCA   That's not true!

Hanne   I suppose it was unusual for a woman. Men can be bastards, that's normal. But a woman.

Pause.

I didn't know what I would lose. But finally it was as if I was being covered by a layer of ice that deadened all sounds and blurred all messages coming from outside . . . as if I was . . . encapsulated. In an ice cocoon. And everything that once hurt me – pain torment, fear, mistakes, anxiety – all the painful things that kept me *alive*, were now a bit . . . distant. Do you know your sore spots, Mr Andersen? Those stubborn, living sore spots that hurt so much, so much, and that remind us of being alive. Without these sore sports we're nothing, simply dead. If they are encapsulated we begin to die.

HCA   Like . . . Hermann?

Hanne   Hermann. Heiberg. Sometimes I can't tell them apart . . .

Pause.

There was a time when I would remember exactly, very clearly, how we'd wronged each other. And the pain kept me alive, reminded me that I had a certain . . . responsibility. But then it began to become encapsulated. It was no longer important. The skin got a bit thicker. One becomes more cynical. Experienced. Not so childish any longer to care about the sore spots. At first I thought it was good. I was so concerned with learning the steps, the game, that I was happy not to feel anything. Slightly thicker skin each day. When it was almost too late I realised I was dying. Yet at times I can still lie awake at night trying to remember the sore spots, trying to remember what it was like when I didn't have the cocoon around me. When I was . . . alive. And I lie completely still in the dark and hear messages coming from outside, voices whispering from the other side of the darkness, as if something out there was attempting to return home to me, someone crying faintly, in secret. The words can't quite penetrate the ice. Very faint. Like a call through the ice.

HCA   Mrs Heiberg. There are so many of us.

Hanne   Us?

HCA   When I was young, Mama would say: 'Hans Christian, you seem to think that the world disappears when you close your eyes. And that it returns when you open them.' I said: 'Doesn't it?' She said: 'No! No! But if you go on believing that, you will be very lonely.' (*Pause.*) Very. (*Pause.*) Lonely.

Hanne   Ooooh. Yes.

HCA   Perhaps I'm not *frightened* of love. Perhaps it's that . . . (*Silent, he stands with his arms hanging down, looking ahead.*) I can't get . . . out.

Hanne   My God. (*Softly.*) These cocoons.

HCA   I'll leave you now.

Hanne   No, please. Wait.

HCA   I've realised . . . tonight . . . that the speech I was going to make was bad. What I should have said . . . I would have told a tale instead. About us.

Hanne   About us?

HCA   I should have said, I shall now tell you the story of the Snow Queen. About little Hanne and her brother Hans. They love each other dearly; but one day up in the heavens, a wicked angel smashes a mirror. It is the mirror that turns everything beautiful ugly! Everything warm cold! Everything alive dead! And the splinters fall through the sky. And Hanne gets a tiny little splinter in her eye.

Hanne (*mesmerised*)   And she loses the power to feel love.

HCA (*nodding strongly, as if to himself*)   That happens to some. Others only see themselves. But for Hanne it's worse. She travels far away and in the end she arrives at the hall of the Snow Queen. The floor is ice. She is ice. Her heart is ice. She tries to do a word puzzle, out of ice pieces, and she tries to make one word, Love. But she can't, and she sits there until her little brother finds her. And finally, when her little brother arrives, he calls.

Hanne   Faintly, as if through a layer of ice.

HCA   But as she doesn't answer, he starts to cry. And a tear drops on to her heart, and suddenly . . .

He pauses, the room is silent, and she suddenly crosses to him and embraces him, hard almost violently and she cries in desperation.

Hanne   Oh, little brother . . . Oh, little brother . . . Oh, little brother . . .

HCA   Don't cry, little Hanne. I'm the one who cries.

Hanne   Oh, if only you'd come sooner. Oh, little brother.

Pause, she says softly:

I wish you had been my little brother. Then we would always have been together, up there where I was born, Nørrebro, in Little Ravnsborg. And when it grew dark I would fetch the milk. But I was always frightened, because the path led past the Black Pond. And there were always frogs jumping in the dark. But then you would have held my hand and followed me. And I wouldn't have been afraid. I wish it could have been like that.

HCA   Together like two . . . sewer plants.

Hanne   Two sewer plants. And later on we would have helped each other. Perhaps we could both have learnt the game. And still have avoided . . . feeling the layer of ice . . . avoided . . . (*Pause.*) Dying.

HCA   It's not too late, little sister.

Short pause, **Hanne** *breaks free from him, tidies her hair, wipes her face, gradually regaining control of herself and becoming Mrs Heiberg, yes, she's back.*

Hanne (*sternly*)   Yes, Mr Andersen, it is. It is too late.

Lifts the pen, holds it irresolutely before dropping it.

But I can still write. I think I write mainly for Mama's sake. When Papa started drinking she had to earn all the money. She thought of cooking special Austrian blood sausages. Black. And selling them. She had the choice between the poorhouse for all of us or cooking sausages. So she got up at four every morning to prepare things. And would be selling till nine at night. A drunkard and nine children to support. When she came home, she'd sit by the kitchen table, ashen-faced, counting the money. She couldn't read or write. But she could count. She was so tired, she'd sway backwards and forwards. Small piles of five and eight shilling pieces. This one for Papa's schnapps. That one for Hanne's shoes. Incredible how strong she was. My papa, the drunkard, sat in a corner, furious, with his eyes on the money, like a cat. He never dared come close. She would have strangled him straight away.

Pause.

That's what I am writing about. Then I draw the line to the next dot. Seventeen. Eighteen. Nineteen. One night Papa bawled that she was a Jewish pig. That she'd never be laid to rest in Christian soil. The first time I heard it. I'll never forget it. Never. Ever. Twenty-one. No, it's not an elephant.

HCA   A life, perhaps.

Hanne   A life.

Pause, a slight smile.

I usually read aloud to her.

Nodding towards the sleeping **OBW**.

In her compassionate darkness. Afterwards I read to Heiberg. And I'll continue to do so. In the future. And I shall sit with Dr Heiberg most evenings, reading, and he will nod and laugh and say it's interesting, badly spelt, of course, but he will take care of that. Whatever might be common, unsuitable and unworthy, he will cross out.

Pause.

All the filth of life.

Pause.

And in the end I don't think I'll need him any more, I shall know how to write and omit things inside me before putting them down, quite freely. Everything that is unseemly and in bad taste. So only what's proper is left.

Pause.

However, I enjoy reading to her most of all. Sending my writing into her compassionate darkness. Sometimes they seem like . . . delayed questions.

Hanne *sits at the desk, facing the audience. Her voice is low and she looks straight ahead, intensely. Suddenly the* **OBW** *jerks violently, convulsing, but in silence, like an explosion in a vacuum. Only* **HCA** *notices. He stands close to her and sees her tearing at her bonds. When he reaches to loosen her collar, she jerks again, and tears her dress in doing so.* **HCA** *slowly withdraws his hand, his body rigid as he looks at her neck. The dress had covered strange, dark circle-shaped marks, thick marks, as if she had once been branded like an animal.*

She never answers, but that doesn't matter. At times, there are words, phrases, prayers, echoes – small messages from a life . . . from her great compassionate darkness. A life.

Very quiet, **HCA** *puts the collar back, her head lies to one side again, she sits very quietly, her eyes open slightly, looking straight ahead.* **Hanne** *hasn't looked at her all this time.*

HCA   She is your mother, isn't she?

He gently and quietly closes her eyes.

Hanne   Not at all. Can't you see who she is? It's myself, Johanne Louise Heiberg. I am reading to myself, just before I died.

HCA   I understand.

Hanne (*forced and almost despairing*)   But no one understands him out there.

Pause, then bursts out.

Mr Heiberg has been wronged!

Pause, silence.

Sitting under his glass dome, under his ice cold friends, the stars. He's become so lonely. I think he longs to be with us.

Pause.

The dead should take better care of each other.

Pause.

He could sit with us. Each under his own glass dome. And then I could read something.

HCA   Shall I ask him to come in?

Hanne   Yes. Let's have him in.

HCA *nods silently, leaves.*

Hanne *carefully orders her papers into two neat piles. Methodically.*

Silence.

Heiberg *still in his dressing-gown, not surprised at the* **OBW***'s deathly stillness, he looks at* **Hanne** *who sits at the desk staring at her papers.*

Heiberg   Why do you want to read now, Hanne? It's late.

Hanne   Mr Andersen has a dream that love should be like this. Like a very quiet evening. Reading to each other. And perhaps he's right, Johan? We could perhaps . . . pretend that he's right? Sometimes, I suppose you have to do that?

Heiberg   Amor Omnia Vincit.

Pause.

Why did you ask for me?

Hanne   Perhaps we need you.

Heiberg   Me?

*He looks at her quietly, sceptically, a quick little melancholy smile before he sits. They all sit, the family group is formed, their faces lit softly by the glow of the lamp. The **OBW** in her extraordinary stillness. **Heiberg** in his armchair. **HCA** with his hands folded in his lap. And **Hanne**.*

We're all comfortable. You may start reading now, Hanne.

Hanne   I think I'll read what I recently wrote.

Lifts the paper.

'I still see the house before me, with its tall flight of stone steps leading down to the street. Alongside it ran a canal, at the foot of the steps lay a wide gutter. At the time I was three or four years old. Lying on all fours rummaging in the gutter with a stick, I became aware of my own existence . . . I remember suddenly looking up guiltily, wiping my hands and thinking: if anyone sees you lying here, it would be . . . shameful.'

She pauses, looking straight ahead.

Heiberg   Read on, Hanne. What is it?

Hanne (*softly*)   What if it is an elephant after all, Mr Andersen?

Heiberg   What do you mean, Hanne?

Hanne   Elephants have such thick skin. Like . . . prehistoric reptiles. They had such thick armour that they became invulnerable, but that was also why they died.

Pause.

I didn't mean to. I didn't mean to become like this.

HCA   Perhaps one has to make oneself vulnerable. Otherwise one dies.

Hanne   Could it be true? Imagine if it is.

Heiberg   Won't you read some more, Hanne?

Hanne   I shall soon understand how it all happened. Now that it's too late. But all the same. I must still continue writing, mustn't I, Mr Andersen? As if it wasn't too late? That's why we must write, isn't it?

HCA   Yes. That's why.

Hanne   I hope this will reach her. Like . . . a call through . . .

Pause.

Do you think she likes it, Mr Andersen?

HCA   I know she likes it very much.

Hanne (*pauses, takes a short deep breath, almost a sob, and she says softly and breathlessly*)   I didn't mean to become like this.

HCA   I know. I know little sister.

Hanne   Yes. You know.

A quick, almost imperceptible smile, she gathers her paper together and says:

So, let's read on. The very last thing I wrote.

She still sits facing the audience. The light closes in, focusing on the little family group; **Hanne** *and her friends and she is reading. A family portrait from 1856. Slow and melancholy piano music begins; it's a calm and tranquil picture.*

'When I sat at the foot of my beloved stone steps, I had noticed how during heavy showers, rain snakes would come crawling out of the earth, I thought the tiny worms longed to be washed, and so to help them as best I could,

in fulfilling their wish, I dug in the earth for hours on
end, collecting as many as possible.'

The light focuses still stronger on them, **Hanne** *still reading
directly at us, simply and softly.*

'I washed these rain snakes with great care and love; why,
I rinsed the rain snakes in so many changes of water that
in the end they were absolutely . . . clean.'

She looks straight ahead with very dark eyes.

The music continues through the silence.

And suddenly: darkness.

The Hour of the Lynx

by

Per Olov Enquist

translated by

Kim Dambæk

In my Grandfather's House
are many mansions:
if it were not so,
I would have told you.
I go to prepare a place for you

And if I go
and prepare a place for you,
I will come again,
and receive you unto myself;
that where I am
there ye may be also.

This translation of *The Hour of the Lynx* was first
performed at the Traverse Theatre, Edinburgh on
2 August 1990. The cast was as follows:

The Boy   Simon Donald
Lisbeth   Carol Ann Crawford
Pastor   Ann Scott Jones

Director Kim Dambæk
Designer Kathy Strachan

The translation was subsequently performed for a BBC2
screenplay, 1991, with the following cast:

The Boy   Simon Donald
Lisbeth   Sylvestra Le Touzel
Pastor   Eleanor Bron

Director Stuart Burge

*The **Boy** sits as usual, on his wooden chair. The chair faces the audience. He sits on the chair with a folded magazine on his lap. He isn't reading it. Both his fists are clenched and with them he presses the magazine into his lap. He rocks gently, almost imperceptibly, backwards and forwards.*

Are his lips moving? Is he singing?

His lips are moving, so perhaps he is singing. He tries stringing a melody together. Not a sound is heard.

*The **Boy**?*

Isn't he older than a boy? Yes he is. A boy is someone under twenty. Doesn't he look older? No, he doesn't. But perhaps he is older.

*We'll call him the **Boy**.*

Now and again to the rhythm of the rocking, he sings something or tries to reconstruct a song.

'Home . . . again . . . home.' Not very good. He tries again. 'Home again . . . home again . . . across . . . across . . . ' The words are almost clear now.

*What sort of room is it? It's a room. There's a chair. When the key turns in the lock, the **Boy** immediately becomes silent. He opens the magazine quickly, but doesn't look at it. Now we can see that it's* Playboy, *good old* Playboy. *He's completely quiet. After a while he starts a silent giggle and looks down at the page.*

The key turns in the lock. The door opens. A man in a white coat opens the door and lets two women in. He leaves. He doesn't lock the door on leaving.

The first of the two women entering is the project supervisor. A woman probably under the age of thirty. Probably? Yes, most probably. Female project supervisors are probably under the age of thirty.

Why doesn't the man in white lock the door on leaving? Perhaps he is sitting outside, waiting. Perhaps there's a chair outside the door as well. One can't see it.

The other woman, who has entered at the same time, is older. She is sixty-two. She'll soon tell us that.

The project supervisor, the younger woman is called **Lisbeth** *and is probably under thirty. She walks up to the boy, almost shyly, looks askance at the* **Boy** *and says, almost embarrassed:*

Lisbeth   How are you?

Boy   Not bad.

Lisbeth   You won't try doing it again, will you?

Boy   Nothing's going to stop me. And anyway, it's what I promised Valle.

Lisbeth   And that's more important to you than if I ask you?

Boy   Valle made sense of everything once more. And someone like that must not be let down.

Lisbeth   Do you understand that I'm disappointed. For both of us?

Boy   (*looks at her*)   Someone like that must not be let down. Ever!

Lisbeth   You just love screwing things up, don't you?

Boy   (*with a coy, almost shy smile – isn't there triumph in it as well?*)   He came back. You won't ever understand that. But no one is going to stop me.

Lisbeth   (*watching him silently, with resolution or sorrow? Then turns to sit on the chair and says*)   Thanks a lot, pal.

Pastor   (*speaks calm and collected and straight to the audience*) That evening was the first and last time that I saw the boy. I was forty-nine then, now I'm sixty-two. I was a pastor in the Swedish State Church then. I am not any longer. It was partly due to what happened then – what is it? – thirteen years ago. Lisbeth had called. She was the project supervisor responsible for the experiment on behalf of the university. She needed help and called me. The first conversation between us in four years. I asked her, rather aggressively, whether she was now in need of a theological instrument for the final analysis of her human guinea pigs. She just said that things were hellish, that the board of the institution were dissatisfied and she just wanted help.

The **Boy** *starts to giggle quietly, almost inaudibly once more. What is he giggling at? He's giggling at what he's reading of course!* **Lisbeth** *looks at him helplessly, but calmly. She sits on her chair. The* **Boy** *at first giggles silently, then gradually can be heard.*

Pastor   While she explained I was thinking: we fear nothing more than gratuitous violence. The kind that just happens. The other, the ordinary kind we think we understand. And are almost at ease about it. He had killed two innocent people. If only he had had a sexual motive, but there was *none.*

Pause.

Lisbeth was the supervisor of the scientific part of the group project – responsible to the institution. The boy had been kept in custody for an indefinite period, ever since he had jumped on the train and gone up to his grandfather's house, somewhere up north.

When his grandfather died, a middle-aged couple had bought the house. No one knows what happened, but apparently the boy had tried talking to them, they had grown tired and tried to throw him out. He panicked, grabbed a metal rod and killed them both. Afterwards he dragged them out and placed them in a snowdrift outside the house, their arms around each other.

He hadn't tried to run away, but sat down in the bedroom to wait and stare out of the window. Severely mentally disturbed. Brought into custody here since then. He was considered a gentle and retiring fellow. Then later he fled up north again. Tried to commit suicide by setting fire to his grandfather's house. Seemed oddly obsessed by the house. Severely disturbed.

The experiment with the cat was set into motion after that. And then everything collapsed and Lisbeth called. She sobbed throughout the phone call, as if something had been shattered.

Is that right?

Lisbeth *silent, staring straight ahead.*

Is that right Lisbeth? Shattered? For you as well?

Lisbeth *remains silent.*

A long chain of violence and yet none of it fitted together. Three days earlier he had tried to kill a fellow inmate by stabbing him in the stomach with a pair of scissors. The following day, he killed the cat and tried to commit suicide once more.

Pause.

It wasn't easy becoming a female pastor then. Everything had to be considered much more carefully than usual. And we had no handbooks with theological explanations of gratuitous violence. I told Lisbeth that when she called.

Pause.

He had attempted to commit suicide in such a disturbing manner that . . .

Boy's *giggling has unnoticeably changed into silent laughter. The* **Pastor** *cuts herself off, looks at him calmly and with expectation. The* **Boy** *points with his finger at a page in* Playboy, *good old* Playboy, *as if he wanted to wake someone up, get their attention or interrupt someone.*

Boy (*enthusiastically*)   This one's good. Dead funny. Really great. See it's a drawing of this guy lying alone in his bed and about to have a wank. He's pulled his trousers down and is holding his cock. But his cock has got other ideas, it's all limp and small and a real sourpuss, with its head hanging to one side – as if it didn't belong to the boy at all. And there's this speech bubble from the cock's head as if it can talk, and it can, and then, complaining, it says to the guy: 'Not tonight, dear. I've got a headache!'

Lisbeth (*quietly*)   You needn't provoke her like that, just 'cause she's a pastor. She won't faint, if that's what you think. She's very tolerant. As far as I remember. (*Pause.*) Very.

Boy (*triumphant*)   'Not tonight, dear. I've got a headache!' Brilliant!

Lisbeth (*very quietly*)   I can't understand why you don't understand that I'm disappointed. Do you understand that I'm disappointed?

Boy (*mechanically after a pause*) . . . Brilliant . . .

Pastor (*turned to the audience again, calmly waiting for the* **Boy**'s *attention*)   After not having been in touch for four years she asks for help.

Pause.

I actually had a dislike for him before I'd even met him. Then I met him and then I was no longer a pastor. Although that was probably the time when I should have become a pastor.

Pause.

Strange.

Pause.

When I came home that night, I wrote down on a piece of paper all the important things. As I remembered them I wrote: 'Valle said that you don't know how to earn forgiveness. Granddad's house, snow and birds in the ash tree. You have to protect the frogs . . .'

Pause.

A good summary.

Pause.

The day before I saw him, he'd taken a plastic bag, pulled it down over his head, lain down on his bed, laid the dead cat between his left arm and body – with the cat's nose pointing up towards him – and he'd tried holding the plastic bag down with his right hand. Obviously, he hadn't succeeded, although he tried several times, and his arms had thrashed about so violently that his fists were bloody from bashing the wall. One of the assistants had heard strange noises, looked in and understood that something was desperately wrong.

Boy (*quietly*)   Not tonight, dear. I have a headache.

Pastor   Eighteen years after I'd been ordained, I didn't know whether I truly believed. But it didn't *really* matter. Once during the course of the evening, the boy called me a 'bread and butter minister', a civil servant, a non-believer. I thought he was unfair. Later, after this evening, but also during the evening, I began to understand something about – the miracle.

Pause.

And love. And I could no longer remain a pastor.

Pause.

Silly, really.

Pause.

I still don't quite know what it was he had experienced and had tried to tell us. But it has helped me to live these past thirteen years and I hope it will sustain me till I die.

Pause.

The quantum physicists didn't get very far either, as long as they only thought rationally, perhaps that is what he meant by the hour of the lynx.

Pause.

The assistant came in and stopped him. The cat was dead. That was the penultimate attempt. I met him, for the first and last time, between that unsuccessful attempt and the final, successful one.

Boy (*monotone*)   Not tonight. I have a headache.

Pastor   Do you think we should begin?

Boy   Not tonight.

Lisbeth   Aren't you well?

Pastor   Do let me know if you're not well.

Lisbeth (*to the* **Pastor**)   *I'm* not well, if you're interested.

Boy   Aching. But it's not Valle's fault. He understood everything straight away, although he didn't let on at first.

Pastor   You don't have to talk, if you don't want to. I can wait and we can come back another time. I don't wish to intrude. This is completely voluntary.

Boy   Do come in! How nice . . . no, no, do come in. Come inside and sit down!

Lisbeth   We are here.

Boy   You see I'd imagined it like this, quite voluntarily: first you'd knock on the door. I'd look up, slightly surprised. Then a puzzled, but joyful smile would cover my face. I would search distractedly for the key in my pocket, then go to the door and unlock it. And who would I see there, but Lisbeth. Dear Lisbeth, who carries out her fine experiments on us animals. And a kind woman with a little crucifix pinned on her lapel. Very sexy. Perhaps I should first start by saying: how nice . . . how nice . . . how nice . . .

Lisbeth   Please stop. OK?

Boy   Well, one always tries to be polite.

Lisbeth   Doesn't one just?

Boy   All right, all right.

Lisbeth   We know how you feel. No, actually, I don't know how you feel – I don't.

Boy   I'm fine. Fine.

Pastor   (*there is an awkward atmosphere of animosity or guilt or resignation. She looks at them*)   Can we do it this way, that Lisbeth tells me, from the start, how things had been planned when you began this joint project between the university and . . . the . . .

Boy   (*very matter-of-fact*)   Madhouse, as we inmates call it.

Lisbeth   (*looks aggressively at the* **Pastor**)   We have a future studies group at the university, examining the grey areas, the non-theological that is, with alternative methods of experimentation in the care programme for the psychically disturbed, and we deal with the borderline cases where we have attempted to outline some simple distinctions: what will the human being of the future be like, what needs will he/she have, where are the black holes in the universe of the psyche, where are the boundaries drawn between human and non-human? All of which can only be observed in the peripheries of civilisation.

Looks at the **Boy**.

In the enigmatic ones.

To the **Pastor**. *Almost furious.*

In the not quite human human beings!! You know, a bit like testing an oyster with a drop of lemon. If the edge withdraws, the beasts are alive! But you can only tell by watching the extreme edge!

Pastor   Is it really necessary to talk like that in his presence?!!

Lisbeth   (*stiff, formal*)   He doesn't mind at all. I've explained it like that before. We don't keep secrets from each other here. It's OK.

Boy   It's OK. Oyster.

Lisbeth   Doesn't everyone have a few drops of lemon squirted on them at some point or other? And withdraw?

Pastor (*after a pause*)   Shall I leave?

Lisbeth   Social workers wouldn't express themselves in quite the same way, but I'm slightly cruder. I haven't got much to lose. We're working with severely disturbed people, we see the damages, but no one knows how they came about. And we've observed that three square meals a day make no difference whatsoever.

Boy (*turning to the* **Pastor,** *explaining helpfully, whilst indicating something small and round with his hands*) Oysters, of course. Something slimy that withdraws when Lisbeth squirts lemon juice on me.

Lisbeth (*hands covering her face*)   That was mean. We've agreed always to be straight with one another. And you promised not to mix us up in this.

Boy (*matter-of-fact*)   I don't mind oysters at all, honestly.

Lisbeth (*straightening up*)   Of course not and you're to be trusted as well, aren't you?

Pastor   Now please, start from the beginning. I want to hear whether he sees it in the same way as you!

Lisbeth (*stiff, but matter-of-fact*)   We pose one fundamental question here: what is a human being? And what sort of puzzling factors cause its disintegration? And if disintegrated, what may re-form it, so to speak? Emotions, intellect, solidarity, warmth . . . the whole catalogue . . . we started from square one and . . .

Boy   They started by bringing in a ficus.

Lisbeth (*distraught*)   Why do you go on about that, it wasn't the future studies group, it was the management at

this place! And it had nothing whatsoever to do with –
this!

Boy They placed an almost two-metres-high ficus in the
corner, it had small, fine leaves, and that was to see how I
would react to it; other way round I mean, how . . .

Lisbeth That's pathetic. And it wasn't us.

Boy (*dogmatically and quietly*) It was meant to coax the
chlorophyll out of human beings, if it was a human
being, that is. I'm not sure they quite knew who was and
who wasn't. That's why they placed that vegetable in here
to keep control. And I stood there, watering it every day,
but it died. So I suppose I was too toxic. Every single
morning, when I woke up at four o'clock, I switched on
the light and there were leaves lying on the floor. Every
single morning.

Pastor Do you always wake up at four?

Boy It depends, if I take two two mil Nembutal and one
Librium then I'm all right till seven. But if I only take one
Nembutal then I sleep till four. Valle was an incredible
sleeper. He was like a lynx, you know, they sleep twenty-
one hours a day, hunt for three, eat in one and then they
sleep again. Jesus, if only I could sleep like that.

Lisbeth I make that twenty-five hours in a day. There
are only twenty-four.

Boy (*confused, wondering*) I suppose that twenty-fifth
hour lies outside somehow?

Pause.

I wonder what that hour's like?

Pause.

Is it outside? Somewhere beyond?

With a scoff.

The doctor said that it was a clear sign of mental

disturbance, the gravest sort, because I'd placed them in the snow drift with their arms around each other. What do you think about that!

Pause.

Thanks all the same.

Pause.

You take Nembutal for the first half of the night and then you sort of bridge over the second half with Librium. Then everything's fine. Valle slept without any pills. It was something totally different with Valle than with the ficus.

Lisbeth   It wasn't the university that placed the plant in here, but it was us that put Valle in here. That's rubbish about the chlorophyll. That had nothing to do with anything.

Pastor   To do with what?

Lisbeth   The experiment.

Boy   I think they wanted to test if I *really* was a human being and so they placed that vegetable in here. But it died. Every single morning, when I woke up, there were leaves on the floor.

Pause.

That's how they tested you.

Lisbeth   You think you're funny, don't you?

Boy   That's how they test you. If the chlorophyll in the vegetable dies, then you're no ordinary person. And when I put their arms around each other in the snow, that was even more proof! What do you think about that! I had no hard feelings, but they wouldn't listen. Even though they had broken in to Granddad's house.

Scoffing.

Then the doctors know what you are. Disturbed! Disturbed!

Pastor   What do you think you are, yourself?

Boy   I suppose, in spite of everything, a sort of . . .
person?

Pause.

What bullshit proof!

Frowns, shakes his head in despair.

I gathered up the leaves each morning and counted
them. But anyone could have seen where it was leading
to.

Pause.

This one's brilliant.

Boy *points at a page in* Playboy. *Strangely enough, he hasn't
turned the pages at all. He doesn't appear to be looking at what's
he's pointing at, either.*

Boy   There's this girl on a beach. And there's a guy
lying next to her. The girl's in a bikini and the guy's got a
sort of cassock on and a weird hat and he's going to rub
suntan lotion on her. And then you see that he's stuck his
hand up inside her bikini and is rubbing her fanny, and
she gets all huffy, her eyes popping wide open and is
about to get up . . . like this. And then the monk guy says,
all cool, 'Well, you never know where Little Brother Sun
might peep in!'

Pastor   I would imagine he's a Benedictine monk.

Boy   Yeh, he's some sort of monk. Do you read *Playboy?*

Pastor   No, but I can recognise monks by their hats.
(*Looks.*) No, he's a Franciscan! How silly of me, 'Little
Brother Sun!'

Boy   So they try it on with Little Brother Sun rather
than etchings?

Pastor   Either way. Either way. But within the state
church I suppose it's mainly etchings.

Boy (*with respect*)   Fuck me.

Lisbeth   A: The plant had nothing to do with the experiment. B: They weren't testing whether you were a person. They placed it in the room, and . . .

Boy   The cell. We usually talk straight. Don't we? 'Oysters.' 'The cell.' OK?

Lisbeth   The cell. The plant had nothing to do with the university. The university isn't comprised of idiots. Not entirely. Anyway, you said you didn't want a new plant after the one you'd watered to death.

Boy (*shouts*)   I watered according to instructions! (*Calmly.*) It wilted if I came anywhere near it. Seventy-four leaves. Not one left. Anyway, I'd wanted to keep the trunk although the leaves had gone, but I wasn't allowed to.

Lisbeth (*very calmly*)   It was dead. (*Pause.*) Dead!!!

Boy   All trees shed their leaves in autumn. There may have been new ones in May.

Lisbeth   On a ficus? Indoors?

Boy (*after a stubborn pause*)   You never know where Little Brother Sun might peep in.

Lisbeth (*close to him*)   Valle-is-also-dead.

Boy (*with a brief, secretive smile*)   You don't know much. You don't know where Little Brother Sun might peep in. Oh no.

Pastor   Listen, can we take this business about the experiment from the beginning, please?

Boy   Why do you call it an 'experiment' we never knew it was an 'experiment', I get a headache when you say 'experiment'.

Pause.

All right. Not tonight, dear.

Lisbeth *goes to the door, opens it. The* **Guard** *looks up, questioningly. She closes the door.*

Lisbeth   You were given a memo about it. We sat here. Alone. Reading it together.

Boy (*looks at the door impassively*)   Why are you scared? He's still out there.

Lisbeth   I'm not scared. I think I've shown you that.

Boy (*dully*)   Ah, that's why. (*Pause.*) Of course, it was safer having the cat later on. Sure.

Lisbeth (*very quickly and matter-of-fact*)   To cut a long story short. The future studies group at the university . . . The idea was to test animals on a particular group in the care sector, i.e. – criminals serving long term sentences, the severely mentally disturbed or long term patients in geriatric wards. To a certain degree, it's all part of the same problem.

Boy   Group. Same group.

Lisbeth   Not at all. Same problem. We should also have included theologians.

Pause.

So, we let them be responsible for an animal to see if it would lead to a personality transformation. We tried to restore the human in them. Tests have also been carried out in the States. But it was originally a Chinese concept.

Boy   In the memo we read it said that whores became well-behaved if they were allowed to play with dolls.

Lisbeth   Do you really have to be so destructive – always?

Boy   That's what it said!

Lisbeth   Not at all.

Boy   Yes, it did! They'd screwed so much that they'd lost all sensations and had become . . .

Lisbeth (*resolute*)   After the revolution, i.e. after the fall of Chiang Kai Check . . . please, shut up! This is actually important.

Pause.

There were millions of prostitutes in China then. And there was something they'd lost. Tenderness, emotions. Childishness. Mao brought them together in large women's camps, led them back to infancy, so to speak, let them play with dolls, restored their childishness . . .

Boy   You're lucky not having to go to whores. 'Cause you've got your own. Like me.

Lisbeth (*quietly*)   Why do you always mock me? Why do you always try to hurt me?

Boy (*looks at her*)   'Cause you never know where Little Brother Sun might peep in.

Pastor   So you were allowed to look after the cat. Can't the two of you at least try to . . .

Lisbeth (*very matter-of-fact*)   We structured it in such a way that we had an experimental group of ten *with* animals. And then we had a control group of ten, *without*.

Boy (*explaining, almost friendly, to the* **Pastor**)   Ericsson, you see, the one who got the scissors in his belly, was control group. He went without. That's probably why he went so strange.

Lisbeth   I would also feel strange, if I got a pair of scissors in my stomach. In any case, we believed that the control group would provide us with just as interesting results as the others who were allowed animals.

Boy   *How?!!* How!!

Lisbeth   The absence itself . . . the reactions to it. They were just as telling.

Boy   I heard that someone in the control group got worms instead. Brought them in the usual way. Like

drugs. Dead secret. (*Pause.*) Joke. (*Pause.*) But someone
like Ericsson was desperate for a cat.

Lisbeth (*looks at him, after a while, she says, friendly*)
Won't you explain to our friend here, why you call him
Valle? Otherwise our friend won't understand a word.

Boy (*jumps up, throws the chair, shouts*)   For fuck's sake,
that nobody's business, you bitch. Shit, I should have
stuck the scissors in you instead!

Pulls the door, it opens, the **Guard** *looks at him impassively
without moving. The* **Boy** *shuts the door carefully, rests his
forehead against it, sits on the floor now very calm with his back
to the door.*

If you were given a cat you had to prove that you were
trustworthy. Somehow prove yourself dependable. You
had been entrusted with *something* and the others with
nothing.

Pause.

You can't treat people like that.

Pastor   Why did you call him Valle? Tell me. Lisbeth
says that I won't understand a word, otherwise.

Boy   After Granddad. Per Valdemar. We always called
him Valle.

Pastor   Why did you get so angry?

Boy (*laughs, then serious again*)   'Thanks all the same.' As
he used to say.

Lisbeth   He was a lay preacher.

Boy (*despairing*)   Won't you leave him in peace.

Pastor   Lisbeth, I think we should leave him in peace. I
only asked why you called him Valle.

Boy   He was no 'bread-and-butter' minister like you, no
way. And he knew everything about Spitfires. (*Starts to
hum mechanically.*) And animals.

Pastor   Have you looked after animals before? Before Valle, that is?

Boy (*matter-of-fact*)   Frogs.

Pastor   Where did you keep them?

Boy (*very critical*)   You can't *keep* them. You can't *own* a frog. They were *in* the well down below Granddad's house.

Pastor   But I said have you looked after animals.

Boy   Yeah.

Pastor   So what did you do with them when you looked after them?

Boy   Protect them.

Pastor   What do you mean?

Boy   Protect! Protect! Don't you understand anything at all??

Pastor   Yes, but . . . don't just say things like that. You've got to help me understand them. What did you do, when you 'protected them'?

Boy   It's very difficult, but it's possible. It depends on yourself, you've got to take responsibility for them, and not just shove it aside. But if you want to, it's possible.

Pastor   But protect them against whom?

Boy   Well, someone like my mum, for instance, that afternoon when she came up to fetch the suitcase and wanted to make an impression by helping to fetch the water. She slopped all the frogs out, so I had to run down and save them.

Pause.

'That's rich coming from him!'

Scoffs after mimicking.

Ten, she tried wiping out, in one single afternoon. She was . . . unbelievable . . .

Pastor   What was this suitcase she was fetching?

Boy   It was one with some letter in it, from some man or other I suppose.

Pastor   And Valle – that was the first time you had a cat yourself? Your *own?*

Boy   Yes.

Lisbeth   Although when you filled in the application form for the experiment you wrote that you were experienced at handling animals.

Boy   Yes. The frogs.

Lisbeth   Of course, the frogs, I understand that and so does everyone else.

Boy   No.

Pastor   I realise it may be irrelevant to the case . . . but isn't it close to animal cruelty, Lisbeth, placing a live animal like a cat, in a locked, single room.

Boy (*in doubt*)   What? (*Pause.*) We experts are of the opinion that it's only the first few years that are difficult.

Lisbeth (*angrily to the* **Pastor**)   Listen . . . first of all it will receive, I mean, we thought the cat in this experiment would receive the best care and attention any cat ever had. Secondly, there's the yard, the exercise yard, where it can be taken for walks, for at least an hour a day, in fresh air.

Boy   For the sake of its coat.

Lisbeth   For the sake of its coat. As well. Thirdly, he was six months old when he arrived and uncastrated, but we operated on him as we should with male cats when they reach the age of eleven to twelve months. In short, we neutered him. Which actually makes life a lot easier for a

cat living indoors or whichever bloody way you want to
. . . for the sake of its coat! You just want to destroy
everything using some pretty damn cheap tricks!

Boy   It wasn't me! It wasn't me! I didn't want him
operated!

Lisbeth   Stop shouting! Just tell me what it is you
want!

Boy   I didn't want Valle operated! He did! He said so
himself!

Pastor   He said so himself? Did he talk to you?

Boy   We argued about it for a whole month! Became
enemies! A week went by and we didn't say a single word
to each other! It was awful! But he said he'd rather be
operated on 'cause it was animal cruelty the way it was!
And he couldn't stand it!

Lisbeth   Easy. Easy. Take it easy. Calm down!

Boy   And I said to Valle: 'It's a crime against nature! You
shouldn't do such things against God's will.'

Pastor   Against God's will? Why? Why did you say that?

Boy   Because He created us as we are and therefore we
don't have to be ashamed and ask forgiveness and have a
bad conscience. Or be operated on. But Valle said it was
unbearable the way it was. He said it was like living on an
ant hill; he couldn't sleep. Just lay there thinking about it.
Like lying on top of an ant hill. Just lay there imagining
what it was like to fuck. All day and all night. That's what
he said! That's what he said!

Lisbeth   OK. So that's what he said. And what did you
say to Valle?

Boy   (*staring straight ahead. After a pause, says a little
awkwardly*)   I said: 'Valle', I said, 'surely there's more to
life than just fucking.' There have to be *other things* as
well.

Lisbeth   In which case you could at least put *Playboy* away while you've got guests. We are actually talking about those 'other things' now.

Boy   He could have said that. Or something similar. 'You've got a nerve saying that, lying there with your *Playboy* magazine.' No, that's not true. He didn't say that.

Pastor   Aren't you well? Can we get you anything?

Boy   It was awful. I was scared he might smash his head against the wall. It was awful to see someone you care for in such a state. It's inhuman.

Pause.

No, I'm all right. Just hungry, I think.

Pastor   Are you?

Boy   No, it just feels that way. Empty, like.

Pastor   *Are* you hungry?

Boy   No, I've just eaten. 'Not tonight, dear, I have a headache.' But I don't suppose you've ever felt like Valle. Like lying on top of an ant hill.

Pastor   No . . . not quite . . .

Boy   No, I don't suppose you're allowed to as a pastor.

Pastor   You are allowed to. And you might even long for it.

Boy (*confused*)   Long for it? (*Pause.*) You're funny. You haven't a clue what it's like. You think you're funny.

Pause.

Neither Valle nor I were allowed a say. We were allowed to talk. But then one morning they came to fetch him. And operated. We hadn't finished talking when they arrived. I screamed to Valle that it was like removing part of the human in him that we had to protect that part, you have to protect your right to be human although it's like

lying on top of an ant hill. And Valle said that then he'd
just run around the room like a lunatic, peeing in the
corners and it would stink like hell, but I said, 'Valle,' I
said, 'we'll help each other! When it gets really bad we'll
talk, mess about, have a laugh,' I said, 'I don't give a
damn if it stinks when you despair and pee in the
corners, I'll stand by you, we'll be together, won't give in
just because it's difficult.' And we almost agreed.

Pause.

He was so damned honest and never asked about those
two up in Granddad's house.

Pause.

I wanted to help. But then one morning, Christ, they just
came in here, take him away and operate, without asking
us. What assholes! What assholes!

Lisbeth   It's animal cruelty not to. And he was given
plenty of care afterwards. Special food and for some
reason or other which you won't explain, a specially
covered cot in the corner to sleep in.

Boy   Valle said he wanted it. He felt ashamed after the
operation and didn't want to be seen. Not even by me.
Not even by me!!

Pastor   You're always saying that . . . that 'he said' and
'said' . . . I think, I understand . . . but what do you really
mean by him 'talking'?

Boy   He just said things. Is that so fucking difficult to
understand?

Pastor   But, my dear, a cat can't talk.

Boy   A cat can't talk. You talk a lot of shit! Just like that.
You also talk a lot of shit about God although you've
never heard him say a word. And your god hasn't even
got a tail. Valle's got a tail, even a moron like you can see
that. And he talks a lot. All the time. All the time.

Pause.

What a load of bullshit!

Lisbeth   Valle *doesn't* talk. He's dead.

Boy   No?!! (*Grins.*) 'Thanks all the same.'

Pastor   Valles's dead. But God isn't dead.

Lisbeth   Really?

Boy (*a small secretive smile on his lips, he manages to suppress it, slaps his knees triumphantly, then sitting quietly*)   'Thanks all the same,' as Granddad used to say. 'Thanks all the same!' And then he got his beer.

Pastor   So . . . I can't quite make it all fit together. He was a preacher?

Boy   'Thanks all the same.'

Collects himself.

He was a lay-preacher, but the district was so vast and he couldn't even afford the bus fare, so he had to bike and then he had to get work in the forests and also as a grave-digger. So that we had something to live on. The days when he worked as a grave-digger were best. Then he'd want me to sit on the edge so that he had someone to talk to. He'd get thirsty and I'd have to sneak over and fetch a beer in his rucksack so that no one in his congregation would notice. And when I came back and handed the bottle down to Granddad, he'd beam and say, 'Thanks all the same!' and then he got his beer.

Lisbeth   May I ask you something?

Boy   No.

Lisbeth   As you please. But I haven't given up on you.

Pastor (*after a pause*)   Did you ever quarrel, you and the cat – apart from the castration business?

Boy (*passionately*)   He never mentioned a word about

those people up in Granddad's house! You *never* felt guilty!

Pastor   Right, right. But did you never quarrel?

Boy   Yes. When he wanted a live mouse for Christmas.

Lisbeth   'The Christmas Eve Massacre' as the board of directors so wittily put it.

Boy   He sat in a corner looking glum and depressed. So I asked him what he wanted for Christmas. And then he said that he only wanted one thing. A live mouse. Which he could play with for a couple of hours and then kill.

Pastor   Kill . . . I thought you were fond of animals.

Boy   Sure, but Valle most of all. (*Pause.*) All Valle wanted, was a mouse.

Pastor   And he got it! How did you get hold of the mouse?

Boy   Easy. You can get anything you want in here, as long as you pay for it. Fifty kroner to the pet shop and three hundred for the transport. They know their price. (*Pause.*) I wasn't keen on the idea.

Lisbeth   Nor were the group supervisors. Once we were told. It's not exactly creative character building. Playing with a mouse and then torturing it, just to have fun on Christmas Eve.

Boy   But it was all Valle wanted, he said! Otherwise he wasn't bothered. He said it wasn't *him* but *me* who decided. If I brought the mouse then I brought the mouse. He'd only *wished* for one. But if I brought the mouse then he wanted to do with it as he pleased. But *I'd* made the decision.

Pastor   Lisbeth, what is meant to be the character building aspect of this experiment?

Lisbeth (*screams*)   It bloody well wasn't us who smuggled that mouse in here!

Boy   I believe that character building was in *my* deciding *whether* Valle should have a mouse or not. But only if I'd said no.

Lisbeth   I think it's cheap to make fun now it's over. I know it was controversial. We did it all the same. The whole experiment was controversial. I've actually learnt a lot in four years. You won't ever be a guru for me again. You haven't a clue how many pathetic creatures roam about and would give anything for a place like this. Bed. Christmas tree. Cat. Individual tree and individual cat. We'd first planned on carrying out the experiment in a prison, but the management said no. They said, the discomfort of the prison sentences must not be reduced to such a degree that half the population longs to be locked up behind bars! That's how they talk!

Pastor   Why did you call?

No answer.

And why exactly animals?

Lisbeth   We had carried out a major research study on the target group, i.e. criminals, the mentally disturbed and geriatrics, for instance. We'd asked: 'What would you prefer, given the choice, a colour TV or a cat?' More than eighty-five percent had ticked the cat. Many at the university thought it was quite frightening in a way.

Pastor   Frightening?

Lisbeth   Yes, *I* didn't. Most of the others did though. They said it was like turning the whole care-sector into a sort of de-intellectualised farm. Nonetheless, we thought that the business of animals as a character developing factor was interesting and carried out the experiment.

Boy   But I was the only one in our group who got a cat. Almost everyone had ticked 'Yes' to a cat, but I was the only one who got one. The others got a hell of a lot a strange animals, cockatoos and tortoises and I don't know what. They would stress different things, they said. But I was the only one with a cat.

Pastor   Why's that, Lisbeth? Why him?

Boy   They said it was because I'd said that I was an experienced animal keeper. Before they understood it was frogs, that is. But I think that Lisbeth found me so interesting because I was so severely disturbed. She couldn't understand that at all. And that really excited her.

Lisbeth (*in a moment of anger*)   You've butchered two innocent people! And she's been polite enough not to ask: why?!

Boy   That's the difference between Valle and the pastor.

Pastor   But I *haven't* asked.

Boy   You would like to though. But Valle found it *unnecessary*. And that was that.

Lisbeth   I think we can be grateful that there weren't any more. Than those two.

Boy (*concentrating*)   I was an experienced animal keeper. It's much more difficult to protect frogs, 'cause nearly everyone thinks they're disgusting, there were at least ten of them in Granddad's well, you had to lift the bucket so that none of them poured out, that afternoon when Mother was up there trying to make an impression, then . . . Oh well.

Pause.

Valle never asked, he understood straight away.

Pause.

But he didn't tell me straight away how it all fitted together.

Lisbeth   OK. That's enough about him.

Boy   If you hadn't put a tick by severely disturbed, I wouldn't have had Valle. (*Grins secretively, then quiet.*)

Lisbeth   That's enough.

Boy   You could raise frogs in jam jars, first they had a tail, then they lost the tail, then you'd hold them like this in your hand, like this, and you could feel them jumping about in there. Like . . . well . . . like tiny frogs.

Pause.

Someone like my mum wouldn't understand that. Slopped them all out.

Lisbeth   Honestly . . .

Boy   No. Honestly – Little Brother Sun never peeps in.

Lisbeth   Listen. Only last week, you tried to kill Ericsson with a pair of scissors. You strangled Valle. And then you tried it on yourself. Our theologian friend here isn't just hanging around. I've asked her to come. And she wants to know what happened. Not what *I* tell her happened but what *you* tell her happened. And I'm responsible for you.

Boy   Well, then I'd like a mouse for Christmas. You take the responsibility, I take the mouse.

Lisbeth   Very funny. Will you cut the animal stories now, please?

Pastor (*suddenly strangely vexed*)   Can't you leave him alone? I want to hear what *he* thinks is important.

Lisbeth (*looks back without expression*)   You want me to shut up? Fine.

Pastor   If only you would.

Lisbeth   He still interests you? Although you're not quite sure what he's on about?

Pastor   Or it could be that he knows something very interesting which he can't put into words. I think he wants to. But he doesn't know how.

Boy   My money's on Lisbeth. I haven't a clue what I'm on about.

Pastor   Listen, I was at the hospital yesterday and had a talk with Ericsson. Lisbeth thought I should. Ericsson should be included somehow. He's better now. But he's very sorry, strangely enough. He sends his regards and asks me to say he's sorry they took Valle away from you. He still doesn't know that Valle is dead and I didn't want to say anything.

Boy   Good. (*Starts rocking restlessly.*)

Pastor   He asked me something slightly odd . . . whether I thought you could ever forgive him. In any case, he was very sorry. I was to tell you that.

Boy   Good.

Pastor   Otherwise he didn't say much. It is actually rather difficult to see any results of your great experiment, Lisbeth.

Lisbeth   Is it really so difficult? A blood bath on mice, Ericsson's lacerated stomach and a murdered cat. I can see them perfectly well myself. The board of directors can also see them. You're to give the theological answers while I shut up. Especially this business of the murdered cat, no one understands that.

Boy (*gets up as if to scream, body tensely stiff, fists clenched, then says monotonously*)   Valle is not dead. He died but came back to take me to Granddad's house. And I've promised no one is going to stop me. Tell Ericsson that Valle isn't dead. Tell him.

Pastor   Do you think Ericsson would believe that?

Boy (*sits quietly*)   I know Ericsson.

Pause.

Ericsson was only jealous. He was control group and anyway, I was the only one in the experiment group disturbed enough to be allowed a cat. In a way, I think, Ericsson went mad. He also wanted a cat, but most of all he wanted Valle. He didn't want to be control group.

Pause.

'I've bloody well always been that,' he said.

Pause.

He thought Valle was so beautiful. Red and white stripes, like a tiger. Pure white under the chin. He always wanted to borrow Valle for a little while, but I wouldn't let him! Anyway, it was against the rules, Lisbeth said.

Lisbeth (*despairing*)   There would be no point in being slack about who was experiment and who was control. Is that so difficult to understand?

Pastor   Was Ericsson allowed to handle Valle?

Boy   No, but there was the exercise session. I always had Valle on a lead when he went for his exercise in the yard. At first he was so afraid of everything that he just crawled on his stomach along the ground, but then I taught him to run. Gallop! And Ericsson just stood there, staring. He was fucking jealous. Sometimes he'd creep up and ask if he could borrow Valle. Just to do a round on the track! Well, I got furious! I was the one responsible! So he just stood there staring after us as we ran. Pretended to jog along himself at times, a few paces behind us. Tried to *bribe* me once. Said he'd have a tart brought in the cell if he could borrow Valle for an hour a day. And he said it so loudly that Valle heard it all! He just stood there mortified with embarrassment! And every day when we took our round of exercise, Ericsson just stood there, staring. You could feel his eyes in the back of your neck. At times it got so nasty that I picked up Valle and ran inside with him. Straight inside. That was awful.

Pause.

It's difficult to forgive.

Pastor (*to* **Lisbeth**)   Couldn't Ericsson have been in another group than the control one?

Lisbeth   Someone had to be control, otherwise we wouldn't have any point of comparison. The whole administrative group decided on that. Not only me, but a cross section of the administration. It's easy enough coming here and be wise after the event.

Boy (*agitated and quiet*)   Trying to swap with a tart! And in earshot of Valle!

Pastor   So what do you want me to say to Ericsson?

Boy (*carefully*)   How is he?

Pastor   Well he's better now.

Boy   How can a person become as sick in his head as Ericsson? It's unbelievable.

Lisbeth   Well, you haven't helped him get better, he'll only get worse.

Boy   I could tell. I saw the way Ericsson looked, the day it happened. I saw he was sick. He stood there in the yard just staring at Valle and me. And you could tell exactly what he was thinking: I don't want to be control group, I want Valle. If I can't have Valle, then *no fucker's* having Valle. Totally mental. But it all happened so quickly that I didn't register anything.

Pastor   What happened so quickly?

Boy   Well, Valle had the lead on and I held it as usual. We were running and it was just before getting dark, so there was still some light and just the three of us in there. Valle, me and Ericsson. I was doing a round of the track inside the walls, I held the lead in my hand and Valle ran a few paces in front. His tail was sticking straight up and his nose pointing forwards, like when he's in a good mood. And I thought, what the hell, he won't give a damn about Ericsson standing there staring. We'll carry on running till it gets dark. Slowly and then in small spurts, 'cause it was Valle who decided and he liked pulling and taking off now and again. And it got darker and darker. And just then Ericsson came up from behind.

Pastor   You hadn't heard anything?

Boy   Nothing. They'd laid turf in the yard. And then Ericsson came running past, snatched the lead and like a giant grabbed Valle and taking a run, tossed Valle over the wall. It's probably four to five metres high. Just one enormous fling and Valle had gone. Then Ericsson ran inside. And I just stood there howling not knowing what to do. You see, everything was locked.

Lisbeth   They increased security on Ericsson immediately. Locked him up.

Pastor   And Valle?

Lisbeth   Well, I wasn't there myself. But the area outside was searched. But Valle had completely disappeared.

Boy (*almost monotone*)   I wasn't permitted outside to search.

Pastor   Why not?

Lisbeth   Because they couldn't let someone loose who'd practically tried to run through the walls, screaming hysterically. That shouldn't be so difficult to understand! You just can't!

Boy (*without any expression*)   It's against the rules.

Lisbeth (*furious*)   There are no bloody rules against that, there aren't any rules that can predict all that, what a load of rubbish about rules, they just couldn't let you loose!

Boy   I wasn't permitted outside to search.

Pastor   What did they permit you to do?

Boy   I was dragged inside. I was not permitted to go out and search for Valle, so instead I was permitted to be dragged inside.

Lisbeth   It took four, all in all.

Pastor (*after a pause*)   But Valle did come back.

Lisbeth   That wasn't the problem. He was gone without a trace for two days. Then some idiot amongst the inmates here just happens to say that Valle's lead had probably got caught on a bush and that a fox was eating him. And then the following happened, which was that in the evening of the second day, after the incident with Ericsson, and they'd relaxed security on Ericsson, this sweet, little thing went out into the kitchen and took a pair of scissors . . .

Boy   It was at the same time, just as it was starting to get dark.

Lisbeth   In any case, you took the scissors from the kitchen, and . . .

Boy (*triumphantly*)   And he didn't hear me coming!

Lisbeth   Just before he was to be locked up. He got hold of Ericsson. They'd relaxed the watch over Ericsson. Which I felt was wrong. Because now he was in the risk group. And then he went for Ericsson and just stabbed the scissors into his stomach!

Boy   And twisted them around.

Lisbeth   And twisted them around.

Boy (*almost distant*)   Twisted . . . around . . .

Lisbeth (*very aggressively*)   Twice.

Pastor (*after a pause*)   So what would you like me to say to Ericsson?

Boy   I don't know . . . what do you say?

Pause.

Can I say that I had three Nembutal two mil. and two Librium, and didn't sleep all the same? Can you just say that?

Pastor   Not such a good idea. Not really.

Boy   All I could imagine was how Valle was caught on a bush with the lead . . . I saw it clearly . . . and was quite certain, someone had said that there were a lot of foxes around here . . . and then I saw the fox coming. And Valle was trapped. And I heard Valle scream like a maniac, 'cause he was fucking scared. And I could hear every word. But I couldn't go out and search, 'cause they'd locked me in! And I screamed back to Valle with all my strength that they wouldn't let me out! That that was why I didn't come. And that I would hack that fucking Ericsson to pieces. But then I heard Valle in the forest say: 'Don't do it, pity Ericsson, he's control group.'

Pause.

Always listen to cats. Valle said: 'Just tell Ericsson no hard feelings.'

Pastor   Shall I tell him that?

Boy   I don't know. I can't really decide. It's fucking difficult.

Lisbeth   It was when the cat returned that he destroyed the cell.

Boy   The room.

Lisbeth   The room.

Boy   It wasn't Valle who ruined the room. It was me.

Lisbeth   I'm perfectly well aware of that.

Pastor   There's something I don't understand, did Valle come back on his own?

Boy   On his own . . . He must have found a hole some place and crept in. But he came the day after all that with Ericsson and the scissors happened. Lisbeth had been to see me during the day and had been a real pain. I suppose she was in deep shit and things were going to change. Ericsson was in a bad state and I'd ruined her dissertation. Or whatever. Things would now take much longer. A shame about Ericsson, but even worse about her dissertation. But I said nothing. Just lay on the bed, weeping. After a while, she went quiet. She was probably writing a new chapter in her head.

Pause.

No, it's nothing to talk about.

Lisbeth   I wasn't the only one who was sorry for Ericsson. The whole staff of the group projects at the university took it very hard. We'd misjudged. We hadn't realised or understood what feelings had been set in motion in these repressed and disturbed people. We had started something which could no longer be stopped. We had. It was almost an attempt to graft emotions and love, graft. As if we were bloody gardeners. Graft something. On something that . . .

Boy   I always thought I was an oyster.

Lisbeth   I won't even bother answering that. We took it quite hard though. All of us who were responsible. We started to realise that we were playing with dangerous things.

Boy   With Valle.

Pastor   Why were you so fond of Valle?

Boy   What?!

Pastor   Why?

Boy   Because he was never disappointed in me, of course! Can't you understand that?

Pastor   Never?

Boy   Never!! He just snuggled into my armpit and lay there like a great big red sausage, and talked about all sort of things until I was quiet. And fell asleep. But sometimes Valle fell asleep first and lay there snoring and grunting quietly feeling just great. Prrrrh. Prrrrh.

Pause.

Ha ha.

Pause.

Why shouldn't I be fond of him? Never having to feel guilty. Never having to prove that you're good enough.

Pastor But he came back, alive?

Boy Yes.

Pause.

Late at night.

Pause. Beats his hands together nervously, nods and mumbles.

I hear something scratching at the door. Then I hear a miaow and I know immediately, that same instant, immediately! Who it is. It's Valle, who's come back. He's standing there and wants to come inside and I can hear by the sound of his voice how miserable he is and what a hellish nightmare he's been through. Maybe he's wounded and wants me to take care of him. I scream through the door that he's to take it easy!! The door's locked, but I'll get help. And he carries on shouting outside and meowing. You can barely hear him, but he almost sounds manic, and it only gets worse and worse.

Pause, long pause.

. . . And I can't see how he is, maybe he's bleeding and the door's locked, the bastards have locked it, it's locked and I hammer at the door, but no one comes and Valle's desperate and want to come in to me, but no one comes. They just think I've flipped and Valle's out there bleeding maybe, and some new Ericsson fucker might come and . . .

Pause.

. . . and fling him over again . . . like . . . so I go completely crazy and start screaming and smashing the chair into the walls . . . and Valle's out there crying and wanting to come inside . . . and . . . and then someone finally arrives.

Lisbeth   Armageddon.

Boy (*hands to his face, barely in control*)   He leaps straight up to me like a red cannonball.

Lisbeth   OK. Take it easy. It was Armageddon.

Boy   He was hungry! And they'd removed the cat food and tray and everything! And the only thing those fuckers want to talk about is the furniture! A lot of bullshit about the furniture being broken! Valle even had a scar behind his ear which could get infected, but all the fuckers could do was moan about the furniture! Great! Can you believe it! Can you fucking believe it!

Lisbeth   It was Armageddon.

Boy   And then you come and tell us the next day, you bitch. Straight to our faces, Valle and me.

Lisbeth   We had to.

Pastor   Who's we?

Lisbeth   All project staff agreed. We realised that this couldn't go on. It was nothing, not science, nor a realistic attempt at true character development. It had become a sort of emotional hysteria that only became destructive. These weren't people who could always handle such strong feelings. Emotions and humanity are also controls, that's the paradox. And the business with Valle had become so eccentric that it couldn't be permitted to continue.

Boy   They had proved that I was an oyster, but I didn't withdraw in the right way.

Lisbeth   No. Listen, listen. I've never said or thought that. But it was necessary to terminate the experiment. At least we did learn something from it.

Boy   Fucking right you didn't trust me! But you could at least have asked Valle if he trusted me! You could have done that, all right.

Lisbeth   OK, fine. We could have asked Valle if he trusted you. But we didn't. We terminated the experiment.

Boy (*furious*)   Terminated! Fucking right, *you* could terminate, but we couldn't. That's the difference!

Lisbeth   OK. But *we* decided that *you* should terminate.

Boy   But *we couldn't fucking terminate!*

Lisbeth   OK. OK. OK.

Boy   And you were a coward! Before you weren't afraid of stepping into the little cell, but now that you had to say something so fucking awful, you didn't even dare go in! Just stood there! In the door. The door opened, wham, and there you stood looking us straight in the eye and telling us! Straight to Valle's face too! He was to recover a little, just for a day! Just for a day, thank you very much! They wanted to take him away! Terminate the experiment, finish, she says, the bitch! We couldn't fucking terminate! 'For fuck's sake, you can't take Valle away,' I said . . .

Lisbeth   Screamed. More like screamed.

Boy   '. . . He's mine for fuck's sake' and then she said that you can't own a cat. And I said, 'I've never said that you fucking can own a cat,' and then, then she said: 'Really?' And then I said that Valle and I belong together! Do you understand?? And then she said that you can't belong to a cat in that way. It says so in every cat book, she said. 'In every cat book!' I said. 'Who the fuck's written them,' I said. And she just said that it's against the nature of cats. And I said that I'm sure Valle hasn't read those books . . . (*Pause.*) . . . So he thinks we belong together. I said.

Lisbeth   Screamed.

Boy (*stares straight ahead silently, then says awkwardly*)
Then she left. And then they locked the door. And Valle
and I just sat there. They wanted to take him the next
day. He was completely shattered.

Pastor (*to* **Lisbeth**)   Was it necessary?

Lisbeth (*quietly*)   Was it right or wrong? I don't know
but it was necessary.

Pastor   It's frightening when a necessity becomes
necessary. Someone should try and see what would happen
if . . . well . . . the reverse. Whether it's unnecessary.

Lisbeth   The supervisors from both the university and
the institution actually agreed he had become too
destructive. Others were allowed to continue, but he had
become too destructive.

Boy   I was the *only one* who wasn't allowed to continue.

Pastor   But the control group was allowed to continue
with *not* having animals, just as before, I imagine?

Boy   Ericsson was control group. Had he been allowed
one and not been in control group, maybe he wouldn't
have flung Valle over. I think . . . (*Pause.*) . . . It was
probably when I stuck the scissors in Ericsson that they
changed me to control group. Not-allowed-to-have.
(*Pause.*) It was probably then.

Lisbeth   We didn't change you to control group.

Boy   I think the error lay in that business with control
groups. Those in control group had *nothing*. But they
didn't realise that until we others had something. Then it
all got too much for them. In control group. Yes, I believe
they changed me to control group after what happened
with Ericsson and Valle.

Pastor (**Lisbeth** *says nothing, it's very quiet, then the* **Pastor**
says)   Then she shut the door. And you sat there.

Boy   Yes, as control group, that is.

Lisbeth   Stop it.

Boy   First I had nothing, and nothing made sense. And it didn't matter. Then I was given *something*. Then they took Valle away and I was to be in the control group, to be compared to the ones who did have. And that was just too much. Yes, that's how it was.

Lisbeth   Stop it. I'm not very well, actually. But I don't suppose you believe that.

Boy   We just sat there when they'd gone. Valle was completely shattered. He looked like he'd been hit by a sledgehammer. And I stretched out on the bed and just stared up at the ceiling and after a while Valle said: 'Did you hear what she said?' And I didn't answer, 'cause what was I to say? Of course I'd heard. And then he jumped up and stretched out next to me like he used to at night.

Pause.

Although it wasn't night yet.

Pause.

His nose in my armpit. And I lay completely still staring into the air. And *that* was when . . . that I heard him start to sob. I heard him sobbing. He cried.

Pastor   Are you sure? I've never heard a cat cry.

Boy   Absolutely. His whole body was shaking and he was crying. And I said: 'Valle, what is it?' And he said: 'I don't want them to take me away. I want to be here with you.' And then he lay there sobbing and it was fucking awful. And I didn't know what to say.

Suddenly furious.

Now I understand!! Don't even try, you fucking slag! You changed me to control group just so that . . .

Lisbeth   Shut up! Shut up, shut up, shut up . . .

Boy   I should have stabbed you with the scissors instead of Ericsson!!!

Pastor   Can you tell me what's going on between you two?

Lisbeth (*calmly*)   No.

Boy (*also very controlled*)   No, no.

Lisbeth   Good.

Boy   But Valle sobbed and said he'd got it sussed. They conned us into believing that we'd be allowed to stay together. *But it was only an experiment.* Which has been terminated. And what the fuck do you say to that? (*Pause.*) Nothing. I just lay there staring at the ceiling. And caressed Valle's hair.

Lisbeth   Coat.

Pastor   And then you slept?

Boy   No, how were we to do that? Lisbeth has just been standing in the doorway telling us that this would be the last night we'd be allowed to be together! You can't sleep then. Valle couldn't either. He just lay there shivering all over and then I asked him what I should do. And then Valle said: 'Tell me about Granddad's house once more.'

Pastor   Did you often do that?

Boy   Yes, almost every evening. Well, what I'd do was tell him what it was like and things like that. And told him about the things that Granddad used to read me, and later, when I'd learnt to read, the things I'd read for Granddad. That's how it was. After Granddad and I were left alone.

Pastor   What do you mean by alone?

Boy (*a bit annoyed*)   Only the two of us! Don't you understand that?

Pastor   No. Only the two of you. What about your mother?

Boy (*scoffs*)   Mum? She was only there once one afternoon. Making a big fuss and a lot of hugging and kissing. But she'd really only come to collect a suitcase that had arrived and which stood in the cellar. A really big one. I followed her down, just to talk, there were just the two of us down there. Then she unlocked the suitcase and there were a lot of sheets and linen, I think. On top of it all, there was a letter, and it gave her a start, she took the letter and opened it, and when she's read it she was fuming and said: 'That's rich coming from him!' And that was all I got to know. Then she left us again that same evening.

Pause.

'Thanks all the same!'

Pause.

When I'd learnt to read, Granddad wanted me to read aloud to him. I had to read a little every evening.

Pastor   If he was a preacher, it probably wasn't the Bible.

Boy   No, it was always old issues of *Reader's Digest*. He'd piled together a whole bunch of old issues. The best were The Book of the Month, the ones that were about the Second World War.

Pause.

He was funny. They were best when there were a lot of Spitfires in there, he used to say. There were a lot with Spitfires. *Raid On Dieppe*, even though it was a little sad. *The London Blitz*. Or the one that was the best one, *Bombing of the Meuse Dam*. I think we read that one five times.

Pause.

There were a lot of Spitfires in that one.

Pastor   He must have been a rather unusual sort of preacher.

Boy   But after we'd read about Spitfires in *Reader's Digest*, he'd always finish off with a prayer he was very particular about that.

Pause.

He was a real pastor, not a bread-and-butter minister like you.

Pastor   Women who become pastors are seldom bread-and-butter ministers. They have to think things through much more carefully. That's what the ones who leave usually say, don't they, Lisbeth?

Boy (*looks at her suspiciously then says shyly*)   Then you ought to understand what happened to Valle . . . Yeh . . . I haven't told you that yet.

Pause, a little nervous, wants to reach her, but is uncertain.

. . . It was actually boring listening to Granddad preaching. Droning on and on. But when he dug graves and I sat on the edge that was great. When we were alone, that is. Then it was something else.

Pause.

Thanks all the same.

Pause.

You could straight away understand what God was like!!! Like a cat, just lying there purring . . . Or like the heavenly harp . . . How God was somewhere beyond – like the twenty fifth hour perhaps . . . But he never said any of that at the prayer meetings. Only to me. I felt almost sorry for them.

Pause.

Valle shivered and cried so badly that I asked him if I should tell him about the *Bombing of the Meuse Dam* once more. With all the Spitfires. But he'd rather hear about Granddad's house and the heavenly harp.

Pastor   The heavenly harp? Did it have anything to do with the Spitfires?

Boy   Oh. You don't understand anything.

Pastor   But Valle wanted to hear about it?

Boy   Yes. 'Cause he always relaxed when he heard about it. And started to purr, like a sleepy, red tiger. And then he'd fall asleep.

Pause.

I actually think he only liked *The London Blitz* because I liked it. But that night was our last night, that's what Lisbeth had told us. And Valle was completely shattered and sad. So that's why he liked hearing about the heavenly harp and Granddad's house.

Pastor   But that wasn't in *Reader's Digest.*

Boy   No. All that about Granddad's house, I told him that myself.

Pastor   So then, you told Valle about Granddad's house?

Boy   (*explaining both matter-of-factly and irritated*)   Yes, 'cause Valle had grown fond of the house after I'd started telling him about it. He . . . He'd actually started growing as fond of it as I was . . .

Pause.

. . . Although he'd never been there!! But was just as fond of it as me! Granddad didn't even have running water. You had to fetch it from the well.

Pause.

But he did have a phone. His telephone number was number three. The telephone wires were connected to

the gable of the house. That's why the heavenly harp was
there. You understand that don't you?

Pastor No.

Boy The first time I heard it ringing was a winter night.
It was incredibly cold, 'cause it was a wooden house and
the phone wires were connected to the gable and
Granddad and I were sleeping in the bedroom upstairs.
And then I woke up in the middle of the night and it was
singing something incredible. It sang sort of like whining,
sort of – almost like when they play on the saw in prayer
meetings. It was just like someone was stroking a bow on
a musical saw . . .

Pause.

. . . Granddad had a fiddle, by the way, but Mum sold it
when he died.

Pause.

Bitch . . . But it sounded just like when you play on a saw,
a bit whining like, a bit scary and weird and beautiful.
And I woke up, wrapped the rug around me and went to
the window. And there was moonlight. It was incredible.
The whole valley was chalk white, it had been snowing
just the day before, so it was all very clear and moonlight,
it was so bright it hurt my eyes. I tell you . . . it sang so the
whole house boomed. It was as if the wires were
connected to the stars and Granddad's house was a . . .
well, a box . . . and it sang. It boomed with a song and I
was both a little scared, and . . . not scared. But then I
heard Granddad was waking up, 'cause he'd stopped
snoring. Ouuuk. Ouuuk. And then he got up and stood
behind me in his long johns. And then he put his hand
on my head. And stroked my hair very carefully. And then
he said: 'do you hear what that is?' 'No,' I said. 'It's the
heavenly harp,' he said. 'Who's that singing?' I said. 'I
think it's God,' he said. 'He sings like that sometimes.'
'Do you only *think* so,' I said. 'Aren't you sure?' 'No,' said

Granddad, 'but I think it's him.' 'So what's he singing about?' I said. 'I almost know,' said Granddad. 'You'll have to learn to listen, then you'll understand what it is he's trying to say. It's difficult, but you can do it.' 'Can't he speak?!' I said. 'No,' said Granddad, 'but he's good at singing so you understand him.' 'That's strange!' I said. 'No,' said Granddad, 'it's perfectly natural.'

Pastor   Was that how he preached at prayer meetings?

Boy   No, never. To me he'd say such things so you'd know precisely how everything actually fitted together. But not to them. Shame really. I don't think he read about Spitfires at the prayer meetings either. He probably thought that they wouldn't understand it. They were more used to sermons and things like that.

Pastor   Why were you so particularly fond of Spitfires?

Boy   'Cause when everything was lost and surrounded by enemies it always said: 'And in the distance could be heard the sound of – Spitfires.' There always had to be a dash before Spitfires.

Pastor   Was that also why Granddad liked it?

Boy   I never asked him about that. But when I told him about how important it was to protect the frogs, he just folded his arms and said: amen. Then you just knew you'd done the right thing. And he was the one who understood that God could be a cat. And what the heavenly harp sang. And that you could understand what God sang. Only Granddad understood all that and made sense of it all. It's easy enough to explain it, but only Granddad understood it all.

Pastor   Is there a difference between the two?

Boy   Of course. (*Friendly.*) Have you got porridge between your ears?

Pastor   So that last night you told Valle about Granddad's house . . . ?

Boy   Right, that night it wasn't to be about Spitfires, but the heavenly harp and Granddad's house.

Pause.

I don't think he was as keen on the bit that went: 'and then, far away in the distance could be heard the sound of – Spitfires' as I was.

Pause.

But as soon as I started to tell him about Granddad's house he stopped shivering. Even though he'd heard it so many times before. So I included everything, every nut and bolt. How the pipes from the radiators were installed. 'Cause Granddad had built the house himself, his father was a smith, so he'd learnt from him. Granddad knew how to do everything. The hall was in the end part of the house towards the prayer meeting chapel which was some distance away. It had a porch and a balcony on top and during the summer, string was tied up to the balcony and it had hops growing thickly all the way up.

Pause.

There was a rosehip bush growing in front of the house, and in the winter you had to go all the way around in deep snow to get to the well. But in the summer I'd find a hole in the middle of the bush and go straight through.

Pause, then almost bitterly.

What a nerve! Just to turn up one afternoon, fetch the suitcase, open the letter, read it and just scoff and say 'That's rich coming from him!' And that was all we got to know, what do you think of that? Just slopping the frogs out and then I never saw her again.

Pause.

'Thanks all the same!' Fucking right. There was a path down the slope to the well, it had a sort of concrete ring around it, and a wooden frame on top. And a lid. And there were two apple trees by the entrance. There was an attic room behind the bedroom, but I was so young when Dad got locked up and Granny died that it was never properly insulated. They had put a heating unit through that attic room and it often froze. And then Granddad would sit there towards evening with a candle swearing so much that even I once heard it. But then he also asked God for forgiveness that same night and I wasn't to read about the Spitfires.

Pastor   Why do you talk so much about Granddad's house? Why is it so important?

Boy (*looks at her surprised or critically, says calmly*)   You have got porridge between your ears.

Pastor   What happened when Granddad died?

Boy (*calmly explaining as if to an idiot*)   You see, the bedroom was on the first floor and Granddad had built an iron ladder up to the bedroom window, in case of fire. That was the same gable the phone wires went into. And in front of the gable he'd planted a good luck tree, an ash. When you stood by the bedroom window, there was first the gable with the fire escape, then the phone wires and then the rosehip bush. Then came the slope down to the well with the frogs. Then there was the meadow and then the main road. Finally there was the forest on the other side.

Pause, thoughtful.

In the winter there was snow and berries on the ash and also a lot of birds.

Pastor   And that was Granddad's house.

Lisbeth (*almost to herself*)   And there he took the lives of those two. And placed them in the snowdrift outside. Their arms around each other.

Boy (*seriously*)   But they understood nothing of Granddad's house. *And then you get scared.*

Pastor   But what about Valle? Did he understand everything?

Boy   Everything. Long before I did too.

Lisbeth   I would just like to remind you, that you yourself burnt down Granddad's house. I wonder how Valle reacted? Especially to that.

Boy   I thought he'd fallen asleep. While I talked. But then he lifted his head, all calm and quiet and said: 'You know, I think Granddad's house sounds wonderful. Imagine if you and I could move there together.'

Lisbeth (*almost silently*)   Burnt down.

Boy (*smiling secretively, shaking his head stubbornly*)   But that was before Valle had explained *how things really happened.*

Pause.

I said to him: 'My little Valle, we can't move. I've stabbed Ericsson in the stomach with the scissors. And I'll never get out of here. And they're coming to fetch you tomorrow morning and then we'll never see each other again. And Granddad's house . . . but Valle . . . Granddad's house . . .' I've already told you!! I was so fucking sorry and stupid and wanted to finish everything. And those asshole ideas . . . that I didn't want any strangers dirtying Granddad's house. And that I'd hoped to sit in the bedroom upstairs and listen . . . to the heavenly harp . . . and understand the song . . .

Lisbeth   But surely that wasn't why you ran away and set fire to the whole damn thing?

Pastor   Will you shut up!!!

Boy (*as if he hasn't heard them, very quietly*)   It's difficult for anyone who hasn't seen Valle to imagine how beautiful he was, a little tiger. And then he had such mild, friendly, slant eyes – which you were never quite sure of. And then I lay there talking about Granddad's house. About how impossible it all was. But then he sat himself on top of my stomach, laughing almost. And then he said: 'Shall I tell you what really happened when I was out in the forest?' And I said: 'What? What are you trying to tell me?' And then he said: 'What really happened. About the miracle.' And I said: 'Miracle? What the hell are you talking about?'

Lisbeth   OK. You're tired and a bit hyper. Let's carry on tomorrow, same time. OK?

Pastor   No. I want to hear it now.

Boy   And that little cat smile. You know, a bit sad, as if he was afraid that I'd have porridge between my ears and not understand the things most difficult to understand. He'd kept quiet about something.

Pause.

It's really not until a cat like Valle smiles like that, that you understand that God is beautiful.

Pause.

But maybe that isn't important to a pastor like you; that God is beautiful? You don't think of it very often, do you?

Pastor   Is it so important then, that God is beautiful?

Boy   No. But you can be a little touched by it.

Pastor   I've never thought of that.

Boy   You've never seen Valle smile, either.

Pastor   Perhaps it's wrong that I haven't thought of it.

Boy   You can be sort of touched by it.

Pause.

Then Valle explained what had really happened. Ericsson had grabbed Valle around the waist and flung him over. And Valle had been really scared.

Pause.

Imagine if God can be scared. I like that idea.

Pause.

And then he'd run straight into the forest with the lead trailing behind. He'd run like mad. And then . . . well then it got darker . . . and darker. And he didn't really know where he was. But he'd started to walk. And walk and walk and walk. And meowed and cried for me. But I couldn't hear it. He knew that I couldn't hear it, but he was so scared that he'd cried for me even so. And then he got caught.

Lisbeth (*very quietly*)   Listen. You don't know any of that.

Boy   Of course I do! He got caught, he told me later. His lead got caught in a bush and he couldn't get free! And it was dark. And it was some bush or other. And the more he tried getting free the more entangled the lead got. Until in the end he was almost completely strapped down. And he sat there tugging and pulling all night, until it started getting light again. And then he'd seen the fox.

Pastor   The fox??

Boy (*quietly*)   And then the fox had killed Valle.

Lisbeth   OK, OK, OK. Let's stop, shall we.

Pastor   He'd killed him?

Boy   You can imagine what that felt like.

Lisbeth (*to the* **Pastor**)   Let's go.

Boy (*doesn't hear her, too engrossed in the story*)   And then I said to him: 'But Valle, how can you be sitting here then? It's completely mad?' And then he said: 'But can't you see *that I am sitting here*? It was *natural*' he said. 'It was really quite natural!' And I said: 'Natural, what do you mean, it doesn't make sense.' And then suddenly I understood everything. It all made sense. That's just how things are.

Pastor   But I don't understand. I don't. I'd like to though.

Boy (*confused, wondering*)   Don't you understand how it all makes sense? All the things that have been so strange. I'd been so stupid. The horrible fact that I got so mad at the two who tried to throw me out of Granddad's house. And that I went up there and burnt the house to the ground. Just because I hadn't understood!

Pause.

I was so terrified of everything and it was so simple.

Pause.

Valle helped me. With Valle I didn't even feel ashamed for having been so fucking stupid. You didn't have to earn forgiveness. He just looked at me and smiled and then he said: 'I've come back to take you with me.'

Pastor (*strangely disturbed*)   And that makes sense?? What was it? The ladder? The ash . . . the snow and the berries . . . and the birds in the ash? And the rosehip bush . . . and . . .

Boy (*explaining helpfully*)   And the frogs. If nothing makes sense then you go mad. And that was when Valle rose from the dead and I started to understand everything.

Pastor   And that God was a ginger cat which you needn't ask for forgiveness?

Boy (*scoffs*)   And when you think of all the frogs I've saved from being slopped out!

Thoughtfully.

If only I'd had a little less porridge between my ears. And a little sooner! Then maybe I would have understood all the things that Granddad talked about. Although it isn't easy to know what a heavenly harp is singing, as I said to Valle. So meanwhile you make your mistakes.

Pause, smiles slightly.

'Thanks all the same.' But even Granddad wasn't sure
that it was God singing. Or that he could be a cat.

Pastor Valle was to take you where?

Boy To my Granddad's house.

Pastor But that had burnt down??

Boy As if I didn't know! And first of all I thought that
Valle had gone funny after the business with the fox. No
wonder. Imagine being trapped all night. And just as it gets
light, he sees the fox approaching. Imagine just seeing the
fox's eyes! And then he probably stands there staring.
Silent. For a long time. I don't know. I've never been
trapped with a fox next to me. But then he gets a bit closer.
And closer. And then Valle knows for sure that he'll be
killed. Just imagine what that feels like.

Pastor And yet Valle was alive and wanted to take you
back to Granddad's house a few days later!?

Boy That's what I said. You know how it is, I said.
They'll never fucking let me out of here. But then he
said: 'Don't you know that there is a way of getting free?'
'No,' I said, 'whatever I say they'll never buy it. I've done
so much shit! They won't even consider me!' But then
Valle said: 'There is another way. And no one can stop us
getting free. And when we're free, we'll both move up to
Granddad's house and live there together. You've burnt it
down but it's come back.'

Pastor Did you believe that?

Boy (*seriously*) Valle never lied to me. Why should he
do so now? Why shouldn't I believe it?

Pastor (*tonelessly, walking up and down*) But . . . you've
got to see . . .

Lisbeth Yes, what has he got to see? Can you make that
clear? I've tried for four years now.

Boy (*after a moment of silent confusion*)   And straight away
Valle said: 'We can go together. Then we're both free and
can live in Granddad's house up there. We can both stand
by the bedroom window when the heavenly harp sings.
And then you'll hold me and stroke my fur. And
everything will make sense once more. The phone wires
connected to the gable of the house and the heavenly
harps singing and Granddad's fire escape ladder hanging
on the wall, in case anything should happen and in front
there's the ash, which is a good luck tree. And in the
winter there'll be snow and birds eating the berries. And a
bit further away the rosehip bush. And the slope down to
the well and there are frogs that we protect. And
everything will make sense once more.' But then I said:
'Are you quite sure, Valle, will everything make sense?' '*It
will all make sense once more*' he said. And then I said to
him: 'Valle, I would love for us to do that. But I don't
know if I dare. I'm so scared.'

Lisbeth (*walks over to the* **Pastor** *and faces her*)   You
know, listening to you I feel quite ill. If the fox killed
Valle, then he can't come back. You must explain that to
him. A house burns, but it doesn't rise up again. It's your
job to explain that to him. Otherwise you'll only harm
him.

Pastor (*sits on the floor with her hands to her face, isn't she
crying?*)   Yeees . . .

Lisbeth   Because a living being cannot die and then rise
from the dead, it's impossible. Tell him!

Boy (*with a secret smile*)   Ask her once more.

Lisbeth   Yes? Will you tell him then?

The **Pastor** *just shakes her head disconsolately and slowly,
without being able to say a word.*

Boy (*calm, almost mediating*)   You see, Lisbeth.

Lisbeth (*after a pause, to the* **Pastor**)   You're insane.
You're the one who should be locked up.

Pastor (*removing her hand from her face, yes, she's been crying, and she says to the* **Boy**)   You mean that God came to you and it was Valle.

Boy (*speaking calmly, lightly and easily*)   He came back to fetch me.

Pause.

We lay whispering to each other all night, 'cause later they were coming to take him away for ever. And towards the morning we mostly lay there quietly just looking at each other. And then I decided. I said to Valle: 'I think I dare do it now. You go first and I'll do it this time.' And he said: 'I know you got scared the last time when you set fire to Granddad's house. But now it's *different*,' he said.

Pause.

Yes, 'cause I did get so scared that time. And I was so ashamed afterwards. First to escape from this place and run off all the way up to Granddad's house. I'd thought of standing by the bedroom window looking out over the ash and the rosehip bush and the well while it burnt down, 'cause the house was empty then, but then came all the suffocating smoke and it was all so awful. And then I opened the window and climbed down the ladder.

Pause.

But Valle just said: 'It's so easy, you don't have to be afraid. It's so easy to die. And then we'll be free and live together in Granddad's house.' And then I said: 'That's agreed then. I'll see you there. I'm not afraid any more.' And then he lay down, digging his nose well into my armpit, turned his head a bit to face me, lay there purring awhile while I stroked his head and fur. He was so warm and beautiful like a little tiger. And then he died. I stroked my hand over his head and felt that he slowly stopped purring and went quiet. And then he was dead. He'd come back to fetch me. And then it was my turn.

Pastor (*still sitting by the wall. No longer crying, nor* *hysterical, just very sad*)   And then you took the plastic bag.

Boy (*quietly, but determined*)   Yes, that wasn't much of a success though. But Valle's waiting for me.

Pastor   Oh, my dearest, don't make me despair.

Boy   What? There's nothing to despair for. 'Where you go, I shall go too,' I said to Valle. I made a promise. And I'm keeping it. He knew how easy it was. You dig your nose into his armpit. Then you lie there purring for a while. Then you sleep. Then you're free. And now Valle and I can live together in Granddad's house.

Lisbeth (*rises with determination, walks over to the* **Pastor** *who still sits over by the wall, stands in front of her looking down at her for a while. The* **Pastor** *looks up at her*)   Shall we go? Shall we go now?

The **Pastor** *only shakes her head quietly, almost shyly.*

Lisbeth   You are insane. And I'll never listen to you again. You are insane.

The **Pastor** *thinks and then nods.*

Boy   No one can stop me; 'cause Valle's waiting for me.

Lisbeth *leaves, alone and resolute. The* **Guard** *outside looks up, then the door closes.*

Pastor (*looking intently at the* **Boy**'s *back, neither of them has moved*)   Listen, may I stay for a while? I have to know more. I don't quite understand. Or may I visit you again?

Boy (*very softly, friendly*)   No.

Pastor (*sits next to the* **Boy**, *her head in his lap*)   But it's so important – for me.

Boy (*quietly, friendly*)   I've told you everything exactly as it was. Everything. That's how it happened. There's nothing more to say. Understanding it, that's your business. But I've told it exactly as it was.

Smiles almost imperceptibly.

You can't ask like that. Not about Valle.

Pastor   Why not?

Boy   Well, for instance you can't ask where the lynx is that twenty-fifth hour of the day.

Strokes her hair carefully, almost consoling.

It's different.

Pause.

During that hour he's somehow, somewhere outside.

*It's quiet for a while, then the **Pastor** gets up slowly and with difficulty. Is it morning or night? She says calmly and straight to the audience:*

Pastor   Two days later he was dead. They wanted to tell me how he'd done it, but I didn't want to know. I would like to imagine that somehow he'd dug his face into God's armpit, lay there purring for a while, felt a hand carefully stroking his hair and then simply died. What do we need a god for if we can't die in his armpit?

Pause.

It must be easy to die, if you know you've got a cat waiting for you. When this happened I was forty-nine years old and had been a pastor in the Swedish State Church for eighteen years. Now I'm sixty-two. I was ordained when I was thirty-one. It wasn't easy then, for women, things had to be considered very carefully before one started to preach the Holy Gospel and that God was Love, although I probably didn't even understand half of what I said. After that night and after I'd buried the two of them together, I left the Church. Perhaps that was silly. But if one starts to imagine that God is a ginger cat, and that Granddad's house is love, then it's very difficult to stay. But I learnt something that night. And it has helped me tremendously throughout the past thirteen years. And I hope that it will continue to support me until the day I die. Then I'll die just as easily, snuggled into God's armpit, in front of the bedroom window in Granddad's house.

Pause.

The ladder, the tree. White snow and moonlight. The slope down to the well with the frogs. The phone wires singing so that I understand how it all makes sense. And the ash full of snow and birds. When I left that night, he'd started trying to sing Rod Stewart's 'Sailing' once more. That was the year the single was released. Perhaps he was fond of it. It was the last thing I heard.

Boy *has started humming, but just as she has finished talking and moved to the door, he interrupts himself and asks her, without turning his head:*

Boy   Listen, are you going to see Ericsson tomorrow? Won't you tell him there are no hard feelings, for what he did?

Pastor   I will tell him.

Boy   You won't forget now? And that it's from both Valle and me?

Pastor   I'll tell him there are no hard feelings from both Valle and yourself.

Boy *nods silently and resolutely with a flash of an almost joyful smile.   While he sings, she leaves.*

Boy   . . . Home again . . . home again . . . across . . . the sea . . . (*Pause.*) . . . I am sailing . . . I am sailing . . . to be near you . . . to . . . be . . . free . . .

Blackout.

The Image Makers

by

Per Olov Enquist

translated by

Charlotte Barslund and Kim Dambæk

Preface

Bengt Forslund describes in his magnificent biography of Viktor Sjöström the actual events when Selma Lagerlöf and Viktor Sjöström met in connection with the filming of *The Coachman*. Sjöström travelled up to Mårbacka and read aloud to Selma Lagerlöf his entire film script one long afternoon. When he had finished reading and was awaiting her comments with great anticipation a very long silence followed.

Eventually, after this very long silence, Selma Lagerlöf asked him if he wanted a drink. That was all. We are told nothing else.

I too have read this script; it is kept at the Swedish Film Institute; a wonderful, detailed, visionary and remarkably ambitious script consisting of six hundred and five scenes. This would later result in a film that is considered the peak of the silent film era and one of the ten strangest films in history.

However, it was the silence between the two image makers and Selma Lagerlöf's silence in particular which interested me most; what did it contain? And then I wrote this play.

Per Olov Enquist

Characters

Selma Lagerlöf – *aged 62*
Viktor Sjöström – *aged 42*
Tora Teje – *aged 26*
Julius Jaenzon – *aged 38*

Act One

Through the Glass

We will begin shortly.

The room is fairly large, eight metres by four-and-a-half metres, with an opening stage left, leading to an area where a black curtain covers the door.

A darkroom? No, perhaps not. A room for screenings?

But there is no door, just thick black drapes which have now been pulled to one side.

A darkroom? No, not a darkroom, but clearly a kind of lab. Not a laboratory for photographs, film perhaps?

A film laboratory. Part of a horizontal machine can been seen with its lens. The machine is two metres long at least. A suspended reel of film.

A cinematic laboratory. The picture becomes clearer.

Two people.

Tora Teje *and* **Julius Jaenzon**. *She: young, pretty. He: an extremely clever cinematographer and right now hopelessly horny.*

Or what kind of restlessness is he expressing? A fixation with her?

He's not the violent type. He is awkward, no – timid, no – shy. No, not shy but awkward. And she: a cat. There is nothing more enchanting than a cat who is unapproachable in her calm, childlike solitude.

Not enchanting. Frustrating.

They know each other. They have worked together. They haven't been lovers.

She should be going, she thinks. But she won't be.

We will begin shortly.

Tora   What? Shitting yourself? Because of her?

Julius   Surely you understand why I'm scared. The national monument is about to be wheeled in. And we have been tinkering night and day for months and . . . you just don't know . . .

Tora   Must you say 'tinkering'. It sounds so . . . blunt.

Julius   Tinker. Tinker tinker tinker. No no. You must be . . . *humble.* Keep a low profile. But deep inside you're thinking that you're making pictures which . . . well, it is almost as if you were helping little grey birds of clay to fly. The pictures become a little magical . . .

Reaching out.

Come here, my sweet little darling.

Tora   You're not going to tell the woman herself that she's turned out some stone dead birds of clay.

Julius   I know my place. I'm just a humble image maker. Tinker. Tinker. But scared all the same.

Tora   Bloody sucking up to that . . . an overweight, antiquated bumble bee like her . . . surely that's nothing to get . . .

She frees herself with practised ease.

Get off!

Julius   . . . Won't you . . . please . . . ?

Tora   I don't want to.

Julius   Very well. (*Resigned.*) Well . . . I'm used to that.

Tora   I've said I don't want to. Please, Julius. Don't sulk.

Julius   You're cruel. That's what you are. You belittle me.

Tora   Rubbish. I *just don't* want to.

Julius   It's torture! Every time I'm near you I'm like a pressure cooker, I think I'll explode!

Tora   You're scared. Don't be scared. She won't eat you alive.

Julius   I have to walk home bent double. That's dangerous! It can make you ill! You can die! Sooner or later I'll burst and then you'll be sorry! Sorry! And then you'll . . .

Tora   Regret it? Yup. (*Pause.*) Whatever you do, you always have regrets.

Pause.

How much will she watch? Not the whole film, surely?

Julius   We daren't do that. We haven't finished cutting yet . . . Listen!

Changes to his confiding voice which has sometimes resulted in success.

I want to make a confession. It is terrible never to be relieved. You go mad . . .

Tora   Stop bloody pestering me!

Julius   That's how it is. I'm telling you the truth. Honestly! I'm telling you!

Tora   'Honestly . . . honest, honestly . . . ' Every time you're horny you talk like that.

Julius (*dramatically*)   Every time I have a wank I think of you!

Tora   Really!?

Julius   Yes! Every single time!

Tora   How sweet! God, how sweet!

Julius (*sulking*)   I don't think so. Air swimming, that's what it is.

Tora   It's what . . . air swimming?

Julius   Yes. Something theoretical.

Tora (*with a certain newly discovered interest*)   I see. So . . . you're imagining that we are doing it . . . and *every time* I'm there . . . like . . . well, I'm there, but it's like . . . wait a moment! . . . But I avoid having to do it?

Julius   Avoid!?

Depressed, sits down on the table with the script.

Avoid.

Pause.

Yes.

Tora   But, at least you are *thinking* of me. Thank you! Perhaps that is a good thing? Imagine if your entire life was like that. That everything happened mostly in your imagination.

Matter-of-fact.

You could do it with . . . everybody. As if you were . . . everywhere! . . . And you could do it with as many as possible. You could *be* someone for everyone!

Julius (*sulking*)   Well, I actually imagined that it should only be me!

Tora (*now more quiet, enchanted by the thought*)   It would be like . . . well, when Viktor and you make a film and I'm there on the screen for everybody, but I don't actually have to be there. . . . As if life were a film!

Snatches a page of the script from him, he lets it happen, stares darkly at her attractive but so unapproachable arse.

What is this? Is it Viktor's script?

Julius   No, hers. This is from the book. But can't you understand how bloody frustrated I get, when you fantasise and fantasise and fantasise but . . .

Tora   . . . Oooooh. . . . oh, how beautiful . . . imagine being able to write like that . . . even though you are as old, fat and ugly as her . . .

Julius (*irritated*)   What? You're just trying to avoid the issue! The issue is . . . the issue is . . .

Tora   . . . Why I don't want to. God, how beautiful.

Julius   . . . Beautiful! That you don't *want* to do it with me?

Tora (*reads quietly*)   'Do not think my body is worthless. It is the home of my soul, just like yours and other people's bodies. Do not think of it as firm or heavy or strong. Just think of it as a picture which you've seen in a mirror and imagine it has risen through the glass and can speak and move.' Is this in the film?

Julius   Nooo.

Pulls himself together.

Well, we had this idea that we would double expose the film. When the coachman arrives and the drunkard rises from the dead body. I exposed the same take four times and when you double expose . . .

Tora   ' . . . a picture which you've seen in a mirror. A picture which you've seen in a mirror.' As if you're raising something. From the grime of life. And it becomes beautiful.

Julius *looks at her quietly, suddenly she is very beautiful and pure and young, after a while he says:*

Julius   Indeed. The bird of clay can fly.

Tora (*glances at him, says gently and almost apologetically*)
' . . . Do not think that my body is worthless. It is like a picture which you've seen in a mirror.'

Julius (*sits down next to her*)   How are you really, Tora?

Tora   Well . . .

Julius   I mean . . . is it over between Viktor and you or what's going on?

Tora   Don't know.

Julius   Edith is in Helsinki, I hear. Does she know about you?

Tora   He doesn't say very much.

Pause.

Yes. She knows.

Julius   Is that why you didn't get the part in *The Coachman*? Was it Edith who blocked it?

Tora   I think he's scared of me. But not of her. I don't get it.

Julius   Of course.

Tora (*puts on her coat slowly, seeming to freeze the movement*) I must go before they arrive. Viktor will go mad if I'm still here.

Pause.

He probably doesn't want me to meet Selma. (*Pause.*) Probably thinks I'll say the wrong thing. He thinks I always say the wrong thing and I believe he's ashamed.

Julius   No, no, I'm sure he doesn't think that at all . . . it's more that . . . well, with you two . . . and Edith in Helsinki . . .

Tora   So one gets dumped. *Just like that!* It is just so disappointing.

Pause.

Air swimming!

Julius   Don't you at least want to have a look at Selma . . .

for Christ's sake, you don't run into a Nobel Prize winner every . . .

Tora   . . . Sure, sure . . . well . . . he'll only be ashamed, I always screw up on such occasions . . .

Pause.

I think he is ashamed of me, but he's never ashamed of Edith. I suppose that's the difference. That is the difference . . . I suppose. That is the . . . Julle!

Discovers the bottle of whisky on the shelf.

You stingy bastard. You haven't said a word!

Julius   Didn't think it appropriate since we're making a film about a drunkard.

Tora (*sits down on the stool, her coat half off, takes a sip from the bottle, picks up the script, re-reads the page thoughtfully*)
You wonder what they really *are like* those who can write as beautifully as this. Where they find it. And *why*! I mean, there has to be a reason. It is marvellous when you think about it. 'Do not think my body is worthless. It is the home of my soul, just like yours and other people's bodies. Do not think of it as firm or heavy or strong. Just think of it like a picture which you've seen in a mirror and imagine it has risen through the glass and can speak and move.'

Selma *stands in the doorway, she has been listening to the last bit, she is impressed, wears a hat, smiles a little.*

Selma   That was beautiful.

Tora   Christ! You scared me.

Selma   I didn't mean to. Who wrote that?

Tora   You did! The doctor did! Sorry, Christ, I'm so nervous, it is . . . your text, isn't it . . . Julius said that . . .

Selma   Oh yes. Though when I heard it, it wasn't mine, but someone else's. Good afternoon.

Tora . What? It was only me. Hi, Viktor.

Viktor (*he is visibly embarrassed, he is the Nobel Prize winner's escort and was not expecting* **Tora**, *he tries to regain control*) Well, this is Tora Teje, actress and Julius Jaenzon who is the cinematographer and . . .

Tora He spells it J – A – E – N – Z – on, not because he wants to be flashy, he says but . . .

Viktor (*repeats irritably*) . . . who! is! the cinematographer! And he's done an amazing job with the night shots and the trick photography, we filmed the background first, then he ran the same reel through the camera, then we did the ghost, *the spirit*, difficult, twice, a work of precision, you make very precise chalk marks for each person and . . . we are very proud of the spirits' consistency.

Selma Consistency?

Viktor (*enthusiastically*) You must be able to see *through* them. Amazingly Julle has achieved it. Chairs in the foreground must naturally block your view. But you have to be able to see through the spirits all the same.

Julius I lit it in a way so the spirits wouldn't become flat and dim, but three dimensional! It has to . . . fly!

Viktor Quite. Quite.

Selma (*dryly*) So he is responsible for the spirits in this masterpiece.

Tora (*laughs nervously*) That's a good one! Spirits! Did you hear that?

Pulls herself together.

Oh, I beg your pardon, but I'm so nervous and I just thought that it was so great! So great! That you could crack a joke . . . I mean . . .

Viktor (*doesn't see the funny side*) Would you fetch the reels, Julius?

He looks at **Tora**, *glances at the bottle on the table and says.*

I see. I didn't know you were here, Tora.

Tora (*quietly*)   Relax. I'm going.

Viktor   Right, then.

Tora   Don't need to be told. I know my place.

Viktor   Stop it.

Tora   Just a little disappointed, perhaps.

Selma (*who has been watching* **Tora** *intensely all the while*)
What a shame you have to go . . . I think I recognise you
from somewhere . . . weren't you in the film based on
Jerusalem . . . what was the name of that film, they gave it
such a funny title . . .

Viktor (*very strict*)   *Karin Ingmarsdotter.*

Quietly to **Tora**.

Don't blame me.

Selma   But you're not in *The Coachman?*

Tora   Nah.

Selma   Why not?

Tora   Mrs Sjöström blocked it. The wife is jealous.

Selma   Indeed?

Pause.

Indeed.

*Pause, she takes her hat off, wanders around the studio,
everyone watches her nervously.*

It clearly requires a great many machines to create
dreams.

Looks sharply at **Tora** *and adds:*

When one is young and pretty and intelligent like you,

one should take care of oneself. As well as other people's marriages.

Tora   Indeed!

Selma *has stopped in front of her, they glare at each other in silence for a while, then* **Tora** *explodes and goes to the chair where she has thrown her coat.*

Well, kiss my arse.

Julius (*quietly and nervously, stands in the door with the reels in his arms*)   Holy shit.

Tora   Yes, indeed. So I'll say what I always say. Goodbye.

Selma   Why?

Tora   'Cause I'm bloody well not taking any more of this. Not from anyone. You can sit here and admire one another, but I say goodbye, farewell, go to hell; I'm not taking any more of this. The young, pretty and intelligent girl says goodbye and I'll take care of myself, but nobody puts my nose out of joint. Honestly all this is getting up my nose. Which isn't all that big. The end. With these simple words, I . . .

Julius *still stands in the doorway with the reels in his arms, he has been listening to the tirade, with horror beaming from his eyes.*

Tora   . . . Don't stand there like a sheep. Stop cringing!!! I've screwed up. I told you I should have left before they arrived. I just screw up. *Stop cringing, you'll ruin the film.*

Julius *sits down quickly on the stool, he laughs nervously, this must be a bad dream.*

Tora   Good. I'll go now as I've just said in my . . . *exit line.*

Julius   Holy shit. Holy shit!

Viktor   Tora! Apologise!

Tora No bloody way! She doesn't have a clue what she's talking about!

Selma Heavens above . . . what did I say? I've only just come through the door.

Tora No, no. She's been here a long time! Her spirit has been here for weeks. Her spirit! The monument! Three dimensional! Not two! They're terrified. Look at the boys. Julle was so scared of her that he had to have a drink every hour. Scared! That's what they are.

Selma Of whom?

Tora Of you! Because you were coming!

Julius Holy shit.

Selma Yes, but you don't seem very scared, my dear friend.

Tora (*close to tears*) No. Not of . . . her . . . not of . . .

Selma But . . . my dear, little . . .

Tora . . . not of . . .

And suddenly she begins sobbing violently and throws herself in **Selma**'s *arms.*

Julius Holy shit! What are we going to do?

Viktor I do beg your pardon, Dr Lagerlöf. I don't know what to say, but Miss Teje is unbalanced and it is absolutely inexcusable . . . I mean inexplicable . . .

Tora (*furious*) Shut up! There's nothing inexplicable here. If you don't shut up, I'll explain! Is that what you want?

Viktor Please . . .

Julius Holy shit.

Selma (*sharply to* **Julius**) Stop sitting there like some parrot, get the girl a glass of water and a hankie, and hurry up.

Tora (*brightens up suddenly*)   Did you hear what she said! Hurry up!

Viktor *follows* **Julius** *off-stage panic-stricken, the two women are alone together, they look at each other, look in the direction of the panic-stricken men and suddenly they begin laughing. Then silence once more.*

Selma   It's better to get angry than run away.

Tora (*lively*)   Yes, exactly. And they have been scared shitless of you . . . they don't actually like the author turning up because they want to be on their own tinkering with the . . . what's it called . . . what's it called . . .

Selma   The film.

Tora   No, the spirit. The spirit. The spirit of the masterpiece. They want to tinker on their own because they believe you think you have created the soul of the book and they want to tinker with it.

Selma   I like your courage, my friend. Not even the King would dare doing away with my titles.

Tora   . . . Well, I'm informal with you, doctor, but only because I'm so all over the place that I'm quite irresponsible! Do you understand? So it is excusable and then I thought what I was reading was so beautiful . . . that the body is like a picture which you've seen in a mirror . . . and then I thought . . .

Selma   That?

Tora   That if you can write like that, then you must be able to understand everything. Me included. That's why I got so mad at you. I was expecting more! After all, you understand. YOU UNDERSTAND!

Selma   Yes. Indeed. Yes, you perhaps.

Pause, then to herself:

But certainly not everything, my friend.

She pulls herself together, **Julius** *enters with what is required for the rescue operation, she takes the handkerchief and resumes her previous behaviour.*

Blow your nose now and sit down.

Tora   Yes, but I'm supposed to be going . . . I'll . . . retire . . .

Selma   Sit down. You're not going. When I want you to go, then you'll go. Not before.

Julius   Holy shit.

A sharp glance from **Selma,** *for a moment he looks as if he would prefer the Earth to swallow him up, then pulls himself together and straightens up.*

Julius   I should be loading the camera. That's why we're here, isn't it? We're supposed to be looking at the takes, aren't we?

Tora (*now quite happy again, keen to preserve the mood*)   Oi, Selma . . .

Viktor (*boiling with rage*)   Tora! One does not address Dr. Lagerlöf in that manner. Apologise immediately.

Selma   That's quite all right. We've dropped all formalities.

Tora   A name in hand is better than two titles in the bush, so I'll say Selma, because Selma absolutely insists . . .

Looks triumphantly at **Viktor,** *no one interrupts or corrects her.*

. . . So, Selma, tell me why did you, Selma . . . actually write this book! *The Coachman.* Truly?

Selma   My dear friend. I have learnt one thing in a lifetime of idiots coming to ask me about my books. If a journalist asks me why I – truly – wrote a book, then he hasn't read it. Then I have to reel off a lot of things which he couldn't be bothered to read for himself.

Tora   But for Christ's sake, I *have* read it! Every bloody page! I liked it!

Selma   Well, of all my books it is the one closest to my heart.

Tora (*lively*)   You hear that, Viktor! D'you hear that!!! You got so mad at me when I said it was amazing and it was her best book and you said that it was a potboiler with some cinematic potential, but that, honestly, it really was . . .

Viktor (*panic-stricken*)   Tora! That's enough!

Selma (*calmly*)   Yes, many people agree. I'm not offended.

Tora   But he has bloody awful *judgement*, doesn't he? Doesn't he have bloody awful *judgement?* Saying that about a masterpiece which I quite clearly recognised as a masterpiece . . . lousy *judgement!*

Pause.

In all areas.

Julius (*incredulous*)   Which is closest to your heart? Well, I didn't expect that . . . I mean of all the great works which you have written, it is perhaps not . . .

Selma (*dismissively*)   Aren't you going to start soon?

Julius   Start what?

Selma   The screening!

Julius (*delighted and nervous*)   Of course! Please forgive us for . . . please forgive us for . . . well, what with so much going on . . .

Tora (*she stares curiously at* **Selma** *and will not let the question pass*)   Why?

Selma   What do you mean?

Tora   Why is it closest to your heart?

Selma Well that is an entirely private matter. Which I won't divulge.

Tora Won't divulge?

Selma To outsiders.

Tora (*enraged*) Outsiders! And I suppose you mean me? Well, let me tell you. How can you *talk* like that? You just can't say that. I have read it! So how can I be a bloody *outsider*! Come again.

Selma (*irritated*) How do you mean?

Tora 'An entirely private matter,' and then you dump me, that's what you've done. You *dumped* me. Though here I come and I am pleasant and I like your book and I think it is a masterpiece. I actually think so. So you can't just dump me like that, leaving me in the lurch, arse over tit . . . *I don't get it* . . . and then you say that there is something *secret*, but it sure as hell isn't something for little me to worry about . . . so you won't tell me.. you won't tell me! And it feels as if I'm . . .

Julius Air swimming.

Tora *Precisely*! That's it, Julle! You hear, Julius thinks the same as me. Now you've got to get a grip and not dump us like that. Surely you can't write such a completely moving book and then say that something is so private that I can't be let in on it . . . you have got to stop dumping people like that, Selma!

Selma (*agitated, but somewhat confused as she has never before met anyone who has contradicted her in this way*) But, my dear friend . . . what do you mean?! Surely you understand that a writer has . . . an inner core . . . the deepest layer . . . which he or she can never divulge? Surely you understand that?

Tora Absolutely not! It sounds quite mad!

Selma Quite mad! But it is obvious that the core of a work of art must be protected!

Tora   Protected? Against me who reads the book? Why should you, the author, sit there guarding what's most important, while I, the reader . . . have to listen to shit like that . . . 'private' . . . 'outsider' . . . what is this? Just what is this! I've never heard the like!

Selma (*pleading*)   But surely you know, it is well known, practically every expert on literature agrees on this . . . you can read as many critics as you like . . . the essays always say that one has to be sensitive towards the writer's innermost secret, it must be protected, respected, it is well known and . . .

Tora (*appalled*)   Not by me it isn't! I never knew it! Not by me it isn't! I've never read that! Have you read something like that, Julle?

Julius (*cringing*)   No.

Tora   There you are! He's never read it either! No, it's just something you're making up. You've got to do better than that. When someone is a writer like you then there are no 'outsiders', least of all those who *like* your books. Like me! Viktor is an outsider, he didn't like this book, you can dump Viktor, not me.

Selma (*with difficulty*)   The respect for a writer's inner motive and the forces which drive him is something which . . .

Tora   Yes, but Christ Almighty you wrote the book so that I would be interested in this innermost thing? Didn't you? You can't hide like . . . like . . . what am I trying to say, Julle? Like a . . .

Julius (*sits with his face buried in his hands, rocking backwards and forwards*)   Holy shit.

Tora   Precisely! Like some holy shit! Thank you, Julle!

Viktor (*his face white with anger, controls himself only with the greatest of efforts*)   I must ask you to leave now, Tora.

Resolutely, decisively and categorically I ask you to get out. You are coarse and unreasonable. Go.

Tora (*triumphantly*)   You're not in charge here! You're not in charge! Selma is!

Viktor   Yes and I'm sure that Dr Lagerlöf would be . . . unbelievably . . . relieved if you left! Isn't that so?

Selma   I don't know.

Viktor (*close to pleading*)   Isn't that so!??

Selma *is silent, watches* **Tora** *with curiosity.*

Viktor   Isn't that so?

Tora (*very quietly, her face turned away*)   Say it.

Julius   It's loaded.

Selma   Yes, it really is . . . but . . . but . . . what were you talking about?

Julius   It is loaded. Ready to roll. I've put the reel in place. So if it pleases you, Dr Lagerlöf . . .

Tora   Say it.

Selma (*determined, suddenly in the best of moods*)   Now I think it would be wonderfully entertaining to see what the boys have . . . what's it called, Tora, what is it they have done to my so called masterpiece, what's it called. They have . . . ?

Tora   Tinkered.

Selma   Tinkered! I want so see what they have been tinkering with. Tora will please sit down on this chair and not utter anything stupid for several minutes, if she can manage that, there. And Viktor will tell us what he and his friend Julle have been tinkering with! There! No sour faces! Happy faces! You must have that when watching this misery –

Viktor *looks at her darkly, she changes quickly.*

– and I'm not talking about the film or the tinkering, but the terrible story I have written in my terribly pretentious potboiler which Tora loves and that's why, that's why she'll sit there. Stay there.

Tora (*quietly*)   Thank you.

Viktor (*jaw clenched*)   Julius. If you've loaded the projector, then I think it's time. To put an end to this ordeal.

Julius   Oh, dear God. Of course. Of course. This is scene thirty-six b take three.

Viktor   Well, we don't have a pianist here. There should be piano music. Perhaps we could use the gramophone . . . no?

Tora   Why does it need music? I've always wondered about that. It always sounds so rinky dinky dink.

Viktor (*with great self-control*)   To create the right atmosphere!

Tora   But there's no piano in the *book*.

Viktor (*with irony*)   An observation both correct and astute, Tora.

Tora   There's no piano in the book and it still works. That piano music doesn't know what is going on, really, does it?

Viktor   About as much as I do, at any rate.

Tora   Well, that's just it. That's what makes me nervous, but that's not your fault. Because Selma won't tell us why this . . .

Viktor   She has told us in her book, my dear friend. *everything*!

Tora   . . . why it is closest to her heart . . .

Viktor   May I *continue*?

Pause.

This is the Salvation Army Sister, played by the Danish actress Astrid Holm, she's on her deathbed and . . .

Tora   Not played by me as Mrs Sjöström blocked it. *The wife!*

Viktor (*pretends not to hear her*)   . . . and she has been praying that David, the alcoholic whom she's been trying to save will come to visit her. However, it is David's wife who turns up at the sick bed. I tell you, I had a vision here, I wanted to create a scene, this is from the beginning of the film which enabled me to establish the young girl's . . .

Selma (*abruptly*)   I know what happens in the scene.

Viktor   Pardon?

Selma   I know the story.

Viktor   Of course. Of course.

Selma   I even wrote the book.

Tora   She means that it is her book, Viktor. Not yours. You're just tinkering with it.

Viktor   Right, right.

For a moment he stands completely still, as if the subtle insult hasn't reached him, at least not the one from **Tora**, *but perhaps* **Selma***'s, was it an insult? And he says with a subdued voice:*

I realise film is a young art form which cannot compete with the great arts. Nor am I trying to. Julius.

Julius   Yes?

Viktor   Roll it.

Julius   First sensible words I've heard all day.

Julius *turns the lights down, starts the projector, it shudders alive, and images appear on the suspended screen. A bed can be seen, a young woman in the bed. She is clearly dying. A woman*

*comes towards her, they look at each other. The younger woman
in the sick bed sits up, almost in terror, the other woman, the
wife, bends over her, raises her hands, claw-like, as if she wants
to attack the dying woman. They watch each other, then suddenly
the attacking witch, the wife, collapses, rests her head against the
cheek of the dying woman. That is all. A flickering on the screen,
then it is blank, the projector hums and eventually goes silent.*

Viktor   Please load scene fifty-six.

Tora *collapses suddenly as if in a fit, hides her face in her
hands, crying.*

Selma   Dear child, what is it?

Tora   I can't bear watching her. I wanted to do it myself.
I desperately . . . desperately . . . wanted to play her.

Enraged.

And then I realise that her up there is damned good as
well.

Blows her nose.

That's almost the worst thing. Because how the hell could
she know what it's like to have an old man who drank.
She's just acting by numbers. Hasn't a clue.

Selma   A . . . father?

Tora   She is just acting by numbers! Hasn't a clue!
About what she is acting.

Pause.

She's good all the same. Yes, indeed she is. But it
shouldn't be like that.

Julius (*inconsolable*)   Darling one . . . won't you have a
little drink . . . ?

Holds out the whisky bottle, she snivels, takes a gulp, **Julius**
wipes her nose lovingly.

Tora   Oh, Julle, you're so . . . you're so good. You know

what? On your sixtieth birthday I'll give you a present. I
will. The finest you can have. *You know what it is!*

Julius *stares at her happily.*

Yes, I promise. Just because you're such a damned good
person.

Julius (*suddenly depressed*)   When I'm sixty. Right. Then
it will be too late. Then I'll be too old.

Tora (*intensely*)   Not at all. Even if we have to work at it
for several days. Julle, we will work hard and I know it will
be all right. Though you're sixty! Just look at how spry
Selma is.

Selma   What is it you think I would manage?

Tora (*momentarily embarrassed*)   Well . . . difficult to
explain!

Julius   So no air swimming?

Tora   No. Cross my heart.

Selma (*now very tense, says controlled*)   Now I came here
to look at some film, but . . . Can anyone here tell me
what you're talking about?

Julius   No. Bit difficult, that.

Tora   Yes.

Selma   I understand. It's a private matter.

Tora   Yes.

Selma   And that makes everything incomprehensible.
For those who are outsiders. As you pointed out so
perceptively.

Tora (*annoyed*)   But I don't write books about it! Which
become incomprehensible! People who write books
have a different responsibility from the rest of us who . . .
Who . . .

Selma   Responsibility?

Tora   People who write books like you, have a
responsibility . . . otherwise they're just dumping us.
Dumping! And that's a con 'cause that's why everyone has
such *respect* for you, Selma? Selma. We have such respect
for you because . . . well, when I read your books. Then I
know that this is *your* life and then I understand that it is
my life too. So you have a . . . well, a bloody great
responsibility. Actually. Don't you think?

Selma *is silent.*

Tora   Am I wrong?

Selma *is silent.*

Viktor (*resigned*)   This is ridiculous. We have at least ten
scenes which I would like Dr Lagerlöf to watch and we're
not getting anywhere.

Tora   But, Selma, haven't they misunderstood
something here . . . those two women are both trying to
save the alcoholic, so why does the missus almost throttle
the other one? Surely she'd be glad to get some help?

Viktor   May we run the next scene now?

Tora   Why does it say in the book that it is about TB
when it is really about booze? You see, I've never
understood that . . .

Julius (*almost screaming*)   Loaded!

Tora   But I suppose it becomes clear when the film is
finished. It must be fun for you also to see the film . . .
that things become clearer for you as well, or what?

Selma *is silent.*

Julius   Scene fifty-six, take two. Ready?

Confusion spreads, but **Tora** *seems bursting with energy and
paces the room;* **Selma** *sits stony-faced on her chair and says
nothing and everyone looks at her without looking at her.* **Julius**
*fiddles mechanically with the projector, though everything is
ready, but no one gives him the green light.*

Tora   But you're saying, Selma, that you won't tell us why you wrote this book . . . and then Viktor comes along wanting to make a film of it . . . how can he . . . make it clear if you won't . . . 'cause, you have a responsibility to . . . what's it called, Julius?

Julius   How should I know?

Tora   The something of the work of art . . . There's something before. Another word. Julius, you just said it.

Julius   Spirit?

Tora   Yes! Exactly.

Julius   Yes, but we've fixed that . . . we double expose so the spirits become visible . . . an unbelievably difficult . . . an unbelievably difficult . . . technical . . . conundrum . . . to make them three dimensional so to speak . . .

Tora   You hear that, Selma. He has tinkered forth the spirit of the work of art.

Laughs uproariously.

Oh, I see you don't think that was funny. I see that.

Viktor   Tora! May we have the next scene now, please?

Tora   'Like a picture that you've seen in a mirror.' I think that is put so unbelievably beautiful.

Viktor   *May we start now!!!?*

Tora   Ask Selma! She's the one who'll be watching, not me, she's in charge!

Viktor   Right, Dr Lagerlöf, what do you say, may we . . . ?

Selma *is silent.*

Tora   Can't you see she's thinking!

Julius (*grabs the whisky bottle with a quick and practised movement*)   I think I'll help myself to a wee drop though it might seem a little inappropriate . . . Would you like

one, madam? I actually think we've got some glasses
somewhere . . .

Selma *with an almost imperceptible movement, shakes her head,
no, she doesn't want any.*

Julius   No, of course.

Tora   There's something strange about this girl in the
book . . . why does she love that old tosser so much . . . it
puzzled me . . . and when I read it . . .

Full of curiosity she circles **Selma** *who sits like a stone monument.*

How the hell can anyone love such an old tosser . . . she
seems almost completely . . . obsessed . . .

Julius (*hopelessly*)   Well, I'm ready at any rate.

Tora   An old tosser who could be her father . . . and the
missus could be her mother . . . and yet this nice girl won't
dump him . . . of course, it's clear that she's religious, but
she's not the type . . . isn't that strange, Selma . . . or am I
just being stupid . . . you must tell me if it's just me being
stupid . . . Selma!

Selma *is silent, shakes her head quietly.*

Viktor   Roll it!

Julius   Ay, ay, captain.

Tora   But Selma hasn't said what she'd like! Perhaps she
wants to say something about the previous scene?

Viktor (*with exaggerated politeness*)   Perhaps you would
like to say a few words about the previous scene, Dr
Lagerlöf?

Selma *is silent, continues to shake her head slowly.*

Viktor   *Then roll it!*

Julius   *I roll!*

*And he dims the lights and starts the projector, we see the cart
with the coachman and David, the horizon is dark, the Salvation*

Army sister in her bed, David's spirit kneels in front of it, the coachman by the door, finally he commands him: return to your body. And body and soul are re-united, the film begins to wobble, the screen returns to white and it is over. The projector spins and then goes silent. They all sit silently in the semi-darkness. For a while it is very quiet. The characters are seen as four silhouettes. They're all unusually quiet and expectant, after the preceding hysterical chaos. Then a voice is heard, it is **Selma**'s.

Selma   You can turn the lights back on now.

Julius   Shall I load the next one?

Selma (*very quietly*)   No.

Viktor   Of course, we're all very excited, but if Dr Lagerlöf didn't like it and doesn't want to see any more . . .

Tora   Tell us what you think. They've worked their balls off and they want to know!

Selma   I thought it was good. It was very good.

Viktor   Thank you.

Selma (*gets up*)   I would like to speak with Tora in private. Here and now. There is something I must settle with this young lady. If you want anything, Viktor, I'll be staying at the Grand. I would like for us to continue the screening tomorrow seven-thirty pm, half past seven. But I want to talk to Tora.

Tora (*subdued, almost terrified*)   To me?

Selma   To you.

Tora   I see. Alone?

Selma   But the rest of you seven-thirty, same place.

Tora   Yes. Of course.

And the gentlemen head for the door.

Julius (*to* **Tora**, *close to desperation*)   Do you think she liked it? She hasn't said anything about it . . . flying.

Tora   Dear God. I'm scared.

Selma *sits down, watches her constantly.*

Tora (*doesn't know what to say*)   So, The Grand! Jesus. Not bad. How much are you forking out for a room there?

Selma *is silent, then she gets up and goes resolutely to her coat, picks it up and puts it down again.*

Tora   What is it? What have I done?

Selma   Dear child . . . you haven't done anything. But I've made a mistake. Which I regret. I'll see you tomorrow.

Tora   Oh? Why?

Selma   Yes, we'll cancel, so to speak. For a while I became a little . . . impulsive. That was stupid. Perhaps I was a little impulsive tonight . . . I feel a little insecure . . . and think perhaps it is best that we leave as well.

Tora   You want me to leave? Are you throwing me out?

Selma   No, no, you misunderstand . . . perhaps it is not such a good idea . . . as I impulsively thought . . .

Tora   Isn't it now!

Selma   But since you're here . . . we can converse about this and that . . . your work . . . no, it is probably best if we both leave.

Tora   So here I am getting more and more nervous. Shitting myself. And you throw the boys out. And now they think that I'm going to get a right earful because I've screwed up. And then you're dismissing me like some bloody cab you don't want. Well, I think that's bad form, Selma.

Selma (*irritated*)   I. Have. *Not.* Said that you are being thrown out. By the way do stop that awful swearing. How are you going to act the great tragic roles at the Royal

Theatre if you can't say half a sentence without swearing. You must treasure your language!

Tora   Oi. You get those big parts at the Royal Theatre in quite a different way! I'll have you know.

Selma (*annoyed*)   Do tell me.

Tora   Well, first you ingratiate yourself, generally, and do a lot of admiring and after you've admired the right idiots, you jump into bed with the theatre manager, unless he's queer, you understand and then you mustn't slip up in the small, pissy parts, and then you get a tiny break, but only if you jump into bed with the director, unless he's queer, God bless them by the way and then you need luck. A bloody slog, I tell you. Art and bonking, as we put it. Whether or not you swear in your time off isn't the main problem, let me tell you.

Selma   Deary me.

Tora   What d'you mean, deary me! The theatre is full of dirty, old men who've just decided that one has a remarkable talent and want to teach one to stop swearing and speak properly and with correct pronunciation and then they drag you into the dressing-room and hey presto they've pulled their dick out and want you to suck them off. While you simultaneously recite Ophelia's mad scene. Now that's Demostenes pebbles at the theatre, Selma!

Selma (*mimics her irritably*)   'At the theatre this, Selma', 'At the theatre that, Selma.' If you think I'm going to swoon then you're wrong. Stop provoking me.

Tora (*somewhat more docile*)   It is a battle, though. (*Pause.*) A battle.

Pause.

But you can't know about this because you exist high above . . .

Selma   Above?

Tora (*quietly*)   The grime of life.

Selma   Aha.

Tora *doesn't know how to interpret* **Selma***'s reaction, is silent.*

Selma   And can you then, for example, tell me where you are thinking or hoping to spend the night?

Tora   That's a private matter.

Selma   No, I want to know.

Tora (*spitefully*)   At Viktor's. Actually. Or so I hope. Though I've probably, as they say, blown it!

Selma   I guessed as much.

Pause.

You shouldn't sleep with just anybody.

Pause.

You should stand on your own two feet. And move on. You should stand on your own two feet and move on.

Tora *is silent.*

Selma (*sits down, looks at her sharply*)   And I'm floating around, high up, you think. A spiritual existence. No contact with . . . the grime of life.

Tora *looks shyly at* **Selma***, did she hurt her, perhaps she didn't mean to.*

Tora   I didn't mean it.

Selma   Yes, you do mean it.

Tora   Right, then . . . sorry. I meant no harm.

Selma   No, but you meant something.

Tora *is silent.*

Selma (*very clearly*)   'Holy shit', as that friend of yours has a habit of saying. Holy up there and shit down in reality. And you despise me ever so ever so ever so slightly . . .

Tora (*suddenly on the verge of tears*)   I *have* said I'm sorry! Tell me to go if you want to, but don't upset me!

Selma (*just shakes her head in bewilderment, takes* **Tora***'s coat and hangs it up*)   But let that be . . . why do you need to act?

Tora   Well . . . I feel it burning inside me.

Selma   My. My. Burn. Everyone jumped when the cat farted.

Tora (*angry*)   Well, why do *you* have to write? You could marry a rich man, surely?

Selma (*matter-of-fact*)   Yes, yes. And that would have pleased Papa.

Tora (*spots a way out, grasps it with enthusiasm*)   *God!* I've forgotten to say it, but I must thank you! Thank you for that amazing speech you gave about your old man. When you got the Nobel Prize. They read it aloud to us in school and I bawled my eyes out! It's true! That bit about you talking to him in heaven and thanking him for . . . what was it . . . for making you a writer . . . you *owed* that to him . . . such a *debt*, you *owed* him so much.

Selma   A debt.

Tora   That was why you were so grateful. And it was so moving and fine, I remember it clearly.

Selma (*goes to get her small bag, takes out a half-full bottle of sherry well hidden amongst the papers*)   Let's change the subject!

Tora (*momentarily stunned*)   So you did pack a lunch, after all!

Selma   You want some?

Tora (*disgusted*)   Not that sickly sugary stuff . . . haven't you got any whisky? Julle took his little bottle with him, unfortunately!

Selma   Sweet or not, as long as it's got a kick, as a connoisseur I once knew used to say. Good for your throat by the way. An actress must nurse her instrument.

Tora   Right . . .

Tries to resume the conversation.

. . . This thing about you thanking him for making you a writer. God, how I bawled.

Accepts the glass.

Thanks!!! Why don't you drink champagne, surely it is the academy or the hotel that's paying?

Selma   'Not the same bite.' As Papa used to say. Oh, no.

Tora   Well, this sugary stuff is toothless.

No reply.

Oh, how I remember that speech, it was so fine. That speech. Your father must have been amazing. I wish I had had a father like that. Mine just drank. Imagine living your whole life . . . just surrounded by . . .

Selma   Yes?

Tora   Love. I suppose that's why you can write the way you do.

Selma   Oh. Go to hell.

Tora (*speechless*)   What? What did you say?

Selma (*furious*)   My darling, little friend. You're a stirrer, but I've put up with it, so far. I prefer sincerity to the usual arselicking. You don't do that. I suppose that's why I . . . put up with you. Like you. But I don't like your contemptuous tone of voice. You put on these airs of great experience and talk rubbish about me . . .

Tora   What! Course I don't do that!

Selma   . . . as if . . . as if I were some beautiful little muse who had fluttered down from heaven, *the* *storyteller*!!! And you with your experience of life want to teach me . . . actually I want you to show me respect! *Respect!*

Tora (*quite stunned, sees how* **Selma** *drains the sherry glass*) Have I not shown you respect? I'm practically prostrate on the floor! What the hell do you mean?

Selma   Stop swearing!

Tora   I'm bloody well not going to until you explain. What do you mean by respect!

Selma   That you don't belittle me. I happen to know a great deal actually.

Pause.

About . . . the grime of life.

Tora   That was, that was, the most ridiculous thing I've heard in my entire life. Me trying to belittle you? But, dear God . . . look around . . . everyone is flat on their faces, agreeing reverently with you and prostrate at your feet, howling what a genius you are and . . . how could I! Try to belittle you! How would that be possible? Eh?

Pause, she sits down, stares ahead, then looks at **Selma** *and says almost kindly:*

Anyway . . . that's another matter. You were saying. What is it you know about . . . the grime of life?

Selma   Why don't you leave the theatre, Tora?

Tora   Nah.

Selma   It sounds so ghastly. What you were telling me about.

Tora   Nah.

Pause.

That wasn't what I was asking about.

Selma *is silent.*

Tora   So?

Selma (*kindly, formally*)   And what is your favourite part, the one you would most like to play?

Tora (*enraged*)   Listen to yourself! What a load of crap! It's crazy the way you try to get around things. 'Favourite part.' 'Favourite colour.' 'Which historical character do you most admire?' 'Which book would you take with you to a desert island?' Stop it, please! Talk about no respect! Do you think I'm an idiot?

Selma (*helplessly*)   But I was only trying to be helpful . . .

Tora   Stop it. At once!

Selma (*trying to regain control*)   That tone! No one has ever used that in front of me and I wish to remind you that . . .

Tora   No need! No need!

Selma   . . . that I've actually been translated into thirty six languages and . . .

Tora   . . . I know! I'm going! But I haven't treated you with no respect, I just asked you what you meant about you knowing . . . the grime of life. It certainly isn't the theatre's, at any rate.

Selma   No.

Pause.

Don't go. But do stop shouting at me.

Tora   I'll try.

Selma (*quite flatly*)   I don't think I've deserved it.

Tora   No. No.

Selma   Dear friend. I was not unlike you when I was a child. I mean when I was young.

Pause.

Or perhaps my memory's failing me.

Pause.

Then I wanted to be . . . like that.

Tora   Selma? Can I ask you something which I asked you about a while ago. When they were here. But you wouldn't give me an answer then.

Selma   Yes?

Tora   You were saying. That *The Coachman* is closest to your heart. Of all the books you've written?

Selma   Yes. You can ask. But I won't answer.

Tora   I mean . . . of all . . . what's the word . . . the great works . . . *Gösta Berling's Saga* or *Jerusalem* or . . .

Selma   Well, in most books you write the same story. I imagine it is like that for all writers. There is a kind of ur-story, what's the word, yes, an ur-story. And then you try to hide it. You write an . . . ur-story which you don't want to reveal . . . and then it's all about disguising it. *Cover it!* The inner . . . core. So it rests . . . like a little foetus . . . safely . . .

Tora   Why the hell do you do that?

Selma   But with *The Coachman* I was so close. That's why.

Tora   But them there . . . all the books . . . surely they're not the same story!

No reply.

What's there to hide?

Selma   (*seems to have lost her equilibrium*)   It makes me so angry. There you are . . . tinkering and . . . argghhhhh! 'Spirits who rise out of their bodies.' It's so pretty it makes me want to vomit. And then you . . . I feel sick when I listen to you. 'Live one's life surrounded by love.' When one is as gifted as you one cannot be so idiotic. It's perverse! Perverse!

Tora   What's there to hide! You're so obsessed by one thing but too cowardly to let on what it . . .

Selma   Cowardly! No, my little friend. My dear, little friend.

Tora   But, I read your books, those amazing stories about Värmland and so on and tales, isn't that what they're called? And I read your fine speech about your father and I weep because it is so good . . . and your father . . . and Julle always talks about that amazing story of yours he's read about the bird of clay . . . but what you wrote about your father that was . . .

Selma   (*rapidly, it pours out of her*)   A pathetic misfit who drank himself to death. I hope he burns in hell.

Tora *is absolutely stunned.*

Selma   A pathetic misfit who ruined my life.

Tora   Surely, Selma, you don't *mean* that . . . are you unwell? Shall I get someone . . . dear friend . . . dear, little friend . . .

Selma   Don't say that! Don't *say that*! That's how he used to go on . . . 'Dear friend . . . dear, little friend . . . little darling . . .' and then those runny, glassy eyes and the dear, little darling . . .

Tora *has sat down, the situation is out of control,* **Selma** *paces like a restless tiger.*

Tora   . . . Have yourself a drop of sherry that'll . . .

Selma   (*snatches the bottle from* **Tora**'s *hand and slams it on the table*)   I. Drink. When. I. Want. To. Otherwise. Not. So *no thank you!* Don't try pulling me by the nose.

Pause, she returns to the table, deliberately takes her time filling up the glass, immense self-control.

'Sweet or not, as long as it's got a kick.' As he used to say. *Now* I want to. Thank you.

She drinks.

A place for everything and everything in its place. That's the way it should be.

Tora (*dryly*)   I suspected you'd brought a packed lunch.

Selma   *Well, it's in the blood!*

Pause, controlled joking.

He was so creative, was Papa. Unbelievably so. One could never guess how he was going to cover it up. Mostly it was the artistic temperament. No, he was too refined to hide away his booze, he said. Sometimes he was just raging and then it was get the bottle on the table and get the hell out of here, you little brat and I. Drink. When. I. Want. *To!* And now *I want.* To. And no little brat is going to stop me. But sometimes he was so gentle and tearful and wanted to pat the little darling on her head and make everything all right again. But he covered it up because he was so *fragile* and *sensitive!*

Pause, with a certain sadistic delight.

Would you like to hear a little *tale?* About the boozer who hid his drink in the watering can? He insisted the watering can was to be used by him alone and he used it for *watering* the *flowers* in his room. And one day the lady of the house took it by mistake and watered the flowers. And the following day she heard terrible cries from the study and we rushed in and there he stood in his dirty underpants, sweating and was completely furious, pointing at the flowers. And they had all died. Blaaaaaaaaaaah! Drooping! *Couldn't hold their liquor!!!* Which he'd hidden in the watering can. And then tears and accusations and his own children mistrusted him so he was *forced* to hide the *precious drops.* In the watering can. It was this *mistrust!* From his nearest and dearest. Which drove him towards the deepest despair which his artistic temperament couldn't cope with. He was just so *sensitive.* Like all his artistic friends! Who turned up and then they locked themselves away. *The cavaliers!* And we mistrusted him!

Tora (*quietly*)   That was no tale. You're saying we. Did your father hide his drink in the watering can.

Selma (*out of balance*)   Yes . . . no . . . he meant that he was the master of the house and shouldn't have to sink to hiding . . . *but he did!*

Pause.

No, he hid away in . . . Värmland. He hid away in the lies about Värmland. That was the worst. The tales. The cavaliers.

Tora (*dully*)   Yes, I have read what you wrote about them.

Selma (*stares ahead*)   Yes, when I gave readings about their charming dance on the lengthy shore of Löven the old women were always moved to tears. And I suppose that was right. I always wept. As well. Though for other reasons.

Cheerfully.

Well, you saw most of this rabble when they went outside to piss, when they stood there waving their wands, threw up and went back inside to dear Papa. Real heartbreakers. Never did a day's work. Bloody parasites.

Pause.

Transcribed notes!, as I phrased it in *Gösta Berling's Saga.* What they claimed to have done. I had to think of something that sounded creative. How easily people are deceived. Making a living transcribing notes! How stupid can you be!

Tora   – Yes . . . I always wondered what it was . . . they actually did . . .

Selma *Nothing!* Absolutely nothing. When Papa was holding forth . . . '*Music,* my girl, is *the breath of art* in *the spirit of the world.*' The more drunk he got the more rubbish he spoke . . . I saw these transcriptions . . . I'd like to know who could play them . . . the notes collapsing between the lines . . . it was like a language . . . which . . . fell . . . apart . . . which . . . fell . . . apart . . .

Tora Selma. You must calm down.

Selma He was . . . absolutely . . . useless . . . and he said that I . . . *knew* it . . . knew . . . it . . .

Tora Did you tell him?

Selma (*shakes her head forcefully, then quietly and with intensity*)   And lies, lies, lies. Everything had to be so delicate and artistic because he had such an artistic nature. And they are so sensitive, of course. *Sensitive!* A taste for beauty. Having a glass of wine in the company of friends. A song and a glass of *good wine.* From time to time. From time to time every minute of the day. We didn't understand his artistic temperament. He was useless. *You know what? I hate artists!* And artistic temperaments. And beauty. And *delicacy.* He lay there sweating. Bloated, *bloated!* It was as if his face became pasty-like, squelchy, like on a corpse, you could almost rip off lumps of flesh from his cheeks if you wanted to and I wanted to sometimes. And you had to understand. That he was so . . . sensitive. Dead meat. Bloated like a corpse. Do you understand what it is like to grow up with a corpse? With a dead person?

Tora No.

Selma He hadn't always been like that. He hadn't always been like that. Once he was kind and witty and . . . (*Pause.*) I had loved him terribly.

Tora Loved him?

Selma Before he became a corpse. And before everything fell apart. Him. Mårbacka. Us. And me.

Pause.

Us. The worst thing is that I cannot recall what the others looked like. Mama. And my brothers and sisters. It was as if we stood around Papa in a circle for all those years and saw him rot away and the only thing we saw was him, he was the only one who was important. We stood in a circle and looked towards the centre, but we didn't see each other. How awful. (*Pause.*) How awful.

Pause.

The only thing we saw was a corpse vomiting, wailing, lying, shouting at us and nothing else mattered. If only it had. We would have . . . seen one another. We would have been able to . . . see something other than him . . .

Pause.

I cannot recall what Mama looked like. I cannot recall her. I *cannot recall what Mama looked like*!!! I think she was wonderful. I think she was such a good mother. I should write about her sometime, you know. I have never written about her, but then I cannot recall her. How. She. Looked. Dear, dear Tora. Everything I've written is about Papa, *the emperor of Portugalia who is such a charming fool.* Jesus Christ, lies, and this pasty-faced corpse who stood before my eyes.

Pause.

But Mama who surely. Who surely. Was so good. I've never written about her. Only about this wailing, screaming, shivering, puking infant. Who was my father. And he consumed. Consumed. My entire life. Oh, how I hate him. He was once so good.

Pause, quietly.

I have no children, you know. I have no children, you know. But once I did and it was he. Oh, how I hate him for becoming my child. I didn't want him to become my child. (*Quietly.*) That was why I had to kill him.

Tora (*her hands over her face, in despair*)   Stop it. You don't know what you're saying.

Selma   I had to. It was necessary.

Tora   Stop it.

Selma   But he died so slowly. And when you drink yourself to death then it goes like this . . . all feelings disappear and everything revolves around the bottle and he was in love with it and he forgot everything else. So much talk about how he loved me but . . . he was so moved . . . his runny eyes . . . they said something else . . . he only loved . . . *Everything died for him except the bottle and sweet or not as long as it's got a kick* . . . actually I wasn't *sweet at all.* Wasn't sweet at all. If he had to choose between Selma and half a bottle of booze then I know what he would have chosen. Everything died away . . . conscience and feelings and everything . . . and then he was my *child* at the same time and I saw that I had spawned a monster and I knew that it was my fault. I knew it. *I know it.* I know it. It will never pass. Everything is guilt, guilt, *guilt.* That was what I was trying to say.

Tora   In your speech.

Selma   I couldn't see anything except him. I can't. I only see him.

Tora (*pensively*)   You should have given him a fucking boot up the backside.

Selma   I?

Very quietly.

And I knew that I had to kill him to survive.

Tora   You killed him! It's not true. It's not true.

Selma (*kindly and calmly*)   Oh, but it is true.

Tora   You can't be serious.

Selma   I was twenty-one years old when I made up my

mind. Then I went to his room and said that I would go
and study at the teachers' college for young ladies. And
he just laughed. I knew what he thought. For women to
be educated that was just insane. He thought. 'I forbid
you,' he said, almost without slurring and I saw that he
was scared. I saw that he was scared. 'I'm going,' I said,
'there's nothing you can do.' 'I forbid you,' he said.
'Well, I don't give a damn,' I said, 'you can go to hell.'
That was the first time he heard me swear so he
understood that I was serious. Then he started screaming
because he was scared. 'You have to stay,' he bawled, 'you
know I'll kill myself if you leave. I'll drink myself to
death!' 'You do that, you old tosser,' I said, 'it's about
time, but make it snappy.' Then he tried to get up on his
feet to get hold of me and . . . hit me, but he was too
drunk and stumbled into the desk. So all the papers. So
all the papers. (*Pause.*) Were scattered all over the floor.
And there he lay. And I sat down on a chair and we
looked at each other. We both knew that if I left then he
would die. And we knew that I wouldn't change my mind.
'Papa,' I said, 'I'm going to get up now and leave.' 'You
won't be able to manage that,' he said, 'you can't stand
on your own two feet, you lame cow.'

Tora (*the room is very quiet, she's silent for a while*)   And
what did you do?

Selma   I got up on my feet. And I limped away from
him. And that's what I've been doing these past forty
years.

Tora (*it is very quiet, hushed. Then* **Tora** *goes to her noiselessly
and says quietly*)   Naaah, naaah.

Selma *is silent.*

Tora   Naah, Selma. When you describe this so
eloquently and honestly . . . there's something wrong . . .
naaa, Selma . . .

Selma   Wrong?

Tora   Nah, Selma . . . No, there's something wrong . . .
which bit is not right? I don't believe you. . . . nah.
There's something you're not telling me . . . Naaa,
Selma . . .

Selma *looks at her, gets up, takes her coat and hat, looks at her,
exits quickly.*

Tora (*sits on the chair, stares ahead*)   Naaah . . . naaah . . .

And then suddenly: darkness.

Act Two

The Resurrection

How well we know this room.

It is the scene from Act One. It is the screening room, it is the room of machines, of film reels.

Why isn't **Julius** *here? But perhaps he'll be here soon. Is he in the inner room? No. Not in the inner room. Don't ask any more.*

So who is here? That's the right question as it is the one there's an answer to, the answer is that **Tora** *isn't here. No, we're waiting for her. She isn't here. But were she here one could envisage her smoking a cigarette through a long holder, that the room was enclosed in semi-darkness, that she was at first visible like a silhouette, then as a person, but no, it's not like that, no, we're waiting.*

'We see her in three dimension,' **Julius** *would have said. So why doesn't he? We know why: He doesn't say it as he's not here.*

But whoever is here is playing a gramophone. A tango. Scratchy.

No, what we see more than anything else is the flickering screen. Scenes from The Coachman; *almost the final cut.* **Viktor** *has been working all day.* **Julius** *too.*

The shapes free themselves from each other. On the screen. And elsewhere? Perhaps we should make up our minds?

Yes, we have to. We decide that he sits there. **Viktor** *sits next to the projector. Otherwise darkness. What a wondrous film this is. So mysterious, exact. No one will ever understand it. Then* **Tora** *enters.* **Viktor** *looks at her, but doesn't stir.*

Tora (*she stands still, watches the screen, then goes to* **Viktor,** *kisses his hair lightly*)　　She called to say that . . .

Viktor (*abruptly*)   I know.

Tora   . . . that I should join you.

Viktor   I know.

He stops the film, the projector spins, it goes quiet. He switches on a lamp.

She called and told me as well. And so on and so forth. Yes, I know.

Tora   I'm not trying to gatecrash.

Viktor   You know you're always welcome.

Pause, looks at her critically, hits a button and the film starts rewinding.

And . . . how did it go yesterday?

Tora   Fine.

Viktor   What did she want? What was it you . . . were supposed to talk about?

Tora   Well . . . I actually can't . . . no.

Viktor   Oh, I see. Right.

Looks at her dejectedly, says coldly:

Was she mad at you?

Tora (*quietly*)   Don't know.

Viktor   I've just got the feeling that *The Great One* thinks all this cinematic art is really just about filthy lucre. She despises us *a little*. Ever so slightly. We're not good enough.

Tora   You are tinkering with her . . . life. She thinks. Perhaps. Picking at it, as it were.

Viktor (*with badly concealed aggression*)   To my knowledge we're interpreting her book. And not her life.

Pause.

Oh, I suppose I ought to tell you that your so-called
father came up to see me today. Wanted to borrow a
tenner 'from your salary' for booze. But he was drunk so
I threw him out.

Tora   I see.

Viktor   Just so you know.

Tora   Of course.

Pause.

I suppose you enjoyed telling me that. All I can do is
squirm under your glance.

Pause.

There was no need for you to tell me.

Viktor   Oh, but we should be open about family
matters. You are, as I said, always welcome.

Tora   What a way of putting it. 'You are, as I said, always
welcome.'

Viktor   I haven't given you anything but . . . a little
warning. That the old man is around again.

Very formally.

And you know that you're always welcome.

Tora   And anyway it isn't true. You think it's a bloody
nuisance when I visit.

Viktor   Tora.

Tora   *Jawohl, maestro!*

Can't keep it up, sits on a chair hides her head in her hands.

I'm sorry. I always screw up. Whatever I do.

*He looks at her, shakes his head in sorrow, pulls up a chair next
to her, sits down, clasps his knees with his hands.*

Viktor   Tora. (*Pause.*) We can't go on like this.

Tora   We aren't. You dumped me for the sake of your family. I for my part am unhappy. I don't call that 'going on'. We hurt each other. That's the truth of it.

Viktor   Tora. (*Starts off again, now somewhat desperate.*) You think I'm a bastard, I'm not. *I'm not,* but you don't understand that I'm scared, s . . . c . . . a . . . r . . . e . . . d. And then I get defensive. I'm scared of you.

Tora   AaaaaaaaaH. *Aaaaaaahhh* help. *Ich sterbe!!!* The great one is *scared*!

Viktor   Would you shut up for just a second. I have never met anyone like you. Anyone so gifted, anyone so stupid, anyone so beautiful, anyone so disgusting, anyone so deadly. You're a genius and I hope to spot just a hint of intelligence in you. Most geniuses have none. One day you're inspired on stage, the next you hold forth about corsets in the *Weekly Journal* which makes me want to scream. There is no one more faithful than you and your poor husband, yes, I believe you're married, *it's damn improbable*, but I believe you are *married*, you deceive him. You're as faithful as a chimpanzee. I can't take it any more. It's impossible to make sense of you. Just the thought of us living together scares me to death. *And!* I can't live without you. *But . . .* will you be quiet for just a minute . . . I don't want you to destroy what little I have left. Of my self-respect. And the little I have got left is this bloody film, I think it is wonderful and I am terrified about it, about how it's going to go, about Selma, about . . . my tiny, little self-respect. And every time you enter a room, chaos follows. Chaos. I don't want you tearing me to shreds. Dearest, beloved, girl, I hate the moment. We. *Met.*

Pause.

I have crept inside this film and hidden away. As inside a . . . cave. It is *mine*!

Pause.

When her bloody potboiler has been forgotten they'll remember my film. So I'm not ashamed that I should tinker with her so-called soul.

Pause.

And I won't let you hurt me any more. That was all.

Tora (*it's very quiet for a while*)   Feel better now?

Viktor   Better.

Tora   What a bloody awful monster I must be.

Quietly.

I don't understand why I am the one forced to frighten people . . . I don't understand.

Viktor   Thank your lucky stars that you do frighten people . . . (*Pause.*) . . . You don't know what fear is, that's terrifying.

Tora (*completely quiet*)   I would really . . . like to know. That you *told* me what it is Edith has. That I haven't got.

Viktor   Let's not . . . let's not . . .

Tora   Yes. (*Pause.*) Yes. Let's.

Viktor (*waiting, then he says at last*)   As you wish. She makes me feel . . . completely calm and warm . . . as if she embraced me. Yes. As . . . as if I were a foetus. Snug . . . in the waters of the womb . . .

Tora (*almost without expression*)   . . . Noooo . . . don't say that . . .

Viktor   Yes. And you wanted to know.

Tora   Yes, but not like . . . that.

Viktor   But that's the way it is with her.

Tora   So that's why. How disgusting. (*Almost hatefully.*) So there you lie sloshing around. And won't let anyone in. Anyone like me. (*Pause.*) Outsiders.

Viktor   You tear people to pieces. That's the difference.

Tora   Aaaah, what an idiot I am.

Pause.

I don't feel too well.

Pause.

Great to be so inaccessible, eh. Fucking hell. And then pretty little me who wants to release you. And your secrets.

Pause.

Actually you're a bit alike you and Selma. Though you don't know it. But don't worry. I won't . . . tear you to pieces . . .

Hides her face in her hands.

Viktor   . . . But, I love you . . .

Tora (*furious*)   Shut up!

Now she's really evil.

You and *your* film. *In there!!!* Mustn't be touched by . . . *outsiders*! Like pretty little me.

Viktor   We won't talk about it any more.

Tora   I'll talk about whatever I like! So it's *your* film. You own the very soul of the film. Then you're supposed to be able to tell me what this film means?

Viktor   You know that just as well as I do.

Tora   No, the *outsider* is a little curious! About. Your. Masterpiece!

Viktor   It is actually .. my own business.

Tora   It is . . . *actually* . . . ridiculous.

Viktor   Don't worry your pretty little head about it.

Tora (*she sits down, breathes deeply, starts again*)   So it's war. War.

Viktor   But darling . . . sweet, little Tora . . .

Tora (*furious*)   I know I'm not *in*! Outside! Well, fuck you and Mrs Sjöström . . . What an *idiot* I was! *An idiot!*! But I am an *actress*. And I intend one day to play those great roles and I want to understand and I am trying to understand that I will be standing on a stage. *Phaedra*! Don't laugh at me. *Nora! Chekhov!* And act by numbers. As you're so nicely in the habit of putting it. Then I want to know what the numbers are! *Otherwise I can't make them mine!* But right now I'm just getting more and more . . . angry! Outsider!!! Bewildered!

Viktor   I'm listening.

Tora   I thought I understood.

Pause.

But . . . that which is the . . . *essence* . . .

Viktor *remains silent, confused.*

Tora   But now I don't understand. How can you act it when you don't understand the person who wrote the numbers . . . their *thoughts*!

Viktor   I write the numbers and I tell you if . . .

Tora   *You?!*

Viktor   . . . I tell you if you've misunderstood.

Tora (*pensively*)   You can stuff your numbers up your arse because they're not yours.

Pause.

It is actually *her life*.

Viktor (*circles her, watches her pensively*)   One day I'll make a film about you. About how burning hatred can turn into . . . art . . . grime can be transformed into . . . beauty.

Pause.

Into art.

She sits on the edge of the chair like a little girl with her toes turned inwards, what is he saying, why is he so aggressive?

Stop doing that!

Tora   What?

Viktor   Your toes! It's too obvious! *I'm not falling for it!* At drama school you've been taught to sit with your toes turned inwards because they told you that you then 'express innocence and vulnerability'. *But you're not fooling me.* You have hurt me. I'm bloody well going to make a film about you . . . and I *promise* you that you won't be in it. Because I'll . . . I'll . . .

Tora   Own it.

Viktor   Precisely.

Tora   Entirely.

Pause.

Yes. It'll be about me. But you'll let someone else . . . play me. By numbers which you. Have noted down. Some new vamp will play me. Unless Mrs Sjöström accepts.

Abruptly.

How long will it be?

Viktor   What?

Tora   The film. *The Coachman.* Or what's the title? '*Patricide*'?

Viktor   (*momentarily confused, what is she talking about?*) 935 metres I think . . . one hour and 55 minutes . . .

Tora   (*unemotionally*)   I see. I wonder how long I'll be. As a film.

Pause.

Chimpanzee.

Pause.

Actually all I wanted to do was to come here, see the film and then disappear. I thought, damn it Tora, just lie low and don't make a fuss. And later on write a sweet little letter which makes Viktor calm and happy. And not . . . scared. Then you can return to the lap of the family so to speak. So cosy. Cluck, cluck, cluck, another cup of tea, darling?

Pause.

But it hurts like hell. Like hell.

Pause.

I'll sit with my toes how the hell I like!

Pause.

No, Viktor . . . it hurts like hell, Viktor. I can't bear it.

On the verge of tears.

Noooo, Viktor, I can't bear it. Wait, I'll be fine, but. . . . no, Viktor . . .

Viktor (*he watches her silent despair completely nonplussed, what is he going to say to her?*)   . . . But I didn't mean it like that . . . you can sit with your toes any way you like darling, little Tora . . .

Tora (*crying, doesn't hear him, looks up*)   What . . . what are you saying . . . ?

Viktor   Sit with your toes any way you like . . . pointing inwards, I mean . . .

Tora (*wipes her nose incensed, irate, surprisingly she's regaining control over the situation*)   I sit with my toes how I like! Like this! I don't give a damn if you think it's wrong turning them inwards! You're *mad*! Why can't people sit how they like with their toes!

Viktor (*desperate*)   Sit how you like! Sit how you like!

Tora   I see? Just now I couldn't sit with them turned inwards . . . didn't you say so?

Viktor   *You can sit with your tosie wosies turned inwards* – I'm losing my mind.

Selma   (*for once she's made an almost unnoticeable entrance, but, in any case, now she's there and doesn't understand a word*)   What's going on?

Tora   (*throws herself in **Selma**'s arms*)   He won't let me sit with my *toes* turned inwards!

Selma   (*holds her away from her for a while, looks sharply at both of them*)   Don't be silly. And I'm not an idiot. What is this really all about?

Viktor   (*capitulating somewhat*)   Well, it's not about toes.

Selma   I can see you've been quarrelling. Was it really necessary?

Viktor   We'll start the screening shortly, Dr Lagerlöf. I'm just waiting for Julius. He is always late.

Selma   (*isn't distracted*)   I want to know what you were talking about.

Tora   (*pragmatically*)   He says that the only thing which matters to him is this film and that he'll creep inside it like a cave which is full of foetus fluid and that I'm like a randy chimpanzee and that I sit with my toes turned inwards.

Selma   I see.

Tora   And then we talked about Father.

Selma   *Who?*

Tora   The old soak.

Selma   (*stiffens*)   And what did you say about him?

Tora   Mine, of course. Not yours.

Selma   Good.

Pause, then very carefully:

I think that was a good idea. I don't discuss my father with anyone – outside.

Tora   Got it.

Selma   Not with anyone.

Tora   Yes. Yes yes yes yes!

Selma   And I demand your obedience on this matter.

Tora   Yes! Yes!

Pause, angrily.

You don't *trust* me! Isn't that so? You think I'll tell. All I'm saying is: I'm an oyster. You follow? An oyster. And I *don't* think . . .

Selma   (*quickly*)   When will the cinematographer be here?

Tora   (*darkly*)   With the greyhounds.

Selma   With *what?*

Tora   No, no. *Joke!* That was last time. Viktor is upset that I made a fool of myself in the *Weekly Journal.* And he doesn't approve that I said in the *Weekly Journal* that girls should throw away their corsets. I messed up and he wants to scream. He always wants to scream and be ashamed on my behalf. Stupid stupid stupid! What's wrong with throwing away your corset? I said you feel cramped in a corset, it's like at home, five to one room at Horngatan, six until the old man was kicked out on his arse and they thought that was so wittily put. Though they didn't print the bit about the old man. That was . . .

Viktor   Delicate!

Tora   Instead they later photographed me with two hired greyhounds whose breath stank something rotten. How many rooms were there at Mårbacka?

Selma (*dismissively*)   I never counted.

Viktor (*with a hint of irony*)   Darling Tora, one never asks rich people how big their houses are or how much money they have. Bad form.

Tora   Oh well. Wrong again. Just like the corset.

Selma (*sharply*)   I am not 'rich', I've worked for everything I've got, I rebuilt Mårbacka and reconstructed . . . everything. I inherited nothing. I rebuilt it. From the very bottom to the top. And I'm not ashamed of it.

Viktor   But, Dr Lagerlöf . . . it was far from my intention to . . .

Selma   I cannot bear to be considered wealthy!

Viktor   Really?

Selma   Now can we hear more of plucky little Tora's story. You . . . kicked out your father on . . .

Tora   . . . on his arse. Everything was much cosier from then on.

Selma   Just like that? Kicked him out?

Tora (*cheerfully*)   Well, it was mostly Mother who did the kicking. But it got much cosier afterwards!

Selma (*watches her maliciously*)   Aren't you making it a little too easy for yourself now. You who are so . . . sincere.

Tora   Easy?

Selma   Dodging a little bit . . . How do you call it . . . ? Making it a little . . . 'charming' . . . Isn't that how you put it . . . 'charming'?

Tora   I see! So now I'm a liar? Not many people have dared say that to me.

Selma   And you never . . . felt guilt afterwards?

Tora   Guilt? *Absolutely* not.

A strangely hostile atmosphere suddenly begins to emerge.

Should I have done?

Selma   I was just . . . a little surprised. It sounded so . . .
robust.

Tora   Robust? Then tell me. 'Cause you know. How one
ought to behave. Was it wrong of me? Stupid? A little
dumb?

Viktor (*nervous, doesn't understand*)   We actually thought
of filming right in that area . . . to the south . . . Tora
accompanied me for research to her home district and
those streets are just right as location, terrible slums, but
then we looked at Landskrona, as Dr Lagerlöf had
suggested . . .

Tora (*clings like a limpet*)   So it is a little insensitive of me
not to feel guilt.

Viktor   But honestly with per diems it just turned out to
be too expensive to go to Landskrona.

Tora   Not everyone is a great artist. Eh? And they have
such interesting spiritual lives.

Selma (*pensively*)   I admire you. So terribly . . .
frighteningly . . . strong. You are strong. Yes, I admire you.

Tora   Strong? Why? (*Aggressively.*) I'll tell you one thing.
I don't like being made fun of.

Selma   But you have never . . . written.

Tora (*silent, but suddenly furious*)   You're going to have
to explain that one.

Selma   You have never written. I suppose that's why you
can . . . kick him out. And just . . . get on with your life.

With flashes of growing anger.

Bang! Out the door! The old soak! Then off to be
photographed with the greyhounds! Wise words about
corsets! You are quite remarkable, sweet Tora, I give you

that. You have such strength. Interviews in the *Weekly
Journal* with greyhounds. Kick out Papa and tear the
corsets off the girls. Really, what a range! Pretty, slim,
little lady thinks ill of corsets. Very chic. Very. Honestly,
have you thought about how fat, old ladies like me would
keep upright without corsets?

Tora (*angry*)   Have you tried? My mum didn't have a
bloody corset and she kept herself and four kids upright.
And she managed. And *none of us blended in with the
wallpaper!* What's more we didn't have any. Wallpaper,
that is!

Viktor (*smoothing over*)   Tora has probably had other
more . . . robust . . . experiences than the doctor.

Tora (*nastily*)   Robust??? No one knows! No one knows!
No one knows! Because Selma had a happy childhood
with a beloved father, so she tells all outsiders. Though
not in the *Weekly Journal* as it's a rag! There you'll just find
vulgar actresses, but no Nobel Prize winners! Isn't that so!
To outsiders she's aunty story-teller. And there's not a
single bastard on the inside! Not even herself! That's why
she doesn't understand the meaning of robust!

From **Selma** *icy silence.*

Tora   She's never kicked her drunken old man out on
his arse! Hasn't counted the rooms at Mårbacka! Bad
form to count! Darling aunty story-teller!

Selma   I'm not having this. That's enough.

Tora   Liar! Teller of tales!

Viktor   Tora!

Tora   The teller of tales at Mårbacka! Christ, how I
admire you!

Selma   That's enough.

Viktor   That's enough, Tora!

Tora   Is it?

Hisses into his face.

Viktor, isn't it time to find out where Julius is!

Selma (*quietly*)   What do you want, Tora?

Tora   I want him to go and call Julius. Just like I said. Like this.

Hisses and imitates.

Viktor, isn't it time to find out where Julius is! I remember it precisely. It's what I just said.

Selma (*quietly*)   No, you're up to something.

Tora   Viktor?

Viktor (*capitulating*)   What shall I do? What shall I do?

Selma   She wants you to go looking for Julius. But it's just a pretext.

Viktor   For what?

Selma (*sharply*)   Do as she says.

Viktor (*looks at her silently, shakes his head gently*)   That's the second time. I'll have to consider whether it's one time too many. No one wants to see it.

Tora (**Viktor** *leaves. Silence. After a while the silence borders on the unpleasant, she says*)   I seem to recall someone saying 'When I want you to leave, you'll leave, not before.' You've changed your tune.

Selma (*sits down, breathes slowly and heavily*)   Oh, how I regret telling you. Good God, how I regret telling you. Why couldn't I keep my stupid, little trap shut, good God why did I tell you.

Tora   Ohhhh. So that's what you're thinking.

Selma   Why? Why?

Tora   You're thinking that I've got something on you. And I'll exploit it. That's what you're thinking.

Selma *says nothing.*

Tora   You're really thinking that. Really. That I'm a bitch. God, it makes me sick.

Pause.

But I'm not really a bitch. And I like you, Selma.

Explodes.

But I don't understand how you manage to carry on with such a cover up. For yourself. And everybody else.

Selma   You mean that I've given hypocrisy a face.

Tora (*pause*)   Sorry. Stupid of me.

Selma *says nothing.*

Tora   Dear Selma. No war, please.

Selma   No. No war.

Tora   Good.

Selma   Yes, and I suppose it's true. I did write so you would understand what it was like. Almost without it hurting. No one should be able to pick at that. At me. But still understand it. But hardly anyone reads it like that.

Pause.

I always thought they belittled what I'd done. I was so terribly loved. But for the wrong reasons.

Tora (*mercilessly*)   Do you want them to *understand* or don't you???

Selma   Well, exactly. Good question.

Tora   Did you long for unconditional love?

Selma   Yes, I thought so. But I was so scared . . . of being visible. From the very beginning. From . . . the ur story. The drunkard Gösta Berling who smashed everything to pieces and . . . (*With a kind of disgust.*) And

then the unbelievably sweet emperor of Portugalia with
flowers in his hair . . . like Ophelia! Like Ophelia! God,
how the old women wept. And no one understood.

Tora   No. No no. Well, then I didn't read it correctly.

Selma   And no one else either. God, how I hate
Värmland.

Sees **Tora** *laugh and screams furiously.*

If you call me aunty story-teller once more, I'll whack you!

Tora   Peace. Word of honour.

Selma   God, how I hate Värmland. Everything which is
'Värmland'. It's so unbelievably pretty. And all the
parasites who hung around at the manor houses and
played the lute and told stories and were no use at
anything. *Don't you understand that it was Värmland which
killed Papa?* Among boon companions. Stories, so
unbelievably stupid, it was just a load of rubbish, every
time someone drank and babbled then it was stories and
Värmland and fine. Do you understand that he was
terrified that he was no good at anything? Lieutenant,
blaaah. He was no good. He was no good. God, how I
hate Värmland. That bloody countryside took every
ounce of self-respect from him.

Tora   I think you've started swearing an awful lot,
Selma. That's not good. You'll become. Like . . . me.

Selma   Yes, I want to. God, how I wish I could be like
you. Young and pretty and cheeky.

Pause.

No, I could never kick Papa out on his arse. Never. He
stayed where he was. He stayed where he was.

Tora   That's what I thought was so odd . . . yesterday.
Weren't you also a little grateful for that . . . Selma?

Selma   (*on the verge of exploding, controls herself*)   No.
peace. No war now, Selma.

Pause.

But you're not scared of anything. Not scared of anything. No corset. I would really like to be like you.

Tora   And be told that you fuck around like a chimpanzee?

Selma (*looks at her sharply*)   Yes . . . what's it actually like?

Tora   Well.

Selma   Well what?

Tora   Varied. Bit up and down. Can be fun.

Selma (*considers it*)   Well, then I'd probably fuck around like a chimpanzee.

Tora   Oh.

Selma   Though I don't know.

Tora   But . . . (*She doesn't know if she dares.*) . . . You've never . . . you've.. have you . . . never?

Selma *looks at her kindly.*

Tora   . . . Never?

Selma   Never.

Tora   *Jesus Christ!*

Selma   You can say that again. But what good will he do, asked the girl.

Tora   But darling Selma . . . you've written some of the most beautiful . . . the most beautiful . . . depictions of love I've . . .

Selma   You don't write about things as they are, but how you'd like them to be.

Tora (*breathlessly*)   Really. Really.

Selma   Like a spell. That's why you write.

Tora   Really.

Selma *says nothing.*

Tora   I'm not sure I approve.

Pause.

Wait, let me think about it.

Pause.

No, I'm not sure I approve. How would someone like me
. . . you do need . . . guidance. So to speak. And for that
you have to know what it's like as well. See? Not just how
it ought to be. Otherwise it'll . . . bite you on the arse.
Later on. Nah!

Selma (*irritably*)   Now I think we should change the
subject, Tora, dear.

Tora   Oh, no you don't. We won't! So! You read about
how beautiful and wondrous love is and how right it is
while you lie there trembling and then they've got your
knickers off, swissssh and boing, there it is and bang,
straight in it goes and there you lie on your back, cross-
eyed and stuffed and . . . nah. It has to be much better!
Otherwise you're just making a fool of yourself!

Selma (*looks at her for a long time, starts again*)   Do you
know something, Tora. Tora. I've never seen you on
stage. But I do know you're very bright. And you think
for yourself. Yes, you do. But you've never really
understood what it takes to create a work of art. Not at
all. It hurts, you see. And so you have to write . . . a
spell.

Pause.

No, that sounds so . . . but *then it doesn't hurt so much!*
Then it doesn't hurt so much. Yes, a spell.

Tora (*almost childlike*)   So you don't think I'm stupid.

Selma   You know a pearl. First a tiny grain of sand
which hurts so badly. And then mother-of-pearl as
protection.

Tora   Yes.

Selma   No pain no pearl. And without a spell, only sand.

Walks restlessly over to the silent, awaiting film projector, strokes it.

Sand!

Pensively.

You're fortunate you get to stand on stage. And hide yourself in someone else.

Tora (*dances a step pensively towards* **Selma**, *stands up*) Fortunate? Ta . . . dam . . . ta . . . dam . . . fortunate? Ta . . . dam . . . ta . . . dam . . . sometimes . . . when I'm on stage . . . I imagine that there is no world outside the theatre. It's wonderful . . . it almost makes me a little . . . tipsy. Intoxicated! But then I get scared because it feels wrong. And then I think that in order to be able to act you have to embrace *the world*. And if one day I'll play those really great roles, then I have to, like, embrace . . . it. Do you see? I suppose that's what the . . . grain of sand is. It has to start with that. There has to be a grain of sand at the centre. Otherwise it doesn't make sense.

Selma   I think you will act those great roles one day.

Tora   You think so?

Selma   And I suppose that's why I got so mad about the . . . aunty story-teller. I'm sorry.

Pause.

They belittle me and I don't deserve it.

Pause.

They don't see . . . the grain of sand. Which *is there*.

Tora   And which you must take with you. On stage. And not . . . hide?

Selma (*suddenly smiling*)   On stage.

Tora   Forgive me.

Selma   What for?

Tora   For getting so mad. I got so damned upset, no mad, when you said I ought to feel a sense of guilt because Mum threw Dad out.

Very quietly.

I feel no guilt. He's responsible for his own life. I'm responsible for mine. And since then I've had men like Dad around me all my life and if I hadn't learnt to kick them out they would have made mincemeat of me. *Mincemeat!* You have to think for yourself. I learnt that from Mum. And how she. And how she. Took responsibility.

Pause.

It is a great art not to feel guilty.

Selma   I could never do that. Never. Ever.

Tora   You have to defend yourself against men like Dad, you see.

Selma   Viktor included?

Tora *is silent.*

Selma   Viktor included?

Tora   Sometimes he's so delicate. Like a child. And then I get so sad when he's afraid of me.

Selma   Then let me tell you something. Old men who become childlike, they're the worst. If you meet someone like that, then you must run. Then you must run far away and not stop until you can no longer see them. Then you can slow down. *But run!*

Tora   Why?

Selma   Because they can hurt you very badly.

Tora (*sits down next to* **Selma**)   And you never saw him again?

Selma Who?

Tora Your dad. The old soak. The lieutenant!

Selma Yes.

Tora When?

Selma They called. I was at the teacher's college for young ladies. They said he was dying. And so I went home.

Tora How awful. Wasn't it awful?

Selma Nah. He had become so small. That happens when you drink yourself to death.

Tora So you weren't scared?

Selma He was just so small. He'd been vomiting blood and was scared and though we'd hardly exchanged a word since the time I left, I saw that he . . . was awfully glad. I was his favourite.

Tora Yes, that's understandable.

Selma Though it got so . . . awful . . . that I was forced to leave. He was more in love with the bottle, I thought. But when he was dying he became so awfully small. And scared. He lay there and was small and curled up and I saw then that he was sober. It's like they shrivel up in a small heap when they can't drink any longer and he knew that. Sometimes he coughed up some yellow phlegm. Then I sat down by his bed. And there I sat until he died, except for a few hours when I lay on the floor.

Tora What did he say?

Selma Well, it was mostly about how scared he was. And later about how he felt. The thing about him being no use and that he was scared. And then he asked all the time how I would remember him. He went on about that. He couldn't put that aside.

Tora How would you remember him?

Selma   Some nights he slept mostly. But that was when I told him about the Resurrection. That it would be like a miracle.

Tora   Resurrection?

Selma   I told him not to be scared, because I would ensure his resurrection. I would be the assurance of his resurrection. I would . . . I believe I told him about Michelangelo, the creation, you know God who points his finger at man and the spark of life . . . and he would come alive . . . from the grime and the clay . . . grow wings . . . fly . . .

Tora   Calm down, Selma, you must calm down, surely you're not *God* either . . .

Selma   It didn't matter how everything *had been*. I would restore him. *Restore!* It would be my life's work, Papa would be my . . . life's work . . . it is crazy, Tora . . . I'm ashamed . . . I'm crazy but . . .

Tora   Dear, sweet, Selma . . . I don't think you're . . .

Selma   (*tries to pull herself together, now almost composed*) We wouldn't concern ourselves with all that business with boon companions and a glass of good wine and songs and him locking himself in to drink with the hangers-on or . . . the eternal lying. Everything I think of as Värmland. *The lies!* How we were. I would tell a story, I said. I would become a writer and tell it like *it should have been.* Not that we stood around him in a circle. And stared at the corpse. And then everyone would understand what a fine papa he really was. I told him he was a fine papa. Really.

Pause.

Really.

Tora   But, Selma . . . dearest . . . it was for your own sake too . . . you can't say that's why you . . . *really* . . .

Selma   *You have to believe me even when I am lying, Tora!*

Tora   I believe you. I don't believe it is so
straightforward.

Selma   And I would write books about it and everyone
would remember him for what he really was. So fine. Like
a flickering flame. And though it . . . *in reality* . . . was
hard to keep the flame alive he would be reborn. And I
would be reborn. Yes, it is true, Tora, me too. And then
everyone would read about him and then I would get
rich and Mårbacka would be fine and happy again. But it
all rested on him, it was thanks to him, because I would
rewrite everything, not just write it as it was. *Not just write
it as it was!* Rewrite it to how it really should have been.

Pause.

We were to be merciful towards each other. And
transform. The grime of life.

Tora   The grime of life. To what it ought to be.

Julius *stands in the doorway, enters completely unnoticed, says
nothing, listens. But they don't see him.*

Selma   And I saw he listened. And he became
completely calm. And then I described his resurrection.
And then I saw how the flame in him grew dimmer and
dimmer and dimmer. And his breathing slowed down.
And he became completely translucent and beautiful,
like when I was quite little. Then he was beautiful. And
then the flame burned down . . . grew smaller and . . .
smaller . . . and disappeared. And then he was dead. But I
had been able to tell him everything. Everything. About
my life's work. About his resurrection. And everything
which was . . . Papa's true flame . . . which was . . . his true
. . . that would be resurrected in me. And it would be . . .
absolutely clear. For everyone.

Pause.

Mercy. For ever and ever.

Pause.

Resurrection was possible.

Tora   Resurrection.

Selma   His light. His flame. In me. As it should be.

Tora *can do nothing, she just sits watching old* **Selma***, yes, she's old, we can see that now. And she's no monument and she's just trying to calm her almost timid tears.*

Tora   Did you love him that much?

Selma *nods silently and forcefully, but can speak no longer.*

Tora   One day . . . when I'm on stage . . . and I'm acting by numbers . . . then I'll think of you.

Selma   And Papa.

Tora   And your papa.

Selma   That's good.

Tora   (*it is very quiet and something is finished and* **Tora** *knows it*)   Do you want to go home or do you want to watch the film?

Selma   (*stutters, almost like a prayer*)   The film.

Tora   Are you sure?

Selma   The film.

Julius   (*that's the pass word, he is free from his paralysis, tiptoes forward carefully*)   I didn't mean to disturb. But if you want me . . . to show the film . . .

Selma   Ahhhhh . . . you gave me a fright.

Tora   So where's Viktor?

Julius   He told me to stay and run the film. For those who wanted to see his vision, he said.

Selma   (*still doesn't understand*)   Yeees . . . ?

Tora   He has gone?

Julius   Yes . . . yes, he was . . .

Pause, with an almost accusatory tone of voice.

Yes, to be honest he was upset.

Pause, but what he overheard while he was listening has erased part of his shyness.

I think he was upset. You see . . . Viktor had an old man who was an alcoholic and his childhood was hell. And then he wanted to make a film about . . . well, about his life really. Yes, about *his* life. Though it would originate from the doctor's novel. And that's why he was a little scared. That you would think he was distorting it, you see. It had become so personal to him. Slaved over the script. Six hundred and five scenes, describing every angle. And I suppose that's why he got a little . . . upset. He said he wanted to make the first film in history to deal with real life. And he thought he had seen something which he wasn't sure the doctor would like. She'd think he was distorting or something.

Selma   Good God. What had he . . . seen?

Tora   The grain of sand.

Selma   He saw that. Why didn't he say?

Almost childlike.

Why did he keep quiet?

Tora   Why did *you?*

Selma (*almost to herself*)   Then he saw the grain of sand.

Julius   Yes, but a little upset. You see.

Selma   Oooh dear. I didn't mean to. I didn't mean to hurt him. But imagine, he saw it.

Julius   I suppose he was so nervous about what you would think. And then it seemed as if you didn't . . . have the time.

Pause.

I think we're still wondering a little . . .

Almost kindly.

Do you hate us?

Selma (*covers her face with her hands*)   How can you ask that?

Julius   Well . . . film is not. . . . an art form. Many people say so. A little bird . . . a bird of clay.

Selma   I don't know if I can take much more. Tora and I . . . it's been so exhausting. Please.

Julius   Yes, yes.

Selma   But I want to see the film. I do . . . I want to see what you . . . saw.

Julius   Can I tell you something?

Sits down beside her.

I didn't plan on telling you but . . . since it's become so . . . strange. Well, I read a short story by you, Dr Lagerlöf, when I was a boy. It was the one where Jesus and Judas were children and were making birds out of clay. And Jesus made such fine and amazing birds . . . *effortlessly!* He just put his hand in the muddy water and it filled with colours . . . shimmered like *mother-of-pearl,* I believe . . . while Judas' birds were lumpy and ugly. The colour of mud. It just wouldn't happen for him, ugly and lumpy . . . and then Judas got so bloody angry that he stamped Jesus' birds to pieces, one by one, but Jesus just clapped his hands and said . . . fly! Fly! And the birds of clay came alive and flew . . . and saved themselves . . . They came to life!

Selma   Yes. I remember.

Julius   And I got so angry. And upset. With you who had written it. Honestly! I was bloody angry. Because then Mary turned up and said to Judas, who was just a child, you follow? something about Judas being completely thick and how he would never amount to anything if he 'undertook to compete with he who paints with sunshine and breathes the spirit of life into dead clay.' And I got so upset. And angry. If Doctor Lagerlöf will excuse me. How the hell could Mary know what talents that boy Judas possessed. Given the chance. Later in life. I'm bloody sure that his birds of clay . . . well . . . why should anyone belittle them. *Despise them!* No, perhaps they were just . . . fine. Would fly eventually. And . . . I believe the important thing was that he tried. So why did he have to take that shit from Mary.

Pause, explanatory.

And I found that you were a little . . . arrogant towards that boy, Dr Lagerlöf. Perhaps that boy Judas was a kind of artist as well?

Selma   That's true. How stupid of me.

Julius   There's no need to be arrogant!

Selma   No. True.

Julius   And later I often thought about that story. And I thought that . . . How *wrong* you were.

Pause.

Yes, later I thought I wanted to be an image maker. *An image maker* – you see. Create images. And then later on I became a cinematographer. Though that is perhaps also a kind of image maker.

Shyly.

Well, never mind. (*Pause.*) Never mind.

Selma (*watches him in pain*)   No. I hadn't thought of that. What a stupid way to end a story.

Julius   Well, it . . . sort of stuck with me.

Selma   The Image Makers? A good description. Such a good description. Perhaps I'm an image maker too?

Julius   Well, it's not so straightforward. When you think about it. To be an image maker.

Selma (*pensively*)   I know. I'm beginning to realise that more and more.

Julius   Shall we begin? So this is *The Coachman*, reel five.

Pause.

I want you to know, Dr Lagerlöf, that we've worked night and day for months.

Pause.

We haven't just been tinkering.

Selma (*nods strongly*)   Will it be called *The Coachman?*

Julius   *The Coachman?* What else?

Selma   For a while I thought of '*Resurrection*'.

Viktor (*has opened the door almost unnoticed, stands like a silhouette*)   Of course it will be called *The Coachman*. Then you know what the film is really about.

Selma   Oh . . . you're back, Mr Sjöström . . . I'm glad . . . I've been so stupid. I'm sorry.

Viktor (*doesn't understand, doesn't move from the door, makes a sign, the film can begin*)   Julius. We'll start now.

They sit down, but just before **Tora** *sits down she goes to* **Selma**, *caresses her cheek and says:*

Tora   Selma. Don't be sorry. You're the finest and sweetest little bumble bee I've ever met.

Selma (*close to laughter, she waits and then she says quietly*)   Thank you. (*Pause.*) No one has ever said anything as nice to me in all my life.

The film begins. The resurrected spirit rises from the dead body.

The tango has been added.

The four characters as silhouettes. The image makers see their images rise out of the story.

And then suddenly darkness.

www.ingramcontent.com/pod-product-compliance
Ingram Content Group UK Ltd.
Pitfield, Milton Keynes, MK11 3LW, UK
UKHW040639280225
455688UK00001B/4

9 780413 772008